ACCIDENTAL OCCIDENTAL

ACCIDENTAL OCCIDENTAL

Economics and Culture of Transition in Mitteleuropa, the Baltic and the Balkan Area

LAJOS BOKROS

CEU PRESS

Central European University Press
Budapest–New York

Published in 2013 by

Central European University Press

An imprint of the
Central European University Limited Liability Company
Nádor utca 11, H-1051 Budapest, Hungary
Tel: +36-1-327-3138 or 327-3000
Fax: +36-1-327-3183
E-mail: ceupress@ceu.hu
Website: www.ceupress.com

400 West 59th Street, New York NY 10019, USA
Tel: +1-212-547-6932
Fax: +1-646-557-2416
E-mail: martin.greenwald@opensocietyfoundations.org

ISBN 978-615-5225-24-6

Library of Congress Cataloging-in-Publication Data

Bokros, Lajos.
Accidental occidental : economics and culture of transition in Mitteleuropa, the Baltic, and the Balkan Area / Lajos Bokros.
p. cm.
Includes bibliographical references and index.
ISBN 978-6155225246 (hardbound)
1. Europe, Eastern--Economic policy--1989- 2. Europe, Eastern--Economic conditions--1989- 3. Post-communism--Europe, Eastern. I. Title.

HC244.B6744 2013
330.947--dc23

2012040142

Printed in the USA

To Yehuda Elkana
(1934–2012)
president & rector
Central European University
(1999–2009)

Table of Contents

Foreword ix

Introduction 1

1. Communism as an Economic and Societal System in the Twentieth Century 9

1.1. The theoretical model of the command economy and society 9
1.2. The historical evolution of Soviet communism 18
1.3. Three basic models of communism in Central and Eastern Europe 31

2. Transition to Market and Democracy in Central and Eastern Europe 57

2.1. The matrix of structural reforms in transition 57
2.2. Business sector liberalization 59
2.3. Macroeconomic stabilization 70
2.4. Competitive privatization 80
2.5. Public utility and financial sector privatization 94
2.6. Restructuring public utilities and financial institutions 102
2.7. Regulation and supervision of public utilities and financial institutions 113
2.8. Public finance and administration 127
2.9. Subsovereign governments 141
2.10. Legal and judicial reform 154
2.11. Matrix reloaded 159

3. Transition for the Twenty-First Century 167

References 177

Index 189

Foreword

I started writing this book in the course of 2009, in a year which was to be considered *annus miserabilis* from the very beginning. The autumn of 2008 wrought havoc on the whole world. Collapsing banks and insurance companies, financial sector meltdown, global recession, fiscal bankruptcy created unprecedented fear and pessimism in many countries. Governments, some acting in panic, tried desperately to mitigate the consequences of the downturn by implementing extraordinary measures of Keynesian stimuli. *Financial and fiscal socialism*—i.e. state ownership of big chunks of the banking system and profligate overspending—became fashionable once again in a big way. Governments, apparently reluctant to apply the seductive monetary and fiscal shower, were strongly and widely criticized for their lack of imagination and their allegedly harmful inaction.

In such an atmosphere and zeitgeist, nothing seemed more remote and unimportant than the so-called **transition** which had started twenty years earlier in Central and Eastern Europe. The implosion of the vast Soviet empire seemed distant memory and history, having little or no relevance to contemporary events and thoughts. People were celebrating the twentieth anniversary of the fall of the Berlin Wall in a subdued mood and manner. The twentieth anniversary of Tien An Men square tragedy raised more fear than remembrance and not only in the official circles of the People's Republic of China. Although communism seems to have retreated forever, capitalism now appears once again under serious threat; *this time around from within*.

During the 1990s, communism, an inherently non-market system from economic and societal point of view, was replaced by capitalism not only in Central and Eastern Europe—which is the subject of this book—but also in Russia, the Caucasus, Central Asia, China and Vietnam. Nevertheless, in the vast Eurasian mega-continent *capitalism did not bring about liberal democracy*. Instead, a new formation emerged, which can be called **authoritarian state capitalism**.[1] This is a major difference between Central and Eastern Europe and the rest of what had been called the *second world* for more than 40 years until 1989. Moreover, authoritarian state capitalism, embodied first and foremost by *China and Russia*, looked like a viable and attractive alternative to Western democracy as it was producing far higher rates of economic growth. (It was happening not only in China for almost 30 years but also in Russia at least in a short decade from 2000 to 2007).

In the contemporary context this book can be considered as an untimely but salient *defense of market capitalism and liberal democracy*. Celebrating transition today is tantamount to upholding the decidedly superior values and achievements of a market system over a non-market one and that of a democratic system over a non-democratic one. It is definitely not to deny the failures, shortcomings or imperfections of market economy and democracy. Neither do I take the survival of market capitalism and liberal democracy for granted. On the contrary, by highlighting the glorious and painful process of transition and making an attempt to understand its economics and culture, I wish to contribute to the once again badly needed **theoretical** (academic) and **practical** (political) **defense of Western civilization**.[2]

---

[1] Some scholars even predicted that "a successful nondemocratic Second World could emerge as an attractive alternative to liberal democracy." Gat (2007). In light of the still unfolding global economic and financial crisis, which has spilled over to many emerging markets and proved the theory of decoupling liberal democracy and capitalism relevant, it can still be considered a real threat.

[2] Capitalism—and, in a much wider context, Western civilization—has been considered in terminal decline by countless scholars and ideologues, left and right. Marxist communists obviously took the demise and ultimate disappearance of capitalism for granted for 150 years. But conservative thinkers were also keen to predict the destruction of Western culture and civilization at the crossroads of history in the twentieth century. The first attempt to forecast the ultimate failure of Western culture and civilization was made by Oswald Spengler in his groundbreaking book: "Der Untergang des Abendlandes" (The Decline of the West) the first volume of which was published in 1918, exactly when World War I ended. Another famous and thoroughly pessimistic account of Western civilization was written by Arnold Toynbee: "Civilization on Trial" published in 1945, right at the end of World War II. Countless books and publications, including literary works, made the idea of decline a staple food of Western intellectuals for the second half of the

1989 was an epochal year at the start of transition and later it came to be symbolized by the fall of the Berlin Wall. When 1989 began, everything that happened had still been unimaginable. Although the Soviet Union had experienced *glasnost* (enlightenment) and *perestroika* (rebuilding) for a number of years, nobody knew that Gorbachev was going to be the last president of the Soviet Union. Thus, 1989 was "annus mirabilis"—the year of the miracle, the year witnessing the start of several unfolding miracles which culminated in the largely peaceful collapse of the Soviet Union in late 1991.[3]

In addition, to explain and understand transition in the last twenty years, this book is also to celebrate its historic triumph. The victory of miracle over misery. *To learn more about the nature of this miracle to avoid new misery.*

Another imperative for the vigorous defense of democratic capitalism stems from the fact that transition, no matter how irrelevant it is perceived today, is *far from being a closed chapter of world history*. January 1, 2009 marked the half-centenary of the Cuban revolution. Although Fidel Castro has by and large abandoned the commanding heights of the party-state bureaucratic-military machine, communism seems to have outlived him in Cuba quite comfortably. North Korea, another remote outpost of a system which is inherently hostile to both market and democracy, has shown remarkable endurance and even defiance despite the misery and suffering it brought to its own people. Most important, these regimes of economic and political stagnation have gained tremendous support from China, an unlikely ally. This raw autocratic (authoritarian) capitalist emerging superpower, sometimes reluctantly, but often ruthlessly, chooses to prop up

---

twentieth century. (A concise summary of these efforts is offered by Arthur Herman in his book: "The Idea of Decline in Western History.") What is remarkable is not whether Western civilization has been really in terminal decline or not but the fact that the *myth about decline* has become so strong over time that it may become a *self-fulfilling prophecy*. **The idea of Western decline may well contribute to its real decline**.

[3] Famous intellectuals were also predicting the collapse of empire-like structures as a consequence of what can be called "imperial overstretch," i.e. the inadequacy of resources—both human and financial—when a great power undertakes global commitments disproportionate to its own economic and political capacity. Paul Kennedy was forecasting the fall of the American empire citing the experience of the United Kingdom after the two world wars. [Kennedy (1988)] Interestingly and intriguingly, it was not the USA but the Soviet Union which collapsed as an immediate consequence of unbearable imperial overstretch in Afghanistan (and many other factors) as it was more precisely predicted by Emmanuel Todd in his relatively early account "La chute finale" (1976) [The Final Fall (1979)]. See also Brzezinski (1989).

ineffective and inhuman regimes in name of traditional power politics shaping the new multipolar world in the early twenty-first century.

Will these last anachronistic bastions of communism collapse only after the democratization of China or will they finally succumb to growing and unbearable internal pressure? Will this transformation be largely peaceful as it was the case in most of Central and Eastern Europe or violent, with the violence and chaos eventually spilling over to the international arena? These are questions of truly historic importance, relevant even today.

On a personal note: *I am not only an academic witness but also a vivid practitioner of transition.* In Hungary, people most remember me as minister of finance, who designed and introduced a package of stringent austerity measures and some basic structural reforms in 1995 when the Hungarian economy was on the verge of fiscal collapse. Later, I was working at the World Bank between 1996 and 2004, for most of this period as a director of a newly-established Financial and Private Sector Development Department. I was overseeing many projects in the whole former Soviet communist world, on occasion in China and Vietnam. Both in official and personal capacity I was advising various governments in countries of transition in designing and implementing macroeconomic policy programs and structural reforms. I keep doing this until today. My intellectual and practical footprint has been left in many former communist countries, most intensively in Poland, Slovakia, Croatia, Romania, Bulgaria, Serbia, Russia and, lately, Ukraine. (My hope and strong desire is to be called to assist Cuban and North Korean transition when the time is ripe.) Therefore, what is accounted for here in this book cannot be separated from my practical experience in public policy gained throughout transition in Central and Eastern Europe and beyond.

Introduction

The title of this book occurred to me at dawn on Sunday, August 7, 2011 when I was sitting at the eleventh floor balcony of a quite decrepit hotel in Mangalia, a small resort town on the Romanian littoral. While marveling on the magnificent view of the sun as it was rising from the waters of the Black Sea, I was reflecting on my fantastic experience the day before.

I arrived to the coast by train from Bucharest early afternoon on Saturday. Having checked into the hotel, I wished to order a light lunch. The restaurant was overcrowded, but only one large group was enjoying their meal at the spacious poolside bar. When I asked the young bartender what was on offer to eat there, he said that, according to prevailing rules, there were no meals to be had at the poolside bar. When I risked the question how then it was possible for the large group to have a sumptuous buffet, he leaned close to me and whispered that they were *the largest investors of the hotel*.

My memory of the early days of post-communist transition came back vividly. Time seemed to have stopped over the Romanian littoral. In terms of economics and culture, this shocking experience was not without lessons.

First, it was interesting to see that those were the *first to breach the rules* who must have set them up in the first place. Second, they did it not behind the scenes but in the open and plain daylight; and they could not care less about the impact it might have on outsiders. Worse still, many locals must have considered their behavior as completely natural and expected. Third, the owners clearly felt that they were entitled to have, and even demonstrate, privileges. Like in the "good old days" of Ceauşescu, the Stalinist-nationalist dictator of Romania, until the very end of the communist system in 1989, those who happened to be at the higher end of the societal ladder were thinking *in terms of privileges* rather than earned respect in a competitive environment. Fourth, they did not even recognize their own enlightened self-interest: the maximum satisfaction of customers may, by and large, enhance their profit and the value of their precious property. Quite the opposite: they seemed not to have been really concerned about the maximum possible exploitation of the hunger and thirst of the guests in the hotel and around.

Of course, this small incident could have happened anywhere else in the transition world and similar events do occur still quite often in many places. But it is revealing in a distinct way that nascent or renascent capitalism has **different rules in economics and culture in this part of world**. It may not be like that forever but it is absolutely sure that it is going to be like this for a very long historical period of time. **Transition is far from over** and even if it was in the narrow and formal sense of economics, it has certainly not been completed in terms of institution building and human behavior.[1]

To use a German word, *Mitteleuropa,* for the subtitle of this book may seem strange and sound preposterous to the scholarly audience nurtured by the recent and prevailing Anglo-Saxon tradition of using cautious neutral words. It is somewhat less dangerous to Central and Eastern European readers. Mitteleuropa is not only a term circumscribing a specific geographic area but a well-known concept coined by Friedrich Neumann almost hundred years ago.[2] This concept reflects a rather *unique culture and civilization* that had existed for almost a millennium before 1900, has survived in various forms ever since and, with remarkable modifications, continues to exist even today. While Central Europe is a mere geographic expression,[3] Mitteleuropa clearly constitutes a unique culture with very special life feelings (*lebensgefühl*). It is a rather pessimistic and introvert culture reflecting several centuries of failure of the peoples of the region

---

[1] My Black Sea experience highlights the peculiar culture of transition, an eloquent illustration capturing the distorted and distorting spirit of capitalism in the region which, in turn, anchors the development of these countries rather firmly in their not fully-Westernized political and cultural tradition. It is exactly this specific cultural heritage and experience which makes transition in Central and Eastern Europe a process which can be characterized in a somewhat ironic way as accidentally occidental.

[2] Neumann (1915).

[3] In strict geographic terms Central Europe includes Germany, Switzerland, Northern Italy, Austria, Poland, the Czech Republic, Slovakia, Hungary, Slovenia, Croatia, Voivodina (Serbia), Transsylvania (Romania).

in attaining **state and status**, i.e. *political and economic development and emancipation despite having had a rather glorious past in the first five hundred years of their stately existence.*[4]

To use the word "Balkan" may also raise some eyebrows. Prevailing and customary political correctness would dictate a reference to the area in neutral geographic terms like "South East Europe" in order to avoid hurting local sensitivities. I deliberately refuse to surrender to this euphemism because I uphold the notion that the culture and civilization of the Balkans is neither superior, nor inferior to any other in the world, but it is clearly different from that of Western Europe, Eastern Europe and Mitteleuropa. *One of the most important objectives of this book is to put the history of recent economic and societal transformation into the context of regional culture and civilization because that is the best way to understand its course, motivations, successes and failures as well as its implications for the future.*

We are lucky not to have this problem with the term "Baltic." Fortunately, the notion has no derogatory connotation in the culture of the three small countries—Estonia, Latvia and Lithuania—which constitute the Baltic region. The term is widely and proudly used by the peoples themselves. This is a neat difference between the two important appendices to the Central European mainland and reveals a lot about the strikingly different history, culture and tradition these peoples have.

The present and future fate of the three distinct subregions of transition covered by this book are very much influenced by their history and culture. As a consequence, the Baltic region, and to a certain extent even Poland, can also be conceived as part of the *Nordic civilization*. The Visegrád countries (V4) with Slovenia and Croatia (V6) are strongly under *German–Austrian and Franco-Italian influence*. Most Balkan countries show the spectacular and splendid rejuvenation of *Greek and Turkish heritage and tradition.*

One can actually see the inescapable power of these cultural conditions within each of the three subregions in the dominance of foreign strategic

[4] "Beyond the rejection of Moscow as a radiating center, a positive content also animated the notion of Central European identity, a reality pregnant with regional import. It portended the emergence of a wider cultural community, somewhat reminiscent of the old Austro-Hungarian Empire and of the nineteenth-century cultural concept of a "Mitteleuropa." It implied the notion that "Europe" was not an entity neatly divided into two entities—a Western Europe and an Eastern Europe with each subject to an extra-European power—but a cultural-historical community with overlapping also distinctive layers of shared experience, values and culture." Brzezinski (1989) 139. See also Szűcs (1983).

investors in commercial banking, one of the most important areas of the new market economy. In the 1990s large foreign banks followed their compatriot non-financial corporations when deciding where to go. It is no coincidence that the Baltic banking landscape is dominated by Swedish, Danish and Finnish banks. The Visegrád countries and Croatia show the overwhelming importance of Austrian, German and Italian banks. In the Balkans Greek and Turkish banks have acquired significant stakes in the financial sector. This tendency undeniably shows the strong influence of culture and tradition which is now resurfacing after the hiatus of communism.[5] People may not always like and even recognize it, but they certainly live with the strong impact of the past and, hence, demonstrate a remarkable substream of predisposition in their historical determination.[6]

I highlight this feature in order to underline my general argument that *there is no such thing as a unified region of Central and Eastern Europe*. Furthermore, despite the common characteristics of communism which were visible in the whole Soviet world, regional and national differences were quite discernible during the whole course of communism. Soviet communism was not the same in Estonia and Turkmenistan; that is common sense. Less obvious, however, is that Poland was quite different from Czechoslovakia, Romania from Bulgaria, even Slovenia from Croatia. Historical influences did not disappear from society under communism albeit the communist system, with all its identical general features, was strongly superimposed on it. Differences in communism—maybe secondary at that time—have outlived their primary relevance and can be traced even today.[7] Long-term original and subsequent historical determination

---

[5] See Bokros (2001).

[6] Actually, the very course of transition itself shows historical determination on several levels. Transition could not have been started without the Afghanistan imbroglio facing the Soviet empire throughout the 1980s. Gorbachev came to power after Soviet gerontocracy had exhausted all its options and Andropov, as well as Chernenko, died in quick succession. The Star War Initiative of the Reagan administration did play a role in creating a sense of desperation and helplessness among the Soviet elite but it is a gross exaggeration to believe that it triggered the collapse of the Soviet Union. As it is clear by now, **non-market systems and non-democratic regimes cannot be destroyed from the outside by peaceful means. They implode from within as a consequence of unbearable tensions created by half-hearted and unsuccessful reforms.** [See Brown (2009) Chapters 24 and 26.]

[7] That is the unescapable conclusion one can draw from reading the vast monograph of Roy Medvedev about Stalinism. [See Medvedev (1989)] While it is now clear that Stalin wasted no time and effort in trying to eradicate all historical differences from the culture of the peoples under his rule, even the system, now bearing his name, could not become

has resurfaced and reinforced its impact enormously in the last twenty years.

In sum, while I attempt to work out a "*general theory of transition*," that will always remain just a starting point. Not for a split second is it possible to forget about huge differences *in economic system, societal structure and dynamics, political events and thoughts, basic values, cultural background, historical legacy and national tradition, etc.* when understanding transition and designing and implementing practical solutions to present problems.

The book is organized as follows. Part 1 is about the communist system.[8] Chapter 1.1 describes the ideal-typical model of what I will call the *command economy* as a "kontrapunkt" to the theoretically conceived pure market economy. Chapter 1.2 presents an overview of the *historical context* which made the creation and functioning of the command economy not only viable but also legitimate first and foremost in the Soviet Union and later in Central and Eastern Europe.[9] Chapter 1.3 analyzes *various forms of communism* which existed in Europe between 1917 and 1989—the classical Stalinist, the modified Hungarian and the Yugoslav models.

---

totally homogeneous in his lifetime and beyond. History has proved to be extremely strong and continues to exert its influence in a wide variety of ways even today.

[8] Instead of using the word "socialism" or "socialist system," I will always refer to **communism** and/or the **communist system**. This is a deliberate choice in order to avoid misleading generalizations. Socialism is a very broad concept which includes a wide variety of parties, movements, ideologies, societal systems and even practical public policy solutions in many Western countries which have never renounced market and democracy. This is the most important dividing line which has distinguished communist parties from social democratic ones and Marxist-Leninist ideology from a wide variety of social democratic thought throughout the last hundred years. The great and historically fatal schism between social democracy and communism occurred at the twilight years of World War I when Lenin formulated the revolutionary ideology of what was to become the credo of Soviet communism in his two famous books: *State and Revolution* (1917) and *The Proletarian Revolution and the Renegade Kautsky* (1918).

[9] In this sense my selection of denomination is even more cautious: instead of talking about "communism" I will almost always refer to "**Soviet communism**." This is warranted for two reasons. First, the geographic scope of my study is Central and Eastern Europe, which was either part of the Soviet empire (Warsaw Pact) or under the overwhelming influence thereof (Yugoslavia, Albania). Second, Soviet communism is clearly identifying a system which is now defunct and discredited forever. No present and future left-leaning dictator will probably ever dare to refer to Soviet communism as a role model for his or her aspirations.

The second part of the book aims to build a *concise theory of transition* highlighting most of those **structural and institutional reforms** which, without doubt, have proved *indispensable* in all transition countries in their quest to establishing a market system. Chapter 2.1 analyzes what I call the **matrix of structural reforms** as it constitutes a suggestive instrument of systematization and rationalization for the hundreds of different measures which have been necessary to transform a still largely non-market economy into a now predominantly market-oriented one. Chapters 2.2 through 2.10 cover the nine separate but closely interrelated components of the matrix highlighting their mutually reinforcing character while bringing back some aspects of the historical analysis as well. It also reveals why some countries managed to charge ahead while others lost another decade before real transition started and became finally entrenched. Political events, policy mistakes (especially that of optimal sequencing and fallbacks), misguided ideological considerations, sometimes chaos and disintegration, other times war and physical destruction made transition an unpredictable and uneven process across the region. Chapter 2.11 takes stock as to *where we stand now after more than twenty years*. In this respect the accession of eight former communist countries to the European Union in May, 2004 and another two in January, 2007 stands out as perhaps the most important historical achievement of this multi-faced and multi-faceted systemic transformation.[10]

The third and concluding part of the book asks the impertinent question whether **transition is over or not**. It summarizes the *economic, political and cultural progress and regress* made by European post-communist societies on the way of transition and highlights the still outstanding task of changing fundamentally many of the values governing everyday economic and societal behavior of most institutions and the vast majority of people. It is absolutely clear that the smooth functioning of the market and democracy requires not only a facade of formal institutions but also self-conscious citizens who believe in these institutions and fill them up with responsible civic activity every day. Unfortunately, in the great majority of cases, it is still not what is happening in Mitteleuropa,

[10] The three small Baltic states, Estonia, Latvia and Lithuania, the four larger Visegrad countries, Poland, the Czech Republic, Slovakia and Hungary, together with the former Yugoslav republic of Slovenia accessed the European Union on May 1, 2004. Romania and Bulgaria joined on January 1, 2007. Croatia will follow them in July, 2013. All these countries belong to the core research area of this book.

the Baltic and the Balkan area.[11] As a consequence, the concluding chapter also contains some *policy advice* for selected transition countries as they intend to speed up real convergence to Western Europe. These issues are crucially important today, in the midst of an unprecedented global economic and financial crisis, which has hugely strengthened populist and extremist movements and ideologies not only in the transition world but in all parts of Europe. It is going to be the first **fundamental historical test of the whole process of transition** whether market capitalism and liberal democracy will hold and survive in the European periphery rather than succumb to the forceful waves of illiberal authoritarianism which, proudly and aggressively, denies the superiority of market and political freedom over arbitrary and predatory state intervention and tries to restore centuries-old paternalism based on incontestable special interests and privileges sanctioned by an autocratic political system.[12]

[11] "In certain countries of Europe the natives consider themselves as kind of settlers, indifferent to the fate of the spot upon which they live. The greatest changes are effected without their concurrence and without their knowledge; nay more the citizen is unconcerned as to the condition of his village, the police of his street, the repairs of the church or of the parsonage: for he looks upon all these things as unconnected with himself, and as the property of a powerful stranger whom he calls the Government. He has only a life-interest in these possessions, and he entertains no notion of ownership or of improvement. This want of interest in his own affairs goes so far that, if his own safety or that of his children is endangered, instead of trying to avert the peril, he will fold his arms, and wait till the nation comes to his assistance. This same individual, who has so completely sacrificed his own free will, has no natural propensity to obedience; he cowers, it is true, before the pettiest officer; but he braves the law with the spirit of a conquered foe as soon as its superior force is removed: his oscillations between servitude and license are perpetual." Tocqueville (2000) 103.

[12] One of the most fundamental political schisms in democratic Europe today seems to be the growing political fault line between what I will call *institutional and populist democracy*. The institutional variant upholds the values of liberalism, constitutionalism and the rule of law while the populist one is characterized by the unconstrained and direct rule of a strongly nationalist *volkspartei* typically led by a charismatic fatherly figure, politicizing, pushing aside, weakening or ignoring societal institutions, which are supposed to provide basic *checks and balances* against illiberal and/or extremist policies and behavior. [See Lukacs (2005).]

1. Communism as an Economic and Societal System in the Twentieth Century

1.1. The theoretical model of the command economy and society

It is extremely hard to describe a non-market economy in positive terms. Contemporary analyses highlighted that in a non-market system there was no freedom of contract, entrepreneurial autonomy, consumer choice, money and profit. All true in negative terms. But it does not make up for an eloquent and suggestive description of what exactly a command economy is.[1]

The command economy is embedded in an *absolutely hierarchical society* where human beings matter—value themselves and each other—only as a function of a *superstructure encompassing the whole society*. The economy and the individuals have no separate, autonomous standing in societal life. People play inseparable economic and societal roles determined by either *tradition* in subsistence societies not striving for material abundance or by *ideology* in self-styled growth-oriented post-capitalist formations claiming superiority to capitalism and thus competing for surpassing it.[2]

---

[1] Unfortunately, we are captive to our narrow mindset formulated by market theory. The powerful stream of classical theories depicting the market as a largely self-regulating entity and backbone of all economies we know have distorted our thinking considerably. We lack plausible notions describing non-market systems. That is a huge impediment when trying to understand economic and societal systems not based on self-regulating markets. By the same token, it is a big mistake to consider the first ten thousand years of human history as a mere introduction to capitalism and the market economy. [See Karl Polanyi (1946).]

[2] That is why *command economy* is an imprecise term; it would be better to talk about a *command society*.

As a result, *the command economy (and society) is always totalitarian.*[3] It cannot be otherwise. Mobilizing society for increasing production, for supporting military efforts with increased production, for symbolic acts in culture (praising the party, the leading person, the ideology, etc.) requires *total control on most if not all aspects of human life.*[4] In negative terms, a command system is completely alien to any kind of individualism, does not allow the development and flourishing of any personal want or desire which is not part of the officially sanctioned set of collective wants and desires.[5]

Command economies, therefore, can be referred to as *state collectivism*. State is key, indeed, although it is hardly separable from society as a whole. All members of society are important insofar as they perform duties defined by the collective as represented by the state and perform them well to the benefit of the collective as defined by the state. It is not only the economy which has no autonomous standing and separate meaning in societal life but *within the economy* there is little or no distinctive functioning of production, distribution and consumption (negative description, once again). Likewise, the legal and judiciary system, church and religion, education and science, arts and culture, or any other sphere of societal life have no autonomous existence either. In this respect, *totalitarian regimes constitute a fallback to premodern societies* no matter how much they claim to represent modernity, or even more, ultra-modernity.

---

[3] Totalitarian societies are always *despotic and dictatorial* and never democratic. In fact they openly and publicly despise Western democracy. In the twentieth century many societies were labelled as totalitarian: Italian fascism, German nazism, Soviet Stalinism, Chinese Maoism and even some Latin-American military regimes driven by ideology. [See Hannah Arendt (1958)] At the same time the "notion of totalitarianism denotes a system of political domination and this is why it defines the socio-economic structure from only one aspect. Quite different socio-economic structures can be totalitarian in the same way." Fehér–Heller–Márkus (1983) 147.

[4] Another way of calling this type of society is political society. "Political society means the primacy of the state over the whole societal life; society is an annex to the omnipotent political state rather than a relatively independent entity." Fehér–Heller–Márkus (1983) 253. "...totalitarianism is identical with political society (submission and liquidation of civil society), with the elimination of any recognized pluralism." Ibid., 147.

[5] "…the substitution of central planning for competition would require central direction of a much greater part of our lives than was ever attempted before. It could not stop at what we regard as our economic activities… It is no accident that in the totalitarian countries, be it Russia or Germany or Italy, the question of how to organize the people's leisure has become a problem of planning." Hayek (1944) 132.

It is obvious from the above that *money does not play any meaningful role in integrating the economy in a command system if it exists at all.* Money always means *freedom of choice*[6] and implies at least some very limited *consumer autonomy*. If people are told what to do, where to work, how much and, likewise, what to consume, when and how much, etc., then there is no point in paying them monetary wages. In subsistence and hydraulic societies consumption was determined and regulated by religion and/or tradition. In ideology-based, growth-oriented totalitarian regimes, like Soviet communism, it is defined and fixed by a more or less overarching *rationing system*.[7] In any case, money does not function as a means of exchange and measurement of value, because there is no trading of goods and services and, hence, value to be measured in market transactions.[8]

Command is a suggestive word to grasp the very essence of such society. The market economy is based on *contract*, which on theoretical level implies horizontal relationships, freedom of choice, autonomy in decision making. The command economy is a clear opposite. *Command* instead of contract. *Vertical,* instead of horizontal societal bonds. No freedom of choice and autonomy in decision making at any level but *subordinated existence* to fulfill predetermined economic and societal functions.[9]

---

[6] It is in the Friedmanite sense that money means freedom of choice. [See Milton and Rose Friedman (1980).]

[7] Rationing systems are usually justified by the lack of sufficient goods for consumption. In fact, such systems operated in market-based economies when there was a need for an extreme concentration of efforts in an exceptional political situation, in case of existential threat (like in Great Britain during World War II.) The above mentioned justification was also used in Soviet times and not only during war. But reality is quite different from ideology. In fact, the rationing system is the only approach to consumption which is **fully consistent with a command economy**. Rationing scarce consumer goods means that the state can prescribe to all citizens what to consume, how much, when, etc. It is the direct opposite to freedom of choice in the area of consumption. It is an absolutely rational extension of totalitarian command from production to consumption. [See Kornai (1992) 241–243.] In such a system, even if there is money, it is largely useless because there is nothing to buy for it and/or it is declared illegal outright.

[8] As we shall see, the (re)introduction of money into a command economy is always a *concession* and implies the admission of defeat with methods much more consistent with the command system. Money, as freedom of choice, surely contradicts to the logic of the command system in the first place.

[9] I deliberately depart from the notion of planning when conceptualizing the antithesis of a market system. I follow F.A. Hayek who argued that planning is part of our everyday life and stems from the desire to "handle our common problems as rationally as possible." Hayek (1944) 85. He clearly understood that the supporters of modern planning had a completely different aspiration. (See footnote 14.)

In this book I concentrate on a *very specific historical variation* of the command economy and society, namely **Soviet communism.**[10] The nascent Soviet Union was never conceived as a traditional, immovable society and its economy was not based on simple reproduction and subsistence without the accumulation of surplus. Just the opposite: the most important driving force and source of legitimacy for Soviet communism was a *special ideology* which praised **economic growth and material abundance**—not necessarily for the individual consumer but for society as a whole. It intended to be a very radical departure from anything traditional. In political sense it strove and pretended to be ultra-modern.

There were at least three elements in this ideology—"Marxism–Leninism"—which implied the need and possibility of **unrestricted economic growth**. First, *communism was defined and always justified as superior to capitalism* because it claimed to liberate the proletariat—the class created by and oppressed in capitalism—from "wage slavery." Second, communism was declared more efficient than capitalism because it was going to be based on *society-wide conscious planning rather than an inherently wasteful market.*[11] Third, while market capitalism was based on profit and material gain as a primary driving force of most private economic activity including, first and foremost, productive investment, in communism the profit motive was to be completely eliminated and replaced by the *universal aspiration to satisfy directly the material needs of society in a close-to-perfect way.*[12]

---

[10] When it started in post-revolutionary Russia, Soviet communism was clearly conceived as a non-market system not only for ideological reasons but also for it had been born out of war. (The first historical form of Soviet communism was later labeled as war communism.) It is important to advance the observation (analyzed in the next chapter in detail) that **war was always the midwife of communism everywhere**. **The suspension of market forces always accompanied the victory of communism in all parts of the world**. Nevertheless, market forces were reintroduced in most places to a variable extent when the inherent contradictions of the non-market system made its preservation untenable. In some places the rebuilding of market relationships reached such an advanced stage that it changed substantially the nature of the system. Such deviation led to the formation of the *Hungarian modified model* and, much earlier, to the *Yugoslav model* based on workers' self-management in collective enterprises. However, these two variations remain to be called *models within Soviet communism* and will be analyzed in Chapter 1.3.

[11] In Marxian ideology the market is considered as an inherently inefficient mechanism to coordinate the allocation of productive resources according to human needs thus leading to anarchy and substantial waste. [See Engels (1894) Part III. Chapter II.]

[12] It is intriguingly interesting to follow the evolution of Marxian philosophy—as it was originally conceived by Marx and Engels—into the very practically oriented ideology of

It became a fundamental—almost existential—question throughout the whole twentieth century either to prove or to deny the validity of these three conclusions. Fierce ideological and physical battles were fought in order to answer these questions of almost metaphysical importance once for all. While history finally demonstrated that Soviet communism was much less efficient and viable than market economy and liberal democracy, and it failed spectacularly in satisfying the ever-growing and ever-diversifying needs of a sophisticated consumer society, at the time of the present global economic and financial crisis and the fast-spreading cultural and political pessimism it is important to highlight the ultimate theoretical arguments for the *superiority of market over command*.[13]

It is worth emphasizing that the truly relevant comparison is not between market and planning, not even between market and central planning. Planning at the *micro level* (i.e. within enterprises, institutions, government agencies, etc.) is almost indispensable and largely beneficial to ensure the smooth, effective and efficient functioning of the organization in question. Planning at the *macro level* also became part of everyday life in several market economies throughout the twentieth century. Planning in itself, even central planning, does not necessarily bring about a command economy. That happens only if the **plan is transformed into a set of compulsory targets to be achieved by way of political command**.[14]

Marxism-Leninism which attained the status of a state religion under Soviet communism. There are many contradictions which came to be presented as natural developments and seamless rejuvenation of the original Marxian thought. One of the most important issues is the *unilinear determinism of history* which predicted communism as an unavoidable destiny of mankind after the stages of antiquity, feudalism and capitalism. That made Marxism an utterly optimistic belief, which happily predicted the decline and ultimate disappearance of capitalism. But if original Marxian ideology had remained unchanged and kept being the guiding force of the Russian Social Democratic Party, it would have never been able to seize and consolidate power and there would be nothing for us now to analyze in terms of transition from communism back to capitalism.

[13] The debate over plan and market gained utmost importance right after the birth of Soviet communism as a practically functioning economic and societal management system. Economists of the famous Austrian school of economics immediately realized the mortal danger this system represented to a weakening market system and a decadent liberal democracy. Ludwig von Mises was the first to grasp the enormity of the challenge and unleashed a frontal attack in his seminal essay "Economic Calculation in the Socialist Commonwealth." It gained prominence only after it was (re)published in English, edited by Hayek, in "Collectivist Economic Planning: Critical Studies on the Possibilities of Socialism" (London, 1935).

[14] In fact, that was the dominant interpretation of (central) planning in all former communist economies, at least at the very beginning. In the classic version of Soviet commu-

In this respect the **mandatory nature of decisions made top-down** in an overcentralized super-bureaucracy is what constitutes the very backbone of a command economy and society, where individual freedom of choice (in both production and consumption) is alien and hostile to the smooth functioning of the system and, hence, it is extinguished to the greatest possible extent.[15]

Two vital questions follow from the above. First, whether the command economy can be **more effective and efficient** in harmonizing ever-changing needs with production.[16] Second, even if the command economy

---

nism—as we will see it in Chapter 1.3—targets of physical production (and, to a great extent, consumption) identified by both macro and micro level plans were *compulsory* and were disaggregated into more and more specific targets along the way. These targets constituted a **hierarchy of commands**, with little or no autonomy for the production units to attain them. That is exactly the reason why it is plausible to talk about a command economy in an idealtypical setting because the ultimate consequence of this horrendous edifice of mandatory planning targets is the creation of a fully hierarchical, totalitarian society. "What our planners demand is a central direction of all economic activity according to a single plan, laying down how the resources of society should be 'consciously directed' to serve particular ends in a definite way." Hayek (1944) 85.

[15] "Eastern European societies… organize social production in principle from one administrative centre, developing it according to the corporate power interest of this unified apparatus and subordinating it to the principle of the maximal extension of the material basis of the domination of the apparatus over society… It primarily takes the form of… restriction of the supply itself… partly in the direct material sense… partly indirectly, through the suspension of demand-supply mechanisms… In its pure form, therefore, this system tends to act as a **brutal dictatorship over needs**." (bolding mine) Fehér–Heller–Márkus (1983) 88–89.

[16] This issue is perhaps less relevant in the context of this book than in light of the contemporary and global economic and financial crisis which may lead to a renewal of the quest for socialism or at least for much more state intervention and regulation in the economy. Either way, it was undoubtedly one of the most important theoretical questions of political economy throughout the twentieth century. Belief in the superiority of mandatory central planning and, consequently, that of the command economy was unquestionable and widespread not only among Soviet and satellite communist leaders but also among Eastern and Western intelligentsia for a protracted period of time. Although compelling arguments were forwarded by Mises, Hayek, Robbins and other academics, these were largely dismissed as reactionary even by mainstream British economists and leftist scholars. (See the Introduction to *The Road to Serfdom*, written by the editor, Bruce Caldwell. The Definitive Edition. The University of Chicago Press, 2007.) After World War II it took more than two decades for the terminal illness of the command economy to become obvious to both Western and Eastern thinkers. Ironically, most people living under the communist system and perhaps even a good part of the nomenclature ceased to believe in the superiority of Soviet communism much earlier than many renowned representatives of Western and Eastern intelligentsia.

proves more effective and efficient in solving the evergreen problem of allocating scarce resources among competing uses, **is it worth sacrificing freedom** in society at the altar of abstract economic efficiency?[17]

The alleged superiority of the command economy was thought to be based on its capacity *to concentrate all information at the level of the state* in order to take stock of and pin down all different needs in the economy and allocate all disposable resources—in quantity as well as in quality—according to the *relative importance* of these needs. It was clear, however, that not all needs can be satisfied immediately, therefore, it was considered imperative that society—or its representative, the state—be empowered to make deliberate choices and formulate an *order of ranking* among these needs.

In subsistence and hydraulic societies, where the spectrum of goods and services consumed was *rather narrow and relatively stable* (i.e. it did not change over time or changed very slowly), these wants and needs were sufficiently well known, fixed and sanctioned by *tradition, religion, societal status, gender, age*, etc. In these societies the coordination of material needs with disposable productive resources was sufficiently simple, and usually happened almost automatically, without any significant deliberate action, *without much intervention from above*. That is absolutely key. Under such circumstances what we have is a system of *classic natural redistribution*.[18] That is effective (simple in process and procedure) and efficient (ensures the reproduction of society) and legitimate (members of society largely accept both the mechanism and the outcome).

---

[17] This question is much more important. Benito Mussolini is said to have claimed already in the 1920s that the reason why his regime was obliged to abolish individual freedoms was that Italian civilization was already far ahead of the Western one. Communists and fascists alike maintained that civilization marching forward would inevitably restrict, if not eliminate, outdated and outmoded individualism. Therefore, it was a matter of principle for those who believed in civil liberties and individual (human) rights to fight against even the stealth advancement of totalitarianism in name of compulsory central planning.

[18] Karl Polanyi discussed systems of reciprocity and redistribution as important historical antecedents to the self-regulating market. He maintained that these principles of behavior were not primarily aimed at ensuring some separately definable economic outcomes. Rather, these principles of behavior were there to serve the **integrity and cohesion** of these societies and, incidentally, they played an economic role as well. [See Polanyi (1946).] That is precisely what I have in mind when emphasizing the *embedded nature of a command economy*. There is no separation among societal spheres of existence, there is no stand alone economy, no independent logic of the economy to determine or influence the functioning of other spheres.

The picture changes fundamentally when considering an *economy*—no matter how underdeveloped it is—a *society*—no matter how preindustrial its stratification looks like—and an *ideology*—no matter how modern it claims to be—defined by the **overwhelming aspiration of fastest possible economic growth, and the ultimate desire to surpass all other economic and societal formations in terms of welfare and material abundance**. Unless we presuppose that this growth is without the slightest modification in the structure of needs or production, it is inconceivable to believe that the *administrative coordination mechanism*, upon which the functioning of the whole economy depends, remains effective and efficient. When needs change, production must change, too. If certain natural resources are no longer abundantly available, needs must also change or at least their *relative importance*. New needs may and do emerge by the day. New production methods are to be developed by science and by technological innovation. **New information is created every single day** and it is supposed to be very detailed and absolutely precise in order for it to be used properly.[19]

Moreover, this knowledge needs to be collected, analyzed and decisions made upon its best possible use should be transmitted to the production units **without delay and distortion**. It must find its way into the great macro mechanism which would keep ensuring the seamless, smooth and optimal satisfaction of needs sanctioned by the plan as approved by the

[19] "In the first place it is clear if central direction is to take the place of the initiative of the manager of the individual enterprise… it will not be sufficient that it takes the form of mere general direction, but it will have to include and be intimately responsible for details of the most minute description. It is impossible to decide rationally how much material or new machinery should be assigned to any one enterprise and at what price (in an accounting sense) it will be rational to do so, without also deciding at the same time whether and in which way the machinery and tools already in use should continue to be used or be disposed of. It is matters of this sort, details of technique, the saving of one material rather than the other or any one of the small economies which cumulatively decide the success or failure of a firm; and in any central plan which is not to be hopelessly wasteful they must be taken into account of. In order to be able to do so, it will be necessary to treat every machine, every tool, or building not just one of a class of physically similar objects but as an individual whose usefulness is determined by its particular state of wear and tear, its location, etc. The same applies to every batch of commodities which is situated at a different place or which differs in any other respect from other batches. This means that, in order to achieve that degree of economy in this respect which is secured by the competitive system, the calculations of the central planning authority would have to treat the existing body of instrumental goods as being constituted of almost as many different types of good as there are individual units." Hayek (1948) 153–154.

state, party, or any other body of supreme command enjoying high societal legitimacy. And this is exactly what is completely impossible.[20]

The vested interests of various state and party organs in distorting information and tampering instructions according to their particular needs should not be underestimated either. There was no omniscient and omnipotent center which would have been able to control fully lower level organizations of economic management. Rather, there was an iterative process within a multilayered hierarchy all parts of which possessed only partial information but all had their own vested interests in using them to their own benefit. Despite official claims, the formally parallel but in reality superimposed state-party structure was not there to eliminate distortions created by human fallibility. Quite the contrary: it had a function **to create distortions in order to justify its apparent role in correcting them.**

The corollary of the above must now be more than obvious: *societal institutions are never neutral channels of information dissemination.*

As a consequence, there was a *basic, unavoidable, inescapable and, ultimately, insoluble contradiction* built into the very system of Soviet communism. On the one hand, it claimed to be a historical, and historic, formation superior to market capitalism in terms of growth-potential and its capacity to satisfy the material and cultural needs of society ultimately on a level higher than anything considered possible under market capitalism. Its aspiration for economic growth—and, for that matter, higher rate of growth than anything possible under capitalism—was a basic pillar of its ideology and its claim for historical legitimacy. On the other hand, it chose a seemingly ultramodern but in reality *brutally antiquated and backward economic and societal model*—i.e. the **command economy and totalitarian society**—which proved to be completely incompatible and inconsistent with the attainment of these solemn objectives. At this level it is easy to conclude that although the theoretical model of a command economy and society is not unfeasible**, it was inconsistent with the self-**

[20] The most important arguments of Hayek describing in detail why central planning—although technically not impossible—**cannot be more effective and efficient than the market mechanism** is contained in his trilogy with the common name: "Socialist Calculation." The first two of the articles appeared first in a book edited by him and entitled *Collectivist Economic Planning* (London, George Routledge & Sons, 1935), the third in *Economica* (May, 1940). All three were reprinted again in a new collection of essays entitled *Individualism and Economic Order* (The University of Chicago Press, 1948). Subsequent editions of this book constitute now the most common source of references, including that of footnote 19.

declared goals of Soviet communism. That is why the latter ultimately proved to be *unable to achieve its own primary objectives.*[21]

This conclusion is less important now, after the fall of Soviet communism. Had it been clear a hundred years ago, it would have been possible to avoid one of the most brutal, expensive, inhumane and futile attempts of building a utopian society. Trying to achieve unattainable goals and pursuing them ruthlessly against the will of hundreds of millions throughout a protracted period of time was one of the utmost tragedies of the twentieth century.

1.2. The historical evolution of Soviet communism

In late 1917 the Bolshevik revolution was victorious in a geographically extremely vast, closed, poor, still very much underdeveloped and largely agrarian economy completely exhausted and pushed into economic chaos and societal disintegration by a historically unprecedented mechanized war. Under these circumstances, to pursue an economic strategy centered on promoting fast reconstruction and growth, especially that of heavy industrial output, was considered important for the new regime not only from the viewpoint of its ideology but it was imperative for sheer survival.

In practice, *Soviet communist economic and societal governance was born from the Prussian–Russian model of the war economy.* That suited the revolutionary party of the Bolsheviks tremendously well. The imperative to win the civil war against the White, assisted by sporadic, but still meaningful foreign intervention, legitimized the extreme concentration and military deployment of almost all natural, financial and human re-

[21] The fact that a societal system is inconsistent with its own declared goals and, hence, proves unable to attain them does not mean that it has to collapse and disappear as an unavoidable historical necessity. First, societal systems may or may not include *goal rationality*. Second, as Max Weber famously recognized, **rationality is not identical with rationalization**. Soviet communism, although lacking *calculative rationality* in its classical variation to a great extent, made extraordinary efforts to rationalizations, especially at the level of its official ideology. Rationalization may be sufficient to maintain legitimacy, especially if the latter does not exclusively depend on ideology. Legitimation can also be provided by tradition, charisma, nationalism, religion, etc. It is noteworthy that Soviet communism turned out to be quite weak on all counts and still it survived more that seventy years. As it is analyzed in the next chapter, *historical conditions and developments on balance* proved to be quite favorable for the system to survive for so long.

sources. **War communism**,[22] was an attempt to create immediately and vigorously a *command economy*, if not yet a fully controlled and essentially hierarchical *command society*.[23] Democratic traditions, almost completely non-existent in Russian society, did not impede the introduction of an extremely harsh regime of rigid overcentralization. Efforts against an existential threat seem to have justified and legitimized the comprehensive militarization of the domestic economy and society.[24]

The three years of war communism—from mid-1918 to mid-1921—was an extraordinary period of war, destruction, famine on the one hand, and chaos, anarchy, inexperience, incompetence in public administration on the other. It is impossible to describe events in this period as reflecting the orderly implementation of a well-designed and carefully thought-through blueprint of *communist economic and societal governance and management*.[25] Nevertheless, ideological considerations did have an im-

---

[22] Oskar Lange, the prominent Polish theoretician of market socialism regarded the whole Soviet system at least until Stalin's death as a *sui generis* war economy. His lecture delivered in 1957 in Belgrade describing the characteristics of the Soviet economy is cited at length by Alec Nove (1961), 161–162.

[23] "War communism is the name commonly given to the period of extreme communization which began in the middle of 1918, i.e., eight months after the revolution had triumphed. It is therefore necessary to trace the events of the intervening period. Did fully-fledged war communism arise out of a series of improvisations, due to the exigencies of war and collapse, or was it consciously introduced as a deliberate leap into socialism, and ascribed to the war emergency when its failure was found to be discreditable to the regime? Both schools of thought exist." Nove (1969) 48.

[24] "So we can identify the following characteristics of war communism:

(1) An attempt to ban private manufacture, the nationalization of nearly all industry, the allocation of nearly all material stocks, and of what little output there was, by the state, especially for war purposes.
(2) A ban on private trade, never quite effective anywhere, but spasmodically enforced.
(3) Seizure of peasant surpluses (*prodrazverstka*).
(4) The partial elimination of money from the state dealings with its own organizations and the citizens. Free rations, when there was anything to ration.
(5) All these factors combined with terror and arbitrariness, expropriations, requisitions. Efforts to establish discipline, with party control over trade unions. A siege economy with a communist ideology. A partly-organized chaos. Sleepless, leather-jacketed commissars working round the clock in a vain effort to replace the free market." Ibid., 74.

[25] Actually, there was no such general or detailed blueprint of how the economic and societal governance and management system of communism should look like. Marx and Engels not only refused to speculate on it, but ridiculed all those people within and outside the Social Democratic movement who bothered to come up with such a tentative blueprint. As a consequence, there was no consistent and detailed plan based on Marxist

pact on what type of policy was adopted and what specific measures were introduced no matter how effective or ineffectual, timely or premature, justifiable or unnecessary these might have been. Nationalization of banking and capitalist syndicates covering strategic industries, such as iron, coal, oil, sugar, were steps driven by both practical necessity and ideological fervor.[26] At the same time, heavy industry, represented by large enterprises, was relatively easy to bring under close administrative control. There was little or no attempt, at least in the years of the war communism, to extend state ownership to the vast majority of the Russian economy, consisting overwhelmingly of small scale industry, trade and agriculture, despite fierce ideological battles and political demand.

It is worth emphasizing that in 1917 the Russian Bolshevik party came to power in an *overwhelmingly agrarian and peasant society*. One of the most important guarantees for its victory in the civil war and the survival of the new regime thereafter was the smart move of *distributing land and entitle millions of peasants to acquire at least de facto ownership of land*[27] which formerly had been in the hands of the aristocracy.[28] Peasants were

---

ideology as to how a new proletarian government should operate from day one after taking power. Lenin made some efforts to draw up some sketches about post-revolutionary economic management but it was just theorizing about what was already available on the basis of wartime Prussian and tzarist practice.

[26] "… we must allow for the interaction of Bolshevik ideas with the desperate situation in which they found themselves. To take one example among many: rationing and the banning of private trade in foodstuffs were essential features of the period, and came to be regarded as good in themselves. Yet both these measures were common enough among belligerent nations, and in fact the Provisional government had endeavoured somewhat inefficiently to do just these things… to put it another way: actions taken in abnormal circumstances for practical reasons are often clothed in ideological garb and are justified by reference to high principles. It is all too easy then to conclude, with documentary evidence to prove it, that the action was due to a principle." Nove (1969) 47.

[27] "The land decree of 8 November 1917, adopted by the Congress of the Soviets and embodied in a law promulgated in February 1918, followed the lines of the programme, in this instance 'borrowed' from the radical wing of the SRs. (Social Revolutionary Party—LB) Local committees and Soviets were to supervise land distribution. Land was nationalized, the right to use it belonged to the peasants. None should have more than he alone could cultivate, since hiring of labour was to be forbidden." Ibid., 48.

[28] Contrary to conventional wisdom, land reform, including a wholesale redistribution of arable land among landless peasants was not a primary objective in communist ideology. Even the Social Democrats, the main political vanguard of socialism in the late 19th century, were quite ambivalent about agrarian reform and the role the peasant class was supposed to play in the historical progress of the industrializing capitalist society. Peasants were almost always considered backward, uncultured, uncultivated and conservative elements in society way behind the working class in terms of their capacity to or-

willing to fight and make tremendous sacrifices during the civil war in the hope of consolidating their ownership of land. They provided an unexhaustible reservoir of manpower to the nascent Red Army.

However, the peasants in Russia were no fans of Bolshevik power and ideology in any respect. Once the threat of outside intervention and restoration of aristocratic land tenure was subsiding, the peasants expected more autonomy in production and much fairer treatment in trade, both internal and external. That was slow in coming, but—surprisingly—it did come.

Instead of installing a full-fledged command economy, the Bolshevik party led by Lenin introduced a *New Economic Policy* (NEP) in late 1921.[29] The NEP was made unavoidable by the catastrophic consequences of war communism and the revolt of both the peasant society and some of the elite troops in the armed forces.[30] The revolutionary ideas of a narrow elite put in practice at the detriment of the vast majority of society proved to be grossly inefficient and wholly untenable just three years after the revolution. It was time to make a wholesale retreat in order to avoid the fate of Robespierre.[31]

Guaranteeing the **food supply** for the troops of the Red Army and for the urban working class was by far the most important and pressing eco-

---

ganize themselves. Their winning over to the proletarian revolution was regarded as a tactical necessity rather than a strategic goal.

[29] There are many descriptions of the NEP wishing to decide whether it was the "true path" of communism or just a deviation, made necessary by practical imperatives. A Hungarian economist, László Szamuely, tried to prove that NEP was the true face of socialism from the beginning, thus making the Hungarian New Economic Mechanism (NEM), which started in 1968, look like more legitimate. [See Szamuely (1971).]

[30] "We have seen how, all the way up to February 1921, Lenin kept stubbornly on the course of all-round nationalization, centralization, the elimination of money, and, above all, the maintenance of *prodrazverstka*. There was no pressure on him from his colleagues to change this policy. Events, rather than the central committee, provided a potent means of persuasion. The first public sign of second thoughts came in a speech at the plenary session of the Moscow Soviet, on 28 February 1921: he saw the point of a delegate's argument to the effect that the peasants needed to know what they have to deliver to the state, i.e. that the seizure of surpluses be replaced by a tax in kind (*prodnalog*); they would consider this proposal. Once this idea was accepted, however reluctantly, it was bound to lead to a reconsideration of the entire basis of the war communism economy. Any hesitations (Lenin) may have had left on the subject were overcome when the peasant risings in many parts of the country were followed by the Kronstadt sailors' revolt." Nove (1969) 83.

[31] In many of his writings, Lenin himself used the analogy of the French revolution when explaining to his own comrades why it was necessary to deviate from orthodox communist ideology.

nomic and social problem in post-revolutionary Russia. It was clearly connected to the motivations and dedicated work of the peasantry which constituted the overwhelming majority of society. The second issue, not very far from the first but still somewhat less immediate, was rapid **industrialization, with a special emphasis on heavy industry, on the production of armaments**. More often than not, *these objectives came into conflict in Russian economic history.*[32] While this conflict need not necessarily present itself in practice, *the specific way of Soviet development shows a remarkable continuity with previous, pre-revolutionary Russian patterns of development in this regard.*

In essence, the main question at the time was **how to overcome crushing economic backwardness in a semi-feudal society where there was little or no market incentive to domestic capital accumulation** and, hence, industrialization—as the most fundamental way of growing out of economic backwardness—could not be based on the voluntary and profitable delivery of surplus food produced by a dynamic and fast growing agricultural sector.

---

[32] "The main reason for the abysmal economic backwardness of Russia was the preservation of serfdom until the emancipation of 1861. In a certain sense, this very fact may be attributed to the play of a curious mechanism of economic backwardness, and a few words of explanation may be in order. In the course of its process of territorial expansion, which over a few centuries transferred the small duchy of Moscow into the huge land mass of modern Russia, the country became increasingly involved in military conflicts with the West. This involvement revealed a curious internal conflict between the tasks of the Russian government that were "modern" in the contemporary sense of the word and the hopelessly backward economy of the country on which the military policies had to be based. As a result, the economic development of Russia at several important junctures assumed the form of a peculiar series of sequences: (1) Basic was the fact that the state, moved by its military interests, assumed the role of the primary agent propelling the economic progress in the country. (2) The fact that economic development thus became a function of military exigencies imparted a peculiarly jerky character to the course of that development; it proceeded fast whenever military necessities were pressing and subsided as the military pressures relaxed. (3) This mode of economic progress by fits and starts implied that, whenever a considerable upsurge of economic activities was required, a very formidable burden was placed on the shoulders of the generations whose lifespan happened to coincide with the period of intensified development. (4) In order to exact effectively the great sacrifices it required, the government had to subject the reluctant population to a number of severe measures of oppression lest the burdens imposed be evaded by escape to the frontier regions in the southeast and east. (5) Precisely because of the magnitude of the governmental exactions, a period of rapid development was very likely to give way to prolonged stagnation, because the great effort had been pushed beyond the physical endurance of the population and long periods of economic stagnation were the inevitable consequences." Gerschenkron (1962) 17.

In this respect, the NEP was clearly a *retreat to more market orientation*, more voluntary cooperation and less terror and coercion, especially, towards the peasants. It was a political imperative as well as an economic necessity. However, any partial rehabilitation of market forces and market coordination represented insurmountable challenges to Soviet power. These challenges appeared at least on three distinct levels.

First, increasing marketable output from agriculture implied the support of or at least a *tolerant attitude towards larger-scale capitalist farming*. But Lenin was absolutely right in pointing out that the dominance of market conditions in agriculture would inevitably reproduce both capitalists and capitalist relations of production by the day and that was quite logically considered a fatal threat to the very existence of the socialist experiment.[33]

Second, leaving a significant portion of agricultural surplus for rural reinvestment and higher level of consumption at the peasant households *would have reduced considerably valuable resources available for industrial accumulation in urban areas*.

Third, the eventual preferential treatment of the peasant majority would have called into *question the legitimacy of Soviet power* based on the promise of fast industrialization, economic convergence, and the primacy of the working class in society.[34] Why should have been there an excessive centralization of political power if there was no need for the excessive centralization of economic power?

It is no surprise, therefore, that the NEP, with all its ups and downs, lasted only until Stalin finally consolidated his iron-fisted grip and unchallengeable supremacy at the helm of the fully centralized Soviet Commu-

[33] "Small production engenders capitalism and the bourgeoisie continuously, daily, hourly, spontaneously, and on a massive scale." Lenin (1920) 1964–1972, 8.

"If a society allows for the existence of a large number of small commodity producers, and if it permits them to accumulate capital and grow over time, a genuine group of capitalists will emerge sooner or later… Without a doubt, the more successful private businesses would begin to accumulate and grow… The sustained growth of private businesses also runs counter to the ideological premises of the system, and will therefore be held in check by a ruling party and government unwilling to tolerate a significant capitalist sector." Kornai (2008) 32–33.

[34] "Private ownership and private enterprise are foreign to classical socialism and in the long term it cannot tolerate them. The centralized, nationalized order of this society is disturbed not only by large-scale capital but the existence of small-scale peasant ownership. Central power, sooner or later, depending on its tolerance threshold, sets about eliminating it. The Soviet Union waited more than a decade before launching mass collectivization." But it finally did. Ibid., 10.

nist Party. **Totalitarian concentration of political power was a prerequisite for launching the campaign of forced collectivization and industrialization**. By the late 1920s and early 1930s, the true nature of the Soviet communist variant of the totalitarian system was revealed; the dynamic forces of the command economy got finally unleashed.

The specific model of industrialization pursued in the Soviet Union was based on late nineteenth-century patterns observable in relatively large, backward, and latecomer European countries, primarily the second German Reich and the Austro-Hungarian monarchy but also late tsarist Russian empire itself.[35] Emphasis on **heavy industry**, including *coal mining, iron and steel production*, *electricity generation*, *machine building* (to produce modern mechanized armaments), *railway construction* (to ensure fast transportation of military hardware and troops) and, increasingly, *chemical and electrical industry* was strikingly similar to the main characteristics of industrialization carried out 40 years earlier. The primacy of producing investment goods led to the dominance of *large-size factories* employing the then *most advanced technology* and thus requiring *highly qualified engineers* on the one hand and relatively few *low skilled workers* on the other. It was almost a perfect match to communist ideology and to command-type economic management.

We should never forget that forced industrialization and collectivization was started in the Soviet Union exactly at the same time when the

---

[35] The second German Reich and the Austro-Hungarian monarchy were large economic units and at least strong rivals if not enemies of tsarist Russia throughout the second half of the nineteenth century, therefore, they provided an undeniable reference point for designing policies to combat economic backwardness in Russia. "The progress of Russian industrialization suffered from relative shortage of capital, as well as from a poorly developed banking system and a generally low standard of commercial morality. The traditional Muscovite merchants, rich and uneducated, were far from being the prototypes of modern commercial capitalism. The situation changed towards the end of the nineteenth century, and particularly during the rapid industrialization which characterized the nineties. There was marked growth of both Russian and foreign capital, and an equal improvement in the banking system. Russian entrepreneurs of a modern type began more and more to emerge. Under cover of the protective tariff of 1891, and with the establishment of a stabilized rouble based on the gold standard, foreign capital received every encouragement. This was particularly the work of Count Witte, who exercised a dominant influence over Russian financial and commercial policy at this time. His public statements and papers make it abundantly clear that he was pursuing deliberately a policy of industrialization, and that the dominant motive was the traditional one that a relatively backward Russia must catch up with the more developed powers, particularly in her potential to produce the means of national power, above all armaments." Nove (1969) 17–18.

developed Western world entered into one of its most dangerous and fatal economic, financial, social and moral crises ever happened in the history of capitalism. It is more than just coincidence. *The Great Depression, which engulfed the developed Western capitalist market economies in 1929–33, provided yet another powerful argument, maybe a good excuse, but first and foremost a brilliant opportunity and excellent justification for Stalin and the whole Soviet ruling elite to undertake an unprecedentedly aggressive and excessive drive for coercive industrialization.*[36]

For rapid industrialization based on violent expropriation of any surplus above subsistence produced in agriculture and focusing on heavy industry represented by oversized plants, the overarching command system was not only a logical way of economic management consistent with the political and ideological prerequisites but also feasible and not difficult to implement. Comprehensive bureacratization and militarization of

---

[36] "The Soviet government can be properly described as the product of the country's economic backwardness… If anything is a 'grounded historical assumption,' this would seem to be one: the delayed industrial revolution was responsible for a political revolution in the course of which the power fell into the hands of a dictatorial government to which in the long run the vast majority of the population was opposed. It is one thing for such a government to gain power in a moment of great crisis; it is another to maintain this power for a long period. Whatever the strength of the army and the ubiquitousness of the secret police which such a government may have at its disposal, it would be naïve to believe that those instruments of physical oppression can suffice. Such a government can maintain itself in power only if it succeeds in making people believe that it performs an important social function which could not be discharged in its absence.

Industrialization provided such a function for the Soviet government. All the basic factors in the situation of the country pressed in that direction. By reverting to a pattern of development that should have remained confined to a long-bygone age, by substituting collectivization for serfdom, and by pushing up the rate of investment to the maximum point within the limits of endurance of the population, the Soviet government did what no government relying on the consent of the governed could have done. That these policies, after having led through a period of violent struggles, have resulted in permanent day-to-day friction between the government and the population is undeniable. But, paradoxical it may sound, these policies at the same time have secured some broad acquiescence on the part of the people. If all the forces of the population can be engaged in the processes of industrialization and if this industrialization can be justified by the promise of happiness and abundance for future generations and—much more importantly—by the menace of military aggression from beyond the borders, the dictatorial government will find its power broadly unchallenged. And the vindication of a threatening war is easily produced, as is shown by the history of cold war years. Economic backwardness, rapid industrialization, ruthless exercise of dictatorial power, and the danger of war have become inextricably intertwined in Soviet Russia." Gerschenkron (1962) 28–29.

the economy made administrative governance of a still primitive economy not only possible but perhaps also relatively effective.[37]

Events followed each other with quick succession. The first five-year plan was adopted in the spring of 1929 and it represented a very ambitious overstretch of resources. Private trade was banned and made a crime of speculation in 1930. Employment for private gain was outlawed in 1932.

The Stalinist system descending upon Soviet Russia in the 1930s was a logical extension and consistent realization of Bolshevik ideology, and, above all, it represented a new, sinister culture, fully compatible with totalitarianism. Collectivization and industrialization were pursued not only with ruthless cruelty but even more so with a **comprehensive fragmentation of society**. One of the most important methods was to instill fear into the hearts and minds of people as a new source of motivation replacing profit, solidarity.[38]

Cultural life was incorporated into the emerging totalitarianism in general. In the cultural sphere Stalin brought about a violent breach of the past.[39] No more dramatic manifestation was imaginable than the suicide of

---

[37] See Kornai (1992) Chapter 15, "The Coherence of the Classical System."

[38] A very typical manifestation of this seismic shift in culture was the "pursuit of the enemy from within." The enemy, real or imagined, of the Soviet system was supposed and suspected to be always there to commit "sabotage" to slow down or hinder the relentless drive to catch up with the more developed West.

"Sabotage everywhere: at tractors, combine harvesters, etc. sabotage everywhere. Is that really true? Why would the peasants deliberately destroy expensive machinery? Members of the *kolkhozy?* Why would they do that? It turns out that there is no any other way for us. Our peasants have known only one single tool for centuries, the axe. We put them on tractors, combines, cars and then they wreck them because they do not know and understand them because they are ignorant. So what shall we do? Shall we wait until the village becomes technically skilled; gets rid of its century-old underdevelopment, until the nature of the peasant, formed during centuries, changes? In the meantime, shall we let him wreck the tractors, combines and cars? We cannot afford it because it took us great sacrifice to obtain them. Neither can we wait because the capitalist countries will suffocate us. **There is only one means available to us: fear**. It is embodied in the word "sabotage." Should you wreck the tractor, you are a saboteur, you get ten years in prison for that… And there is no any other way out for us; we save the machinery, the industry, the country and the future." Rybakov (1987), my translation and bolding.

[39] "The cultural transformation of the age, no less than the social and economic changes, bears little relationship to anything that went before in Russian history—not even to the garrison atmosphere and fierce proletarian emphases of the Civil War period. Proletarian origins and Marxist convictions were losing all importance. Indeed, the Marxist intellectuals who had played a key part in refining Communist ideology and building the new Soviet state became increasingly prime victims in the

several outstanding figures of revolutionary culture, like that of Yesenin in 1925 and Mayakovsky in 1930. That year was really a turning point in many respects. It witnessed the formal abolition of all what had so far remained of private printing. Voronsky, the literary theorist, Deborin, the philosopher, and many others were forced to recant and repent publicly. Their followers were also expelled from official life. All aesthetic and artistic ferment, which was so characteristic to the twenties, died out between 1930 and 1932.

Finally, this was the time when the **state was restored and rebuilt** in practice not only to an extent previously unknown and unprecedented as a totalitarian creature without limits, but also as a sacrosanct and heretofore *fundamental pillar of communist ideology*. Earlier references made by Lenin and others to the disappearance of the state were ignored, put into brackets or left out to dry.

Within the state and the party or parallel with it, a monster was created: the **secret police and the system of forced labor camps**. After the assassination of Kirov, a potential rival to Stalin, on December 1, 1934, state orchestrated terror and repression engulfed the whole society.[40]

And then the moment of grace arrived. World War II was an immense tragedy to the peoples of the Soviet Union. **But it was a blessing for the Stalinist system**. Without the Great Patriotic War, as the German–Russian conflict came to be known in Soviet parlance, Soviet Communism may not have survived for so long and, definitely, could not have extended its rule to a still larger part of the globe.

---

new purges of the thirties, and fanatical proletarian advocates of Revolutionary egalitarianism were denounced as 'levelers' and left deviationists. There was no serious threat to the Soviet state in the late twenties: and by 1930 the depression in the West had made the danger of 'capitalist encirclement' even more remote and contrived." Billington (1966) 523.

[40] "Despite the very severe situation in the Soviet Union in the years 1930–1933 there was no serious opposition to Stalin. No one disputed his role as party leader because first of all, his personal power was very great in the early thirties. He had virtually unchallenged control over the rapidly growing and highly centralized party apparatus but also… over the security organs. Under these conditions opposition to Stalin was extremely dangerous; many who in the past had been quite critical of him now felt frozen by fear. Secondly, many of the miscalculations and crimes that Stalin committed before 1934 were not fully revealed until later, some only after his death. Only a very few people, for example were privy to the secret rigging of the 1930–1931 trials. Moreover, some of Stalin's crimes and blunders were extolled by the propaganda machine as great achievements." Medvedev (1989) 327–328.

This must be a shocking statement. On second thought, however, it is just common sense. There are several reasons for this.[41]

First, the war was clearly a defensive one against an existential threat. It produced an *absolute moral imperative* to fight against Nazi Germany[42] for friend and foe of the Soviet system alike. Under such existential threat it was almost impossible to separate the societal system from the motherland.[43]

Second, all sufferings, hardships, privation and sacrifice quickly gained an *emotionally acceptable ultimate reason*. Thus, **the legitimacy of the Soviet system grew tremendously almost overnight**. There was hardly any need for additional factors of legitimacy during the war.[44]

---

[41] I described this line of reasoning first in an essay published in Hungarian [Bokros (2007) 226–228.]

[42] The Soviet Union under Stalin's leadership was not only a convenient and willing economic partner of Nazi Germany throughout the 1930s, but an enthusiastic supporter and even an admirer of its achievements. Nothing is more revealing in this respect than the language of the infamous Molotov-Ribbentrop pact. Contrary to present-day official Russian explanation, which is still trying to justify the carve-out of Poland and the annexation of the Baltic states as well as Bessarabia, Stalin clearly felt that the restoration of the former borders of tsarist Russia was a historic necessity. The best proof for the true intentions of Stalin was provided by the disastrous winter war against Finland. After the partition and annexation of Poland into Nazi Germany and Soviet Russia, Stalin's greed grew tremendously and the Soviet Union attacked Finland on November 30, 1939, without declaration of war. [See Lukacs (1976) 92–97.]

[43] That is not to say that it was impossible to welcome invading German troops as liberators from Soviet oppression by significant groups of Russians, Ukrainians, etc. especially peasants, at the beginning of the war. But the brutal and inhumane behavior of the occupying forces created disillusionment very quickly. Nazi totalitarianism—like its Soviet counterpart—was also self-defeating in the sense that ideological demands pushed aside rational military calculations. The fact that SS-Sonderkommando forces took over the policing and administration of occupied territories from the Wehrmacht and implemented ideologically driven policies of oppression and even extermination left little choice to the local population but to expect and, by way of partisan activity, support the return of Soviet power. [See "Nazi Conspiracy and Aggression" (1946).]

[44] Nevertheless, Stalin and his comrades felt the necessity to rely upon additional factors of legitimacy throughout the whole Patriotic war. One such institution was the Orthodox church and religion in general. Even the vocabulary of the Soviet leaders was changed to express the all-encompassing and all-inclusive nature of the war effort. People were no longer addressed as "comrades" in public speeches but they were referred to as "compatriots." Russian national symbols were reinstated as well as symbols of other Soviet nations. The high and popular culture of the Patriotic war did not emphasize communist ideology. Instead, it used ample references to former glorious historical accomplishments, like the successful fight of Kutuzov against Napoleon, etc. [See Deutscher (1949).]

Third, *the command economy was fully consistent with the war efforts.* In fact, a war economy was much more coherent than classical communism.[45] Although it could not produce such spectacular growth rates as the classical Stalinist model of forced industrialization, but that was no longer important. The quintessential factor of effectiveness was the fast relocation of factories and reallocation of resources to the production of military hardware and, at the same time, assure the minimum physical survival of the people at large. There was no need for incentives based on mundane material interest, not even for monetary wage commensurate with performance.[46]

Fourth, the Soviet Union was regarded the lesser evil first by the UK then by the US leadership compared to Nazi Germany. *The Soviet Union became an important ally of the Anglo-Saxon powers* after it had been attacked by Germany on June 22, 1941. As a result, Soviet relations to the Western democracies changed for the better almost overnight.[47] The Soviet Union received significant material assistance from its allies, and, furthermore, valuable political and moral support. Its standing and prestige in the eyes of Western public opinion improved tremendously making it impossible to start a war against it.[48]

Fifth, the paramount importance of defeating Nazi Germany made it not only indispensable but also acceptable that the Red Army swept through a number of hitherto independent states[49] and thus created a "fait

[45] Oskar Lange, the most prominent proponent of *market socialism,* described the whole Stalinist system as war economy. He felt that war communism, while coherent, was sustainable only under extreme circumstances of either external threat or brutal internal repression. That was not considered a desirable alternative by him at all. It was the most compelling reason why he felt the need to elaborate the theory of market socialism in 1936–37. [See Lange (1936–37).]

[46] See Nove (1969) Chapter 10. "The Great Patriotic War."

[47] It was far from easy to bring about a turnaround in Soviet-UK relationship after the Nazi attack on the Soviet Union. Previous events, like the Molotov-Ribbentrop pact, the partition of Poland, the annexation of the Baltic states, the war against Finland, etc. did not increase Western trust in the Soviet foreign policy.

[48] That was certainly true until 1950, when the Korean War started. But no matter how tragic and painful this new East-West conflagration may have been, it was just a proxy war rather than a head-on collision between the new superpowers, the nuclear-armed United States and the Soviet Union. And by that time the victory of Mao's army in mainland China made international communism militarily practically invincible.

[49] Most of these countries came to be occupied by Nazi Germany in various stages of WWII; therefore, they cannot be regarded as truly independent states thereafter. The first victim were the Czech lands of former Czechoslovakia, the second was Poland. Yugoslavia was dismembered in 1941 when the German army was heading towards

accompli" on the ground for the subsequent extension of communist power in the Baltics, a very large part of Mitteleuropa and the Balkans. *The successful Western offensive of the Soviet army in 1944–45 "liberated," willingly or otherwise, friend and foe* alike and the occupation left them no choice but adopting and, adapting to, communist structures of economic and societal management.

Sixth, after having acquired the nuclear bomb, the *Soviet Union became a military superpower* matched only by the United States. Its geopolitical weight, prestige and importance increased tremendously. The West was no longer in a position even to contemplate the liberation of peoples living under communist rule. The maximum ambition of Western powers could be to block the further advancement of Soviet rule. The new geopolitical strategy was labeled by the slogans of "*deterrence*" and "*containment.*"[50] This was a sea change in both strategy and perception compared to what had prevailed between the two world wars.

The apogee of Stalinism as a global politico-military undertaking and imperial power was in 1948–50, exactly in the middle of the twentieth century. The Soviet Communist empire reached its largest territorial extension. Apart from Titoist Yugoslavia, which remained a rather insignificant outpost from geostrategic point of view, the expanding communist world was unified by the unchallengeable dominance of Stalinism which at that time was readily accepted by the recently victorious communists in mainland China as well.[51]

By 1948–50 the post-war reconstruction period was largely over in the Soviet Union and in the new satellite countries of Central and Eastern

---

Greece and occupied some parts of it. Hungary came under direct German rule only on March 19, 1944 in order to prevent its eventual switch to the Western powers in the final stages of the war. Romania and Bulgaria remained free from German troops all along.

50 George Kennan was the father of this concept. He sent his famous long cable to the Secretary of Defense of the US in 1946 in which he set the framework of, and a justification for, a new American policy to temper the spread of communism. It was reformulated in a pseudonymous article (The X Article) entitled the "The Sources of Soviet Conduct" published in *Foreign Affairs* in July 1947. After an elaborate and in-depth analysis of the genesis and nature of Soviet power, the key conclusion of Kennan reads as follows: "In these circumstances it is clear that the main element of any United States policy toward the Soviet Union must be that of long-term, patient but firm and vigilant containment of Russian expansive tendencies."

51 "Between 1917 and 1950, the Soviet system represented an ideological threat to the West, while the West presented a military threat to the Soviet Union… Henceforth, the West will be an ideological threat to the Soviet Union and the USSR a military threat to the West." Todd (1979) 111.

Europe. The vastly expanded communist world initiated rapid economic growth and contemplated further military expansion. The ill-advised Korean War started on June 25, 1950 and, despite massive Chinese and Soviet assistance, it ended in a draw with an armistice signed on July 27, 1953. *There has been no further significant, permanently successful territorial expansion of the Soviet communist system any more.*[52]

1.3. Three basic models of communism in Central and Eastern Europe

In 1950 and beyond the classical (Stalinist) model was unquestionably considered not only as the *only acceptable* model of communism from ideological point of view, but also as the *only conceivable* universal application of the true orthodox design throughout the vastly expanded world of Soviet–Chinese Eurasia. Although deviations started to emerge in the fringes of this huge landmass rather soon, there was yet no sign of any of them developing into a viable alternative model of communist economic and societal management.[53]

The classical (Stalinist) model, as it is best known today, had the following major characteristics:

1. *Exclusive state ownership of most, if not all non-agricultural means of production.* That was much more than simple legal expropriation of assets of companies formerly in private hands. It meant that the **whole economy was functioning as if it were just one single large enterprise**.

[52] The only exception was Viet Nam. After a more than 30-year long ferocious armed struggle, first against the French colonial power, then against the United States, the whole territory of Viet Nam fell under communist rule in 1975 and has remained governed by the Communist party ever since. But Viet Nam today has a fast growing, rather successful, although still overregulated and somewhat arbitrarily governed *capitalist market economy*, which by no means can be labeled as a Soviet-style command system.

[53] When Tito broke with Stalin in 1948, it was not because Yugoslavia had already adopted a markedly different method of domestic economic and societal governance. Yugoslavia was pretty much a classical Stalinist state until 1952 in all respects. The reorganization of the economy started as an urgent necessity **after the break with Stalin's empire and leadership**, but it did not form a coherent mechanism until the economic reforms of 1952 and 1956. The theoretical model of Yugoslav workers' self management was developed only later by Edvard Kardelj, a Slovene, Vladimir Bakarić, a Croat, and Milovan Djilas, a Montenegrin. Even then, it was not more than a desperate attempt of rationalization for building socialism in a small, open economy compelled to rely on the Western world markets for trade and survival.

Individual firms were frequently relegated to the level of an administrative unit of production as if they were merely workshops within a sole immense macro-monopoly.[54] Later state owned organizations acquired some autonomy but the assets they possessed never belonged to them, but directly to the state.[55]

2. After the collectivization carried out ruthlessly in the early 1930s, most agricultural land was in the hands of what came to be called *kolkhozy*, i.e., collective farms operating, at least nominally, as a form of a cooperative. The collective farm statute, which was approved in 1935 right after the completion of collectivization and remained in force without much change until 1958, determined that agricultural land, nationalized in 1917, was transferred to the use of *kolkhozy* without paying rent in perpetuity. One of the most important characteristics of Soviet *kolkhozy* was that **peasants were remunerated as a collective on a residual basis** after all costs and taxes, originating or imposed from outside, were met.[56]

---

[54] Kornai rightly calls it "the bureaucratic state-owned firm". Kornai (1992) 71. While these firms can clearly be regarded as bureaucratic units, they were hardly enterprises at all.

[55] "A state enterprise belongs to the state. From this apparently tautological statement of the obvious flow a number of consequences which are perhaps less obvious. In essence and in law, the enterprise is a convenient unit for the administration of state property. It is a juridical person, it can sue and be sued, but it *owns* none of its assets. The director and his senior colleagues—the chief engineer, who acts as his deputy and the chief accountant—are appointed by state organs to manage the state's assets for purposes determined by the state. This is why there was no charge made for the use of the enterprise's capital, since it belongs to the state anyhow. This is also why the state is entitled to transfer the enterprise's profits to the state budget, save for the portion which the state's regulations or ad hoc decisions permit the enterprise to retain. That is why it is within the power of the state organs to take away any of the enterprise's assets, if they think fit, without financial compensation." Nove (1961) 31.

[56] "When all the expenditures had been met, the remainder was available for distribution to the peasants, along with produce set aside for the same purpose. This cash and produce was then paid to peasants in proportions determined by their contribution to the work of the farm. The proportions were measured in conventional work units (*trudodni*, literally 'workdays')… Firstly, it involved no definite scale of payments. The amount available (in cash and kind), divided by the total number of *trudodni* earned, determined the earnings per unit of work. It is because the amount available could not be known in advance that the *trudodni* system was invented. Secondly, there was no fixed or minimum scale of payment. The **amount distributed was not a wage, it was a residual**… In most farms at least until 1958, the payments to peasants were irregular, often occurring only once or twice a year, as well as varying widely from year to year and from farm to farm." Ibid., 56–57.

3. *Economic management was realized through administrative command*, represented by comprehensive macro and detailed micro planning targets and variables expressed in natural (physical) units. **Hierarchical (vertical) relationships in production, distribution** and, in most cases, **consumption were dominant.**[57] At times there was marginal autonomy for *individual job selection, collective salary setting and personal consumption.* In extreme cases, not infrequently, forced (slave) labor and rationing were prevalent.

4. *The economy and society were incorporated into a totalitarian state.* It was closed and alien to outside initiative, foreign and domestic alike. *Autarchy, self-sufficiency* was achieved and lauded at macro/micro level. External trade was marginal and carried out by specialized monopolist state administration (quasi enterprises). Monetary prices were primarily used for **aggregation in planning, accounting and management as means of extracting revenue and reallocating surplus among economic agents.**[58]

5. *Classical communism used prices, taxes and budgets at various levels of the state.* These important instruments of economic management, all even appearing in monetary form, however, did not represent either a reference point for, or a reflection of, economic policy but were designed to determine and limit the scope of activity of both state and non-state economic agents. They constituted **another mechanism of control over the economy and society both within and outside state ownership**.[59]

---

[57] A comprehensive analysis of the classical system is given by Kornai (1980), (1992) and (2008).

[58] Prices were widely used in classical Stalinism. It was not a system of natural redistribution although many ideologues, especially during war communism, vigorously advocated for the immediate introduction of a completely moneyless system. In 1920, before the end of the civil war, a system of natural redistribution was almost achieved by turning a necessity into a virtue. Then it was abandoned during the NEP.

[59] In a pure natural redistribution system there are no prices, taxes and budgets, i.e. balances of revenues and outlays to envisage some kind of a virtual equilibrium between income and expenses. When the war economy was abandoned in Soviet Russia in 1921, the most important novelty of the NEP was to substitute a tax in kind for the seizure of food surpluses (*prodrazverstka*). Likewise, as private trade and small crafts were permitted, their control was most effectively achieved by frequently adjusted punitive taxes. In urban areas non-agricultural taxes soon acquired a monetary form. At a later stage of development not only state-owned firms but even subsovereign government entities started preparing budgets in monetary form. But it is important to realize that all these "innovations" represented **concessions** from the coherent classical Stalinist model and at the same time shed more and more light on **its irrational and wasteful nature**.

6. *Economic growth was pursued for political* (catching up with the West militarily) and *ideological* (surpassing the West with a superior civilization) reasons instead of improving living standards and conditions continuously. Emphasis was put on heavy industry, production of and investment in coal mining, oil and gas extraction, iron and steel, machine building, electrical engineering and chemicals. Other sectors were largely neglected to the point of decay. **The law of imbalanced growth was in full blossom**.[60]

7. *The economy was made incapable to coordinate its own movements.* Chronic shortage was not merely an unintended byproduct of demand made independent from supply (expressed in Kornai's famous term as *soft budget constraint),* but it was deliberately created by the day in order to reinforce **the supremacy of administrative control over consumer needs**. Money was made useless primarily not by inflation (that would have been more or less just a market phenomenon), but by fragmenting its internal purchasing power and eliminating its domestic convertibility. Money represented not a right to buy whatever was available but an uncertain and revocable privilege to get access to a range of products with unpredictable variability. **Arbitrary administrative stratification of society by allowing access to scarce consumer goods according to variable degree of restrictions** was one of the most effective ways of totalitarian control.[61]

8. The legitimacy of the classical Stalinist model was, to a considerable extent, derived from preparing society to the *inevitability of class struggle both within and from outside.* **Stalinism was fortunate to have been born out of a ferocious civil and international war and constantly threatened by outside intervention, real or imagined**. It had always a *war economy*, legitimized by constant existential menace. It established a

---

[60] When economic growth is pursued for political and ideological reasons, it implies that the economy would not grow by itself; there are no internal, immanent motives (like the profit motive) for it to do so. It shows that the economy does not have any independent standing, it has no autonomy, no intrinsic internal rules and laws to govern its performance. It is subordinated to other spheres of existence. From this viewpoint, imbalanced growth is a rather misleading term because there is no reference point in discovering what balanced growth would be—compared to which the practical result looks like imbalanced.

[61] On the one hand, even rationing cards did not necessarily guarantee access to any products within the predetermined period of its validity. On the other, a network of special shops was established where scarce consumer goods were made available only to privileged groups of the nomenclature.

police state, controlling to a large extent even the private life of all citizens in name of creating a new type of human being: the Soviet one.[62]

9. The classical Stalinist model was geared toward creating *an alternative, non-market type world economy.* It did not compete with the Western world market economy by integrating into it, as the Chinese one since 1979, but **was anxious to isolate itself from it**. Economic and cultural ties with the West were kept at a bare minimum, scientific and technological contacts reduced to the import requirements of Soviet industrialization. Information exchange of any kind was very closely controlled, personal contacts were mostly forbidden. Peoples of the Soviet world were deliberately kept in the dark regarding the true realities of the outside, first and foremost, Western world. External demonstrational impact was largely eliminated.[63]

10. *In the 1930s, the Soviet Union was sympathetic towards Nazi Germany.* As the Great Depression of 1929–33 in the Western world provided an excellent justification for Stalin to start the Soviet "Great Leap Forward," i.e. *forced collectivization and industrialization*, the **ascendancy of Nazi Germany created very favorable conditions for the strengthening of the police state in the Soviet Union**.[64] It was also a period of rela-

[62] The continuous existential threat—real or imagined—explained well the necessity of dictatorial internal control. It provided a perfect pretext and excuse for the permanent repression, for the construed show trials, for the Gulag. It was not (only) Stalin's paranoia. The whole system was paranoid—and was in need of a paranoid leader at the helm. [One of the best literary descriptions of the sinister psychology of the regime is offered by Arthur Koestler: *Darkness at Noon* (1940). The most famous non-literary account is that of Aleksandr Solzhenitsyn: *The Gulag Archipelago* (1973).]

[63] In the Soviet Union, which was an enormous geographical unit, even the **internal movement of people** was typically restricted by the system of internal passports, frequent road checks by both the military and traffic police. Luggage was routinely searched, people interrogated. Tickets for trains and flights were largely made available only for those who could produce a "legitimate reason" for traveling. The control on the movement of the people was effectively used as a way of unlimited intrusion into private life. Stalinism tried to take over and nationalize hitherto private spheres of existence as well. (The best caricature of this effort is provided by George Orwell in his book *1984*, with an interactive monitoring device constantly peeping into family life and barking out instructions in every dwelling. Although technology did not make it possible at that time, the pervasive system of internal espionage had the same chilling effect.)

[64] This was the age of strongmen, open or covert (military) dictatorships and nationalist authoritarianism throughout Europe. Benito Mussolini in Italy, Francisco Franco in Spain, Józef Piłsudski in Poland and Miklós Horthy in Hungary were just four typical representatives of this trend. But it is absolutely clear that **the main driving force in the heart of Europe was the parallel, mutually reinforcing, strikingly similar emergence of Stalinism and Nazism**, as an expression of proud and vigorously anti-

tive calm and even progress in foreign relations with the major Western powers until the fourth partition of Poland by the infamous Molotov–Ribbentrop pact.[65]

11. Finally, Soviet communism in the Stalinist period reflected a quite *advanced refinement of an imperial structure of power.* Control was not only totalitarian but gradually re-Russified after an initial period of appeasement and even repentance for previous tsarist imperial domination and arrogance. Consecutive administrative reorganization of territorial management ensured that no horizontal links had a chance to stabilize at any level in the periphery of the empire. **Territorial expansion was pursued as an overriding goal** whenever chances arose by any means without concern for either historical or legal justification.[66]

These are the basic and most important defining characteristic features of the system called classical Stalinism. Apart from basic necessities for mere physical survival, this societal system largely ignored consumer preferences by deliberately excluding autonomous choices from economic calculation. That was clearly regarded as a brutal throwback to dark ages immemorial by the vast majority of the people in some of the newly conquered countries of Mitteleuropa, which used to have had a more advanced and sophisticated consumer society before World War II. It is no coincidence, therefore, that **spontaneous uprisings occurred already in the 1950s**, especially in three countries particularly hostile to the newly installed Soviet puppet regimes: *East Germany, Poland and Hungary.*

---

democratic, morally relativistic utopianisms. [For a fine comparison of the Stalinist and Nazi regimes see Paul Johnson (1991), Chapter 8, "The Devils," Mazower (1999) and Judt (2005).]

[65] The ambiguous desire and hesitation of Western powers to secure Stalin's support in case of war with Germany, however, did not produce tangible results. [See Ormos (1994), Chapter 4, "The Commander."]

[66] "Subsequently, as supreme leader, Stalin was very strongly guided in his foreign policy by traditionalist tsarist perspectives on territorial expansion, geopolitics and power. His leading lieutenant and foreign minister, Molotov, commented later that like no one else, Stalin understood the great historical destiny of the Russian people—the destiny about which Dostoyevsky wrote: the heart of Russia, more than any other nation, is predestined to be the universal, all-embracing humanitarian union of nations. He believed that once the worldwide communist system had triumphed—and he did everything possible to bring this about—the world's main language, the language of international communication, would be the language of Pushkin and Lenin." Molotov added that "my task as minister of foreign affairs was to expand the borders of our fatherland." This was to assert a traditional imperial view—linking territory, expansion and power—with crudity which might even have made Nicholas II's ministers shiver. [Lieven (2003) 295.]

Why Poland and Hungary? The most plausible explanation for the two countries playing a primordial role in challenging the classical Stalinist model is offered by history. At least three aspects are worth mentioning. First, these two countries had a **glorious past of independent statehood** (magnified disproportionately in popular imagination) going back to almost one thousand years. Second, their statehood and independence was several times challenged, threatened and—especially in case of Poland—**eliminated by tsarist Russia**. Hence, their incorporation into the communist Soviet empire was invariably seen as yet another dark period of hostile Russian domination. Third, not independently from these two factors, Poles and Hungarians have had a **strong anti-Russian popular culture and mindset**, reinforced by a rather monolithic church and dominant Catholicism in Poland and resentment in Hungary as a consequence of the Trianon tragedy, i.e. the dismemberment of multiethnic Hungary and the creation of new multiethnic states, like Czechoslovakia, Romania and Yugoslavia, after World War I.[67] Fervent but suppressed nationalism provided a fertile soil for some tacit popular support for any reforms which would then distinguish these countries from the monolithic Soviet communist system prevailing elsewhere in the bloc. These factors are as important as the universal desire of living better, which must have been a factor in all countries of Central and Eastern Europe.[68]

Unfortunately, these revolts against the Soviet system had absolutely no chance of winning[69] but ultimately at least compelled the new local

[67] For Poland see Lukowski-Zawadzki (2001) and Norman Davies (2005); in case of Hungary see Kontler (1999), Molnár (2001) and Lendvai (2010).

[68] The most important factor behind the first ever anti-Soviet revolt after World War II which happened in East Berlin in 1953 was probably the fast-growing bitterness and exasperation of the people following their realization that they would inevitably lose even the relative freedom and modest affluence enjoyed by their fellow citizens living in West Berlin. It was definitely not the absolute level of misery and ruin which made the workers of East Berlin revolt against the Soviet system but the increasingly obvious and widening gap between propaganda and reality. While the population of East Germany had no choice but to accept the occupation of a large part of former German territory by the Red Army as an inevitable consequence of losing the war against the Soviet Union, people were quite shocked that this occupation also meant a fast implementation of another dictatorial regime based on a culture perceived as hostile, alien and backward.

[69] Some scholars suggest that the 1956 Hungarian uprising may have had a chance of becoming successful in terms of bringing about a market economy and a multiparty democracy and maintain friendly relations with the Soviet Union. [See for example Charles Gati (2006).] After all, the four-power treaty allowing Austria to regain independence and declare neutrality in 1955 was a recent and obvious example next door.

leaders of the respective Communist parties to look for **less repressive methods of political rule and more effective methods in economic management**. After much political deliberation, only Hungary managed to escape from the classical Stalinist command economic system of communism and establish a fundamentally different new model which was to be aiming at incorporating *individual consumer preferences and choices* into the functioning of the economic system. That was really a sea change in the history of Soviet Communism and already a sign of its demise and decline.[70]

But for satellite countries even to contemplate any departure from Soviet orthodoxy the first condition was the *weakening of the cohesion of Soviet orthodoxy itself.* That happened right after Stalin's death in 1954–55. The power struggle among leading personalities in the Soviet Communist party, Malenkov, Molotov, Bulganin, Kaganovich, Beria and Khrushchev created a sense of uncertainty almost immediately as to what course the Soviet Union was going to take in the post-Stalin era. That brought about favorable conditions for the more national-oriented communists in satellite countries to gain momentum in implementing some measures of liberalization into the monstrous monolithic edifice of Soviet-type governance.[71]

But after the establishment of the Warsaw Pact in 1955, there was no real chance for any member country to leave the military alliance and, hence, the Soviet communist empire.

[70] There is a striking similarity between Poland and Hungary in the sequence of events which led to the emergence of less orthodox, more nationally-oriented and, at the same time, more popular alternatives within the communist elites. Despite their impeccable pedigree in fighting for Soviet communist ideals, **Władysław Gomułka** and **Imre Nagy** became soon outcasts in their own countries when these were transformed into Soviet satellites in the late 1940s. The local Stalinists, who wished to outbid each other in proving themselves the best disciples of Stalin, were pushing aside their less orthodox counterparts in a ferocious power struggle between 1945 and 1950. One difference between Poland–Hungary and the rest of the communist world in Central and Eastern Europe was that **the losers were not always murdered**, although many of them were imprisoned for long years. When they were admitted back into the communist party after a thaw, they represented more credible and more popular alternatives to the incumbent orthodox Stalinist leaders, like Bolesław Bierut in Poland and Mátyás Rákosi in Hungary.

[71] Władysław Gomułka was in prison between 1951 and 54. Imre Nagy was prime minister for a brief period of thaw between 1953 and 1955. Their personal fate was to become very different after 1956 as well. Gomułka took over the leadership of the Polish Communist Party in 1956 and stayed at the helm until 1970, when another uprising took place in Poland. Imre Nagy became prime minister again on October 24, 1956 and remained in that position until the Soviet invasion of Hungary which happened on No-

1956 was a year of truly historic significance in Poland and Hungary. Events started in Poznań in June with a spontaneous revolt of the workers. The uprising had a shocking impact on the Soviet world and contributed strongly to the outbreak of the Hungarian revolution in October. *The two events had a mutually reinforcing character.* While the power of the Polish communists was consolidated under the leadership of Władysław Gomułka and the Hungarian communist party, after the bloody Soviet intervention, also succeeded in regaining its own unchallengeable rule under János Kádár, the lesson was clear: *Stalinism could not be restored in these two countries.* New ways and means of political, economic and cultural management had to be found in order to avoid a dreadful repetition of an upheaval. Slowly and gradually, after crawling painfully on a clogged path of fossilized ideology, a new and hitherto unknown communist governance model was finally born: **the Hungarian modified model.**[72]

The *New Economic Mechanism* (NEM) as it came to be known later in Hungary was introduced only in 1968, more than a decade after the uprising in 1956. It looks like an inexplicably long period but in reality it was short. First, neither profound theoretical nor comprehensive practical professional work on reforming socialist economic management could have taken place in the aftermath of the revolution in a period of unprecedented repression.[73] Second, the general theoretical foundations for injecting

vember 4. Imre Nagy was held under house arrest in Romania for more than a year and executed on June 16, 1958.

[72] In contemporary literature this model was labeled as "market socialism, goulash communism, consumer socialism,"etc. After the Prague spring of 1968 "socialism with human face" was another preferred name. Unfortunately, none of these designations are precise enough in capturing the essence of the new model. But since this model has only historical importance, there is no need to invent a new and fancy name for it. The more important question is **why economic reforms did not succeed in Poland** in any coherent way despite the fact that the most brilliant theorists of "market socialism"—Lange, Kalecki, Lipinski, Brus and Zielinski—all were of Polish origin. One possible answer to that question is perhaps that Polish society by and large was and remained exceptionally hostile to communist rule all along and reforms initiated from above may have put the remaining integrity and cohesion of the system in jeopardy.

[73] Surprisingly, even in the years immediately after the failed revolution there were efforts in Hungary to rationalize the command economy. An important book was published by the then young economist, János Kornai, entitled "Overcentralization in Economic Administration" (*A gazdasági vezetés túlzott központosítása*) as early as in 1957 in Hungary. It even found its way to publication in the West in 1959. Moreover, there was a high level, even party-sponsored committee led by István Varga, a mature economist of high social standing, which published a set of reform proposals in October and December of 1957 with the unas-

some market forces into the horrendous edifice of the command system were extremely weak.[74] Third, conservative forces interested in restoring classical Stalinist economic and societal management were still formidable and they relentlessly tried to undermine any efforts for reforms.[75]

But in this period, political, economic and societal circumstances changed considerably in the Soviet Union as well. The Stalinist model of economic management became exhausted. **Soviet communism based on the Stalinist version of command economy reached its historical apogee in 1959–61,** after the successful launching of the first satellite into space in 1957. Extraordinary efforts in concentrating and allocating resources in research and development into space technology, largely as a byproduct of the advancement in rocket technology in the military, led to the first manned space flight by Gagarin in 1961. The Soviet Union seemed to charge ahead in many areas of economic, technological, military development and looked like as if it was capable of proving its systemic superiority.[76] But all these fine achievements were in sharp contrast

suming title "Thoughts of the Economic Expert Committee" ("A Közgazdasági Szakértő Bizottság elgondolásai," *Közgazdasági Szemle,* 1957 October and December).

[74] The theoretical foundations of market socialism were first laid out by Oskar Lange in two articles "On the Economic Theory of Socialism" published in 1936–37 in the *Review of Economic Studies,* republished in a book by the University of Minnesota Press in 1938. Additional arguments were provided by another economist of Polish origin, Włodzimierz Brus in his book *The Market in a Socialist Economy* (originally published in Polish in 1961, republished in English in 1972) and Ota Šik, a Czech economist (*Economic Planning and Management in Czechoslovakia*, Prague, 1966.) Nevertheless, these valuable efforts could not reconcile the inherent contradiction between unchallenged state ownership of important enterprises and the autonomous decision making required for leaders of such enterprises to respond to ever-changing market conditions, especially in the area of productive investments.

[75] Mátyás Rákosi, the Hungarian Stalinist dictator, was deposed in June, 1956 and took refuge in the Soviet Union. After the Soviet troops crushed the revolution of October 1956, he made several attempts to return to Hungary and was supported in this endeavour by many former Stalinist comrades. His return and the restauration of Stalinism in Hungary was a quite plausible possibility at least until 1961. [See Kis (1987).]

[76] US leaders and experts were frightened about the perspective of the Soviet Union winning the contest for military superiority and technological prowess which had been unfolding between the two superpowers. The achievements of the Soviet Union in space technology and its primacy in manned flights triggered an equally grandiose and—some say, unnecessary—program to send humans to the Moon before the end of the decade. John F. Kennedy announced this prestige project and the US Congress approved the financing for the Apollo-program in 1962 just one year after the Cuban missile crisis. That was the time when the world was to the closest to a nuclear war ever, a truly existential showdown between communism and capitalism.

with the miserable living conditions experienced by tens of millions of people in the Soviet Union. Furthermore, administrative reorganizations in economic planning and management advocated by Khrushchev and introduced in a convoluted manner produced only confusions and led to economic stagnation.[77]

In the absence and in the growing impossibility of another global military conflagration, some timid reforms, recreating and releasing energies of domestic dynamism in a period of peace, were contemplated.[78]

The Prague Spring, starting in February, 1968, provided an unprecedented but ultimately very favorable international political context not so much for the introduction of the Hungarian NEM but *much more for its survival*.[79] Hungary was duly participating in the Soviet-led military intervention which crushed the top-down liberalization undertaken by the Czechoslovak party and successfully deflected Soviet attention from its own experimentation which was considered strictly technocratic and absolutely non-political. As a consequence, the Hungarian reform miraculously survived and proved its merits spectacularly in the next five years in terms of improving economic efficiency as well as the living standards. The first challenge came in 1973 at the time of the first international oil crisis. Although Hungary imported all of its oil and gas from the Soviet Union, imported inflation became high as a consequence of second round effects in the international markets. As a result of the reforms introduced in 1968, contacts with the Western market economies intensified tremendously in five short years and by the time of the oil shock, the Hungarian

---

[77] The most important was the establishment of *sovnarkhozy*, **regional bodies of economic management**. "The idea was to cope with the problem of ministerial empire-building and insufficient coordination by the drastic expedient of abolishing the industrial ministries altogether, and substituting a regional structure coordinated by Gosplan. Khrushchev was responding to a very real problem… The trouble… was that the cure was worse than the disease. In any case it is in the nature of all-round planning that any organizational solution carries with it certain disadvantages." Nove (1969) 345.

[78] As a consequence, reformist thinking gained ground even in the Soviet Union in the Khrushchev years (1955–1964) and lasted well into the Brezhnev era. Most of the reforms led nowhere but the intellectual legacy was remarkable. A whole host of distinguished economists and mathematicians, like Nemchinov, Novozhilov, Kantorovich, Fedorenko, Petrakov and lesser figures with more controversial views like Kronrod and Strumilin are worth mentioning. [A concise summary of Soviet reformist thoughts is provided by Nove (1961) in Chapter 11. "Soviet Economics and Economic Laws."]

[79] Actually, the official committee working on the preparation of the NEM was constituted in 1964 and the Hungarian Socialist Workers' Party (MSZMP) approved a detailed program of the NEM already in 1966.

economy became dependent on the importation of a wide variety of Western goods and services.[80]

The most important characteristics of the **Hungarian modified model**, which was later in broad terms adopted in Poland, too—can be summarized as follows:

1. **Mandatory central commands for specific targets of production and distribution for individual state-owned enterprises were abolished.**[81] Henceforward state firms did not receive natural (physical) planning targets for production, procurement, delivery, etc. *Horizontal relationships among state enterprises* started to become relevant in shaping the behavior and functioning of more autonomous enterprises and their management.

2. Central planning was **refocused on selected macroeconomic variables** (like GDP, national income, general price level, inflation, employment, etc.) with **enterprise specific targets set primarily in productive investments**. This feature expressed clearly the widely-held conviction that although the market might be efficient in allocating resources for simple reproduction in the short run, *central planning was superior in determining the allocation of resources for the future of the economy.*[82]

3. Instead of disaggregating physical targets for individual enterprises, there was **a hierarchy of disaggregated regulation in financial form.**[83]

---

[80] As it is analyzed later more in detail, the Hungarian government was able to finance the widely emerging inefficiencies of this halfway marketized model of economic management on the basis of a special re-export business, i.e. converting relatively cheap Soviet raw materials into low value added intermediate goods to be sold in the Western markets. In addition, **the country was increasingly relying on foreign borrowing**, basically from Western banks. These latter institutions were more than willing to lend to the Hungarian state—and state-owned enterprises—and were explicitly encouraged by their respective governments to do so. In the aftermath of the Helsinki agreement (1975), it seemed to be a small price to be paid for *détente*. Nevertheless, heavy reliance on fast accumulating hard currency debt had its limits. Hungary reached those limits in the early 1980s and in the absence of a Soviet bailout it was obliged to join the IMF in 1982.

[81] Kornai calls this process "deregulation" albeit in a different sense than it is customarily used in a market economy. [See Kornai (1992) 480.] It is justified insofar as the abolition of central commands was truly comprehensive; it did cover almost all state enterprises and agricultural cooperatives and was implemented immediately at the beginning of the reform process in one shot.

[82] This remained a widely-held and still acceptable view even among most of the so-called Hungarian reform economists almost until the very end of the communist system. [See, for example, Tardos (1981)]

[83] Financial regulation, i.e. prices, taxes and subsidies were tailored according to the specific conditions and bargaining power of individual enterprises. Disaggregated regula-

Instead of introducing proper tax and subsidy systems, affecting universally and uniformly all enterprises at least in the same area of economic activity, *taxes and subsidies were designed in a very specific manner reflecting the bargaining power of individual enterprises*. As a consequence, the modified communist economic management system was still very far from a market economy despite employing regulatory tools in monetary form.[84]

4. Individual wage setting for individual workers was permitted so long as enterprises kept labor costs within the overall wage bill prescribed for them. Individual wage bargaining not only became tolerable and standard practice but also meaningful because **consumer autonomy was largely restored**. With few exceptions workers were no longer assigned to specific jobs in specific enterprises (in specific geographical areas, in specific branches, etc.) *The labor market, with free movement and bargaining, was restored.*

5. The Hungarian reform **recognized the private sector as a permanent feature of the socialist economy** especially in the areas of agriculture, small scale industry and retail trade, but also in a number of consumer services. This created a tremendous incentive to entrepreneurial activity and growth. As a result, Hungary achieved high levels of material abundance by Soviet bloc standards and became an enviable model of good life for the peoples of other communist countries, including even China and Vietnam. That is why the Hungarian model gained the title of *goulash communism* in Western sociology and then this phrase soon became fashionable in Western media and among academics as well.

6. Although exchange of goods within the Soviet bloc remained dominant and its requirements and consequences were internalized mainly through administrative mechanisms, **foreign trade with the world market economy became significant, too.** Importation of modern technol-

---

tion became perhaps the most peculiar characteristic feature of the Hungarian model [See Antal (1985) Chapter 5.3. "Regulatory bargain becomes generally accepted practice" (A szabályozóalku általános és elfogadott gyakorlattá válik) 270–284.]

[84] It was fashionable to talk about convergence between the two systems, capitalism and communism, throughout the 1970s in some circles of Western intellectuals. That was made possible by the Helsinki Accords signed by 35 nations on August 1, 1975, which led to a lasting *détente* between the two competing superpowers as well as the two competing systems. Despite having some striking similarities in heavy state intervention into the interplay of enterprises with the West, nothing was farther from reality. Brezhnev and the whole Soviet leadership gradually gave up all attempts at economic and social reforms.

ogy, machinery, and *even some selected consumer goods* from the Western countries was made possible by massive exportation of food, medicine and intermediate products which, in most cases, represented rudimentary processing of raw materials imported first and foremost from the Soviet Union.

This was a strikingly advantageous and highly profitable re-exporting business based on extraordinarily cheap Soviet raw materials, particularly crude oil. It started to gain prominence right after the first oil crisis and lasted almost for a decade. The Soviet Union was slow to react to the drastic changes in energy prices in world markets. In the absence of allowing domestic prices to adjust freely to world market prices, **the best way for Hungary to defend itself from the negative consequences of the external oil shock was to exploit the rigidities of classical Soviet communism.** Price distortions in energy became larger as a consequence of the upshot of prices in oil and its derivatives in the Western markets. Having kept importing sizeable amount of Russian crude, Hungary re-exported a good part of it after some low value added processing. This was a hugely lucrative business for Hungary and made it possible to plug for a while the growing fiscal hole which was emerging as a result of generous domestic subsidies.[85]

All in all, while obviously significant, especially from the viewpoint of improving the living standards of the people at large, the NEM maintained firm outside administrative control over the most important decisions affecting the future size, structure, production, etc. of state-owned firms.[86] One of the most important features distinguishing the modified Hungarian model from a real market economy can be summed up by pointing out that *albeit acknowledging and even fostering product, service and labor markets,* **it never accepted the rebirth of a capital market.**[87] That was

[85] See Bokros (2007) 234–235.

[86] Kornai highlights the main characteristics of this control under his concept of "vertical dependence." According to his classification, deregulation left in place four crucial components of vertical dependence:

(1) **entry**, (2) **exit**, (3) **mergers and splits** and (4) **appointment of leaders of firms**. "Taken together, points 1–4 mean that the system did not move away from the situation characteristic of classical socialism, namely, that the principle of free enterprise fails to apply in the public sector. Rivalry between firms does not yield a natural selection between either enterprises or leading persons in the firms. The selection is artificial: the bureaucracy decides on the survival or demise of a firm and the promotion or dismissal of its top managers." Kornai (1992) 482.

[87] It is not to say that investment decisions were kept completely centralized. "Partial deregulation occurs in investment decision making. All reform socialist economies see a

the most significant demarcation line never to be overstepped by the communist party and never to be incorporated into any new twist in ideology.

This last point is relevant in the case of the other remarkable deviation from the classical Stalinist communism, the so-called **Yugoslav model** as well. The main characteristic features of this model can be summarized as follows:

1. Instead of direct state-ownership, most enterprises, especially in the areas of manufacturing and trade (considered non-strategic and competing with Western firms) were notionally owned by employees' collectives.[88] The **introduction of the workers' self-management in the 1950s**, the control of employees over the selection of managers meant to cement the rupture with Stalinism and secure the workers' open consent in the fractious multiethnic federal state of Yugoslavia. *It was a system introduced from above.*[89] Nevertheless, as a defining characteristic of the unique way of building socialism, it became ideologically as sacrosanct in Yugoslavia as unified and indivisible state ownership was in the Soviet empire.

2. Workers' self-management was effective in **selecting and appointing managers** of individual firms[90] and deciding on resource allocation,

---

big rise in the proportion of investments on which a firm can decide independently and whose main source of finance is the firms's own savings from retained profits. The proportion of investment covered by nonrepayable finance from the state budget falls, and the role of bank credit increases." Ibid., 485–486.

[88] Not all enterprises were transformed into non-state social enterprises (yet another name widely used in Yugoslavia throughout the Titoist period). Large and very large firms, especially in areas considered strategic such as mining, public utilities, military production, remained explicitly under direct state control. Banks, in turn, were at least nominally owned by the enterprises operating in the same geographic areas. Last but not least, it is also remarkable that primary farming remained overwhelmingly in private hands; workers' self-management, the closest variant of cooperatives, never dominated the Yugoslav countryside.

[89] "The case in Yugoslavia was not that workers in a few firms voluntarily initiated the forms' introduction and others joined until it became general. The idea of self-management arose in the supreme leadership and when the party leader, Tito, accepted it, it became compulsory." Ibid., 463–464.

[90] "Leadership elections are influenced by party and local government organizations in various ways. Potential candidates undergo screening and voters are manipulated, and if a leader disliked by the bureaucracy is still elected, sooner or later he or she is removed. In any case, the firms' workers know it is to their benefit to elect a leader well connected to the party as well as in the central and regional state organizations, who can obtain favorable loans, tax treatment, investment funds, foreign exchange, and other advantages." Ibid., 464–465.

labor and output composition. As a result, market-substituting command-type central planning became impossible and was replaced by horizontal links at least among self-managed enterprises. Firms started to compete with one another, consumers' choices were prevalent and much better served than in any other part of the communist world. *The profit motive, albeit in a very short-sighted form—or even more precisely, the wage maximization motive—dominated the behavior of enterprises under workers' self-management.*[91]

3. Domestic market relations among self-managed enterprises could also be considered as a logical extension of external market forces of the Western world, which fundamentally influenced what was happening in Yugoslavia. For all intents and purposes, **Yugoslavia was a small and open economy** which could not have survived on its own after Stalin imposed what was essentially a trade embargo on it after the schism in 1948. *Yugoslavia had no choice but to open up its economy to Western economic influence.* As a result, commerce with the Western world market economy became dominant and influenced enormously the internal workings of the economy as well.

4. Yugoslavia introduced a *classic two-tier banking system* where central banking was clearly separated from the commercial banking function. Nevertheless, the latter was exercised in an extremely distorted manner. Commercial banks were largely organized on a territorial basis constituting, in effect, regional monopolies. At the same time they were under the strong influence of, or directly owned by, their client enterprises. This arrangement represented an *insurmountable conflict of interest,* distorted decisions for credit allocation, resulted in a galloping amount of interenterprise arrears and thus contributed enormously to the inflationary pressures prevalent in the whole Yugoslav socialist economy throughout its entire lifespan.[92]

In sum, the half-hearted Hungarian and Yugoslav market-oriented **reforms constituted a desperate response to the fast-eroding legiti-**

[91] The extremely strong stakeholder interest and collusion between workers and their elected managers in maximizing wage growth was considered as a permissible substitute for the capital markets, which did not exist in the Yugoslav model, either. [See Soós (1986) 168–171.]

[92] The decentralization of the Yugoslav banking system started in 1954 with the establishment of hundreds of small banks at the community level. The idea was to have financial institutions strongly under the control of local society. Then in 1961 all six republics and the two autonomous regions of the Yugoslav federation established their own head institutions regulating their own banks, which, in fact transformed the Yugoslav banking system into a three-tiered one. [See Ibid., 156–164.]

macy of the classical Stalinist model of economic and societal management. Curiously, it had nothing to do with the theoretical debates around the perceived superiority of central planning over the market which were quite intensive in the 1930s and 1940s in Western Europe. The Stalinist system, victorious in World War II, had the luxury of ignoring these debates completely and no economist living in the Soviet world could afford bringing them up in any meaningful way. Once the communist party decided to implement certain market-oriented reforms, then and exclusively then official economists attempted to rationalize the new approach by selectively referring to seemingly convenient theoretical antecedents.

When reforms occurred in Hungary and Yugoslavia, they resulted in **lasting deviations** from the command economy and society. In both cases the primary intention was *to avoid the collapse of the system,* the repetition of uprisings and to discover and inject new sources of *energy and political legitimacy* into the rusting edifice of the classical command system. But the ultimate aim of these historical experiments was obviously **to preserve communism as a societal system and perpetuate the "leading role," i.e. the unquestionable rule of the communist party**.

The more socialized, less etatist, light socialist Yugoslav model, based on workers' self-management, and the more mundane, but quite entrepreneurial Hungarian modified model, based on decentralization within the elite, *destroyed forever the universal applicability of the classical Stalinist model*. It had important repercussions to the fate of the latter as well.

The post-Stalin Soviet command economy was increasingly compelled to acknowledge the fast changing and more sophisticated material and cultural needs of an increasingly better-educated society without actually possessing any adequate adjustment mechanism to them. It faced a basic and insoluble contradiction: *it was unable to meet quickly and efficiently the continuously changing needs of the final consumer.*[93] That became a serious threat to its historical legitimacy.

Once a minimum degree of consumer autonomy was restored in order to provide some incentives to more efficient work, the wants and needs of society could no longer be ignored completely. But taking into account more spontaneous market signals was incompatible and irreconcilable with the maintenance of the command system, which was based on the

[93] The description of this phenomenon, consistent with the vocabulary of the market economy would be to say that the **communist system did not have built-in mechanism for supply-side adjustment**.

fundamental ideological consideration that conscious planning was superior to markets.[94]

Consumer preferences, evolving in a spontaneous way, were hardly taken into account by the slow-moving, ineffectual, politically-oriented and, what is extremely important, **largely disinterested planning bureaucracy**. It was a basic distinguishing feature of the communist system throughout its history that **party leaders and planning authorities looked down upon the ordinary needs of the ordinary people**. *This alienated approach to the needs of common people inevitably eroded the legitimacy of the system.*

In most cases it was easy to despise popular wants and needs by the ruling elite because it almost always had privileged and exclusive access to special stores offering scarce consumer goods and services. In fact, the very existence of these special shops expressed brilliantly the strong and almost *feudal stratification of society*. Those at the bottom of the societal pyramid were the landless laborers of the countryside. As a rule, they did not have the right to leave their villages without special permission, they were assigned to administratively determined tasks in the *kolkhozy*, usually they did not get monetary wages, and hence they could not buy anything in free markets. Workers in urban settlements usually had a superior treat with less restricted movement and a monetary wage somewhat more linked to overall productivity and personal performance. As an ideologically perceived ruling class, they received subsidized housing, better schooling, some child and health care. Nevertheless, the real beneficiaries of the Soviet system were the high-level bureaucrats, party *apparatchiks*, enterprise administrators, scientists, artists and sportspeople (if and when they were loyal and willingly performed prescribed roles and rituals to legitimize the system in the eyes of the masses). These latter could be called *nomenclature* and they were the ones who had privileged access to a wide variety of consumer goods and services unavailable for the people at large.[95]

The fast erosion of legitimacy in the twilight years of Soviet communism could not have been slowed down by political intervention of the regime. In the last twenty years of its existence the communist dictator-

---

[94] It was true not only for post-Stalin Soviet communism but for the Hungarian and Yugoslav models as well. [See Kornai (2008) Chapter 2. "The Inner Contradictions of Reform Socialism," 25–47.]

[95] "Members of the apparatus in Soviet-type societies form a unique social group which has no convincing parallels in history and we lack a suitable term even to designate it. Since questions of terminology do not preoccupy us much, we shall call it a corporate ruling group, the pinnacle of which constitutes the ruling elite proper." Fehér–Heller–Márkus (1983) 118.

ship was no longer able to dilute significantly the *intensity of the demonstrational effects* and influences coming from the Western world market economy and consumer society. It was a losing battle during and after the *Brezhnev years of economic and cultural stagnation* which created even more contradictions and set in motion new, destructive forces which, in turn, eroded further the legitimacy of the system.

It was the period when **crime, cronyism and corruption** (the "3C")—while always present in Soviet society—became so widespread and prevalent that the authorities, instead of fighting it, largely accepted and even benefited from it. Some might even argue that corruption was useful and positive because it made an otherwise unworkable system function and somewhat bearable and hence, perpetuated the existence of a system which otherwise should have collapsed already. In any case, the 3C became so firmly embedded in Soviet life that it tore apart the social fabric and basic cultural tenets and pillars of the communist system. One of the most visible consequences of this tendency was the **growing cynicism** not only in society at large, but also among members of the nomenclature. People no longer believed in the superiority of the system even in the Soviet Union. Rather, they resigned to passively tolerate it as an inescapable reality of the post-war bipolar international power system.

It became increasingly clear and then outright obvious that the *command economy was unable to overtake the capitalist system and prove its systemic superiority in peaceful competition.* The growing gap between ideology and reality created tremendous amount of cynicism which further undermined the faith of the people in the regime and destroyed the remaining enthusiasm which was regarded as an important incentive to work in the absence of clearly accepted material incentives.

By the late 1970s and early 1980s the Soviet communist system, its economy, society, politics and culture became tired and exhausted.[96] *From this perspective, its collapse seems to have been almost inevitable.*

---

[96] "The Era of Stagnation was the name given in the last years of the Soviet Union to the period between 1964 and 1982 when Leonid Brezhnev was the leader of the Soviet Communist Party and the most powerful politician within the Soviet state. It was in many ways a fitting description, for this was a period of a declining rate of economic growth, no political reform worthy of the name, and a conservative Communist regime led by the cautious Brezhnev. The term, though, can also be misleading, for Soviet society changed during these years in ways that were not and could not be controlled from above. Moreover, in spite of the censorship and ideological pressures for conformity, there were struggles between different political and intellectual tendencies going on below the surface of politics." Brown (2009) 398.

If that is true, then the real question is not why the communist system finally collapsed but **why it lasted so long** in the Soviet Union and in European countries.[97] That is not an easy question to answer. But probably the best guess is that in the short twentieth century,[98] the state re-emerged, was reconstructed and rejuvenated as a formidable force in post-war Russia, a country of late modernization, and assumed the role of carrying out a *highly accelerated, inorganic, unbalanced industrialization* compressed into a very short historic period of time in order to ensure *first the survival then the undisputable global dominance* of a political system which was totalitarian and imperialistic and derived its own legitimacy by claiming economic, societal, cultural and military superiority to Western civilization. Obviously, internal repression and terror was not for nothing. It served the purpose of eliminating any dissent arising from disgruntled members of society. But repression alone could never have been sufficient in prolonging the existence of the system for more than seventy years. It was just an integral part of any totalitarian architecture making it impossible to destroy the system from outside rather than inside. So long as the built-in contradictions and inherent weaknesses of the totalitarian com-

97 "The main, though not exclusive answer to the question of why Communism lasted so long in most European countries lay in the political resolve and military power of the USSR. Soviet leaders, until the late 1980s, were determined to sustain the communist systems they created or helped create. Even in Albania and Yugoslavia, where Communism was not Soviet-imposed, the example of the party-state, developed in the USSR, was hugely influential. And every other European Communist state would have broken with Communism earlier had it not been for Soviet overlordship. Stark reminders of this reality were issued from time to time, whether in East Germany in 1953, Hungary in 1956 or Czechoslovakia in 1968. That is not to imply that there were no internal sources of stability within the East European communist states. Although, however, policies and institutions which kept the Soviet Union itself quiescent operated in Eastern Europe too, on their own they were not enough. To the extent that the regimes were deemed a foreign imposition, they were not sustainable without Soviet support. That leads naturally to the question: why did Communism survive in the Soviet Union itself for over seventy years?" Ibid., 574.

98 After the collapse of the communist system in the Soviet Union and Central and Eastern Europe, it has become quite fashionable to label the period between 1914—the outbreak of World War I—and 1989—the fall of the Berlin Wall—as a period of the short twentieth century. [See Lukacs (1993).] In a way, it is a fitting concept, because WWI clearly altered drastically the course of history by unleashing forces of war, destruction, revolution, political and cultural violence (communism, fascism, Nazism) in such a brutal way that had been absolutely unexpected and unprecedented in light of the seemingly successful and glorious advance of global capitalism in the previous "long 19th century" (between 1815 and 1914).

mand economy and political system were concealed by achievements gained at the early, and without doubt, simple and primitive phases of forced industrialization, and so long as it was possible to maintain the perception and/or reality of a credible and existential threat coming from a hostile world outside the realm of the Soviet empire, **the legitimacy of the system was strong enough for it remain unchallenged from within**.

The collapse of the Soviet communist system and the Soviet empire was not without serious antecedents. In the international political arena the two most important events that must have speeded up the decline and ultimate fall of the system were the *botched Soviet intervention in Afghanistan* starting in December, 1979, and the *birth of Solidarity as an independent trade union and later as a giant political movement in Poland* in August, 1980.

The Afghanistan *imbroglio* drained the country, already in economic stagnation, of precious material and human resources without providing an acceptable rationale for the tremendous sacrifice and, even more importantly, without the perspective of ever winning the war. Afghanistan destroyed forever the myth of invincibility of the Soviet Army and its hitherto unchallenged heroic social status in the eyes of the Soviet people.[99]

In Poland, the emergence of an independent trade union which quickly turned into a huge alternative political movement with a membership of ten million represented a mortal danger to the monolithic rule of the Polish Communist Party and it was only a matter of time to lead to a massive showdown between the two power blocks. After much hesitation on the part of the Polish ruling elite, martial law was finally declared in December, 1981. Western response, coming first and foremost from the Anglo-Saxon world, the most important Western allies during World War II, proved to be significant, albeit in itself far from decisive.

In May 4, 1979, Margaret Thatcher came to power in the United Kingdom with a *radically liberal and conservative agenda* for her homeland, which set a clear example for many other nations, including the transition economies of the former Soviet empire a decade later. Likewise, the elec-

---

[99] Stories about total lack of military discipline, no will to fight, widespread corruption, including trading arms with the presumptive enemy by Soviet officers and even rank and file were abundant and crept back soon to the hinterland. When the first coffins arrived, mothers of the fallen soldiers were not given adequate information and they were treated in a coarse manner. Wounded soldiers and veterans did not get either surgical or psychological care in a decent and acceptable way; they were treated with contempt at best and with shame at worst. Growing groups of Soviet society started looking at the ruling class as their enemy.

tion of Ronald Reagan in November, 1980 and subsequently his eight years as president of the United States contributed hugely to the assertive reinforcement and reinvigoration of the mightiest superpower on the face of the earth after the seemingly weak years of the Carter administration.[100]

And finally Gorbachev. Without doubt, Mikhail Sergeyevich Gorbachev played an immensely significant and remarkable role in bringing about what can be considered as the single most important factor in triggering transition: *the largely peaceful collapse of the Soviet communist system and empire.*

Gorbachev is widely considered to be a controversial figure even today. When he was General Secretary of the Soviet Communist Party and President of the Soviet Union, he did not want to abolish the communist system, nor wished to oversee the disintegration of the Soviet Union. He was thinking about *improving* rather than abandoning the communist economic and societal management system, to make it more efficient and more humane. At the beginning of his rule he had only rather vague concepts about reforms which he conveniently bundled into old-fashioned party propaganda slogans: *glasnost* (enlightenment) and *perestroika* (rebuilding). More often than not, **he was reacting to events rather than shaping them**. That is certainly true in case of the most significant political undercurrents within the Soviet Union: the *rebirth of nationalism and aspirations for secession.* Nevertheless, his greatest achievement is exactly this: not to intervene by brutal force, by repression even when it was still possible; and the armed forces, the police and, first and foremost, the KGB were still under his more or less firm command and control. **Sometimes it is a great historic achievement to allow events to unfold without intervention**. Gorbachev knew that he was in the position to stop the course of history but he chose not to. He knew that the price to do so

---

[100] The Carter presidency was considered ineffectual and weak after the failed attempt to free the American hostages from Iran in April, 1980. But it is best remembered by the significant changes it brought about in American foreign policy. "President Carter returned the Panama Canal Zone to the people of Panama… The abolition of the Canal Zone was a symbolic sign of the end of a short century of Yankee colonialism. In July, 1979, the army of the Sandinist Liberation Front marched into Managua. Since the Cuban revolution, this was the first case when the United States did not intervene to save a corrupt rightist regime… The US understood that Latin America, always considered a natural sphere of influence under the Monroe doctrine, could no longer be held merely through militant anti-communism and an anti-Cuban approach. A fight was to come, for the heads, the hearts and the souls." [See Bokros (2005).] *With these changes the US regained the moral high ground in the battle for the hearts and minds of many people in the communist world, too.*

would be enormous in economic, political, human and moral terms. He felt that it was not worth paying that price. He realized that the communist system and the Soviet empire were not worth preserving against the will of the people—after all the ultimate legitimate goal of having both was to serve the people. Gorbachev came to understand that insoluble contradiction and decided to give up both the system and the empire. That is why he is, in my personal view, *the greatest historic figure of the short twentieth century*.

What happened was far from inevitable. A totalitarian regime can survive for quite long even after having lost all its internal legitimacy. A privileged group of party officials, bureaucrats, secret police and armed forces can keep an iron grip on society for a long time even in a situation when the economy stagnates or is in decline.[101] More questionable, however, is to what extent a *superpower status* can be preserved under such circumstances. Andropov, who probably knew that the Soviet communist system had already exhausted most of its energies by the beginning of the 1980s and, to a lesser extent, Chernenko in his short tenure made desperate attempts to conceal the internal weaknesses of the regime. Gorbachev, who was elected General Secretary of the Soviet Communist Party three hours after the death of Chernenko on March 11, 1985, decided to change course. Instead of hiding the inherited grave problems, he allowed the sunlight in and hoped to unleash constructive forces (material incentives as well as fervent social, cultural and moral enthusiasm) to play a key role in the revitalization of both the economy and the political process.

But a totalitarian system, once its monolitic structure gets decomposed, can no longer stay static because it has little flexibility to absorb external shocks and no internal equilibrium point.[102] Reforms, however timid at first, let the genie out of the bottle and, in the absence of a violent reversal, events started unfolding according to their own dynamics. It got

---

[101] North Korea and Cuba are cases in point. In both countries the economy has long ceased to function as an engine of growth and source of legitimacy. The North Korean regime has built its survival on nuclear blackmail, illicit trading with rogue states and fear from its collapse in the South. Ironically, the Cuban regime is strongly legitimized by the US embargo and supported by remittances of the Cuban exile community in Florida, significant amount of foreign investment into "apartheid" tourist enclaves, constant revenues from tourism, cheap oil from Venezuela and lately, loans from China on concessionary terms. In both cases, no organic growth in the domestic economy is detected and still the regimes survive.

[102] "In the Soviet Union reform produced crisis more than crisis forced reforms." Brown (2009) 598.

harder and harder to stop the process; the real choice for the ruling class was either to prepare for an **orderly transition to a market economy and more open society and try to secure a relatively competitive position for its own members** or to allow chaos and anarchy to prevail. In the Soviet Union, by and large, the first alternative was realized until the botched *coup d'état* of hardline communist forces which happened on August 19, 1991. Following its failure within two days events unfolded in quick succession. Central party and state control was rapidly and visibly lost. After the dissolution of the USSR on December 26, 1991, and with the resignation of Gorbachev the next day as the last president of the Soviet Union, the second alternative became dominant in the newly independent Russian Federation and in most of the former member states for several years with the notable exception of the Baltics.

By that time, however, the economic and political transition was in full blossom in many former satellite countries in Central and Eastern Europe. *Two years is an extremely long period in case of tremendous and tumultuous, sometimes terrible, other times terrific events of truly historic proportion.* On October 3, 1990, East Germany was legally swallowed by the West German state. By 1991, *Wiedervereinigung* (German reunification) had already been an irreversible historical fact despite tens of thousands of Soviet troops still stationing on the soil of the new German Bundesländer. Poland, Czechoslovakia, Hungary and Slovenia had already advanced on the road of economic and political transition at a fast pace and with considerable and impressive self-confidence. Unfortunately, the newly independent Croatia was at war with Serbia on its own soil and in Bosnia-Hercegovina. Sadly, the whole Western Balkan area was in danger of being engulfed by the flames of armed conflict and civil war. But Soviet troops were still present not only in the Eastern federal states of the new Bundesrepublik, but also in Poland, Czechoslovakia and Hungary, and in the small Baltic states. *Had the* coup d'état *in Moscow in August 1991 been successful, the course of events might have taken a very different, truly catastrophic turn again.*[103]

[103] François Mitterrand, then president of France, recognized the new putschist leadership in Russia almost immediately. Whether he did it out of fear or as a reflex of realpolitik, it is hard to know. But it shows eloquently that the *West was in no mood of either political or military intervention at all even in 1989.* The status quo created and sealed in Yalta and Potsdam and, hence, the division of Europe was still considered unchangeable almost two years after the fall of the Berlin Wall. It is also highly remarkable that both Mitterrand and Margaret Thatcher, then British prime minister were very much against *Wiedervereinigung*, at least at the beginning, apparently for fear of a too strong

Ultimately the August 1991 Moscow putsch and its rapid failure turned out to be extremely favorable for the future of Central and Eastern Europe. The *coup d'état* was quickly declared high treason and the glorious Soviet Communist Party was banned. The remaining legitimacy of the fast disintegrating Soviet Union evaporated almost overnight. Formally existing national communist parties collapsed in all member states of the Soviet Union in quick succession. Member states of the Soviet Union, even those which had been completely unprepared for this turn of events and where the ruling elite did not really wish to secede from the USSR, declared independence one after the other.[104] *The Soviet Union, the Soviet empire, its military might and the Soviet Communist Party with its antiquated ideology represented a hindrance and obstacle no more for the marketization and democratization of Mitteleuropa, the Baltics and the Balkan area.*[105]

and dominant new Germany emerging in the heart of Europe. (The latter famously quipped: two Germanies are preferable for me than just one.) Ronald Reagan, the US president, was much more sympathetic to the idea of German reunification. But it took the courage, steadfastness and skillful diplomacy of Helmut Kohl, then Chancellor of West Germany to persuade not only Mitterrand and Thatcher, but first and foremost Mikhail Gorbachev that a reunified Germany would never pose any threat to anybody, including the Soviet Union. Some material sweeteners coming from Germany greatly helped making a good deal for both sides. The material support was not only related to the relocation and housing of retreating Soviet soldiers, but also in helping Soviet cities to survive harsh winter conditions by getting adequate fuel supply. [See Kohl (2009).]

104 The Baltic states managed to regain their independence already in the spring of 1990 largely by peaceful means although the Kremlin had first, tentatively, reacted the only way it knew: by sending in the tanks. The successful departure of Estonia, Latvia and Lithuania blew a big hole into the wall of the Soviet Union and made other peoples start thinking the previously unthinkable. No surprise, therefore, that the most important objective of the leaders of the *coup d'état* in August, 1991, was to block the further disintegration of the Soviet communist commonwealth. Nevertheless, its failure speeded up not only the dissolution of the Soviet Union, but also the collapse of the whole communist economic and societal management system.

105 Nevertheless, it is important to note that, apart from the Baltic states, real political and economic transition started in the remaining former 12 member states of the Soviet Union only in 1991–1992.

2. Transition to Market and Democracy in Central and Eastern Europe

2.1. The matrix of structural reforms in transition

Transition from a command economy to a market-oriented one and from a totalitarian societal system towards a democratic one has been, and still is, a **historically unprecedented endeavor**. Furthermore, as the collapse of the communist system was almost completely unexpected and unforeseen, nobody had prescribed what to do in case of its demise in a systematic way. When the time for rebuilding the shattered economy and society arrived, there was *no blueprint, no model, not even a vague set of guidelines* to follow. No wonder, therefore, that transition has proved to be and still is a quite *chaotic, disorderly, unruly* process with pitfalls and setbacks along the way.

Twenty years later there is now a vantage point from which it is possible to *construct the political economy of transition*. Since the communist system had many common characteristics, i.e. it was primarily a non-market system even in its modified variants and, without doubt, always a one-party dictatorship until the very last moment, *there must be a compelling reason for transition to have common characteristics* as well. Experience shows that, despite widely different historic circumstances—initial conditions, stratification and capacity of the new ruling elites, resurfacing national ideals and political imperatives, etc.—many of the structural reforms implemented along the way were **almost identical in origin, nature and purpose**. Governments in all transition countries had to *liberalize* their economies at one point or another in order to free it up to private entrepreneurship. Since communist economies were extremely unbalanced from a financial point of view, macroeconomic *stabilization* inevitably had to come to the agenda sooner or later. A market economy based on free enterprise—in addition to being built upon new private ventures—

always required a fair degree of *privatization*, too. In all states, old and new alike, *a completely new set of rules and regulations* for the economy but also for the society were much in order and demand. Public administration—central, regional and local—had to be rejuvenated or, not infrequently, rebuilt from scratch. Legal and judiciary systems could not be left untouched either; they were reconstructed everywhere. **Comprehensive institution building has always been key**.

If political economy, i.e. the interdisciplinary study of interrelationships between political institutions and economic systems, has ever made sense, it is exactly now. Hardly any better example of mutual influence and co-determination between political action and economic behavior can be conceived than the historic transformation of a politically supercharged and embedded system into an economically more autonomous and predisposed one. While in communism the political sphere was more important than the economic one, it is not to say that in capitalism it is exactly the other way round. *The interplay between politics and economics in capitalism is more subtle, stochastic, nuanced and balanced.* What is important here is that transition, as a process of transforming a closed and exclusionary totalitarian system into an open and more inclusive, democratic polity, involves the **restoration of relative autonomy for institutions in all spheres of societal existence**, economy, politics, science, education, culture, law, religion, ethics, etc. Structural reforms, implemented throughout the protracted and still ongoing period of transition, have been aiming at achieving this delicate separation by a *tremendous amount of deliberate institution building* which requires highly professional and deeply political societal governance.

One of the most hotly debated issues in the process of transition was the *sequencing of structural reforms*. Has there been an optimal course for the reforms to be followed? That was largely a theoretical discussion which, at that time, had little or no impact on actions on the ground. These latter were determined, first and foremost, by *political imperatives* (both domestic and foreign), by the declared and/or underlying *values and ideology* of the newly-formed ruling parties, governments, political, cultural and business elites and their degree of *acceptance* by the general public. In the first period right after the first democratically elected governments came to power there was more room to implement even painful reforms as the people, by and large, were more willing to accept the hardships associated (in most cases wrongly) with the reforms themselves.[1]

[1] It was an exceptional time of grace what Leszek Balcerowicz, the father of early Polish reforms, aptly called the period of "extraordinary politics." [See Balcerowicz (1995).]

Nevertheless, the *timely introduction and enhancement* of specific reforms as well as their *endurance without reversal or significant dilution* proved to be immensely important from the viewpoint of success.

Of course, it is hugely important what we ultimately consider success. The separate impact of individual reforms is hardly measurable. But it is less of a problem if the *cumulative impact* of reforms manifests itself in the most remarkable proof of success: **regaining fast, sustainable and sustained, economic growth** which is broadly based enough to include the majority of society and lift most boats. That is also indispensable in order to maintain the political momentum behind the reform process especially after the sharp initial fall in the living standards as a consequence of the steep decline in domestic economic activity and output.

Last but not least, it is important to highlight that individual reforms are very different not only in terms of their political and cultural acceptability but also in terms of *how much deliberate action and administrative capacity they require in design and implementation.* Liberalization, on the extreme, might need only the lifting of existing administrative barriers and not much else. Public finance reforms, conversely, demand enormous intellectual, legal, regulatory and administrative input and much political capital to be spent on convincing people and secure their active and steadfast cooperation. As a consequence, most of those reforms which required enormous political capital and administrative capacity were either carried out at a later stage of transition or implemented in stages. In order to ensure lasting success of the structural reforms and maintain momentum, it was imperative for the new political elite to take into consideration these constraints.

In light of the intricate interlinkages among individual reforms and also taking into account their most logical timeline and increasing complexity, the following **matrix of structural reforms in transition** is conceptualized (see Table 1).

2.2. Business sector liberalization

Although it sounds like a curse for many politicians, intellectuals and sometimes even for ordinary people today, liberalization was almost an automatic byproduct of the sudden collapse of the communist system. As

But it was extremely short and did not occur in all countries which stepped on the long and bumpy road of transition. Politics came back to rule very soon if it was not there all along.

Table 1. The matrix of structural reforms in transition

BUSINESS SECTOR LIBERALIZATION	MACROECONOMIC STABILIZATION	COMPETITIVE PRIVATIZATION
UTILITY & FINANCIAL SECTOR PRIVATIZATION	CORPORATE RESTRUCTURING	UTILITY & FINANCIAL SECTOR RE-REGULATION
PUBLIC FINANCE ADMINISTRATION	SUBSOVEREIGN GOVERNMENT	LEGAL & JUDICIAL REFORM

a first generation reform at the early stages of transition it could be interpreted as a wholesale *removal of administrative barriers* which, even in the best of circumstances, blocked the resurgence and organic evolution of the market economy. Liberalization was clearly understood and greeted as *restoration of freedom in economic activity*. It was by and large popular, rather easily acceptable and accepted. Wherever and whenever transition started with a comprehensive liberalization, it was implemented almost overnight.[2]

Liberalization had several components.[3] From the viewpoint of systemic change, the most important was the **liberalization of entry and exit of new ventures** in the economy. It involved the *restoration of private ownership and the freedom of entrepreneurial activity*, the two basic and indispensable pillars of the market economy. By this step—which, obviously, never could have been made by the communist system—*capitalism was reborn*, indeed.

If new ventures were allowed to be established in most areas of economic activity, that meant that *entrepreneurial competition*—another inherent feature of a market economy—was to reappear. That implied that it was no longer for the state, the party or/and any other central administrative body to decide who were to win and lose in the economy. *The relative autonomy of the economy was thus restored.* Henceforward economic activity was clearly distinguishable from politics and other spheres of

---

[2] Liberalization was one of the very few reforms which could be conceived and implemented either in a gradual manner or in one shot. Nevertheless, this unique feature of liberalization triggered a full-blown debate about gradualism and shock therapy, as if speed had been the quintessential element of all reforms.

[3] "The substantive content of the liberalization requirement is far from self-evident. In fact, it has quite a number of components; I list only the most important ones here.

- Freedom to establish a firm; free entry into the production sphere.
- Free prices, based on free contract between the buyer and the seller.
- Unrestricted right to rent out privately owned assets…
- Unrestricted right to employ people…
- Unrestricted right to accumulate, sell, or buy any article of value…
- Unrestricted right to accumulate, sell, or buy foreign currency…
- Unrestricted right to take out and bring in domestic and foreign currencies.
- Free foreign trade activity, in which the member of the private sector has the unrestricted right to export and import.
- Unrestricted right to lend money, with credit terms freely agreed upon between the creditor and the debtor.
- Freedom of financial investments in the private ventures of other individuals.
- Freedom to sell and buy, at free prices, any privately owned apartment, real estate or other asset." Kornai (1990) 39–40.

societal existence. The influence of the economy on the political institutions was to be as important as the reverse impact. A delicate and dynamic balance was gradually forming (or re-established) between the economy and society.

For competition to be transparent, thus effective and, hence, legitimate, there was an absolute need for a further component: **the comprehensive liberalization of prices**.

Prices constitute the most important factor in transmitting indispensable information for the effective and efficient (re)allocation of scarce resources in the market economy. By and large the freer the prices, the more effective and efficient the allocation of goods and resources might be. Capitalism proved its ultimate superiority over the communist system by fostering open *market competition based on relatively free price formation*. Relative prices are always there to absorb and reflect information on the relative importance of wants and needs and that is exactly which makes the market economy much more flexible than the command economy.[4] Restoring this kind of built-in flexibility into economic life was a major achievement to minimize the gross misallocation of resources and eliminate the enormous distortions created in the economy by the wholly intransparent and rigid communist management system.[5]

Price liberalization could not be complete without freeing up the price of the most important integrating factor in the market economy: that of **money**. *Internal and temporal prices* (interest rates) as well as *external and spatial prices* (exchange rates) of money had to be made free in order to achieve two fundamental goals: to express the *time preferences of savers and investors* (the function of free interest rates) and to make sure that allocative efficiency is based on the relative scarcity of goods and services *in the world market* as an ultimate reference point (the function of free exchange rates).[6]

---

[4] Hayek (1948) 77–79.

[5] As the communist system was insensitive to consumer preferences (and the nomenclature was looking down on the needs of the population at large), resources were not allocated to productive uses according to these preferences. As a consequence, **chronic shortages** of consumer goods were unavoidable and—as Kornai so eloquently proved—constituted an integral part of the communist economic management system. From the viewpoint of the market economy it represented a major, constant and structural weakness: a *permanent misallocation of resources and, hence, a permanent distortion in the structure of the economy*. [See Kornai (1980) and (1992), especially Chapter 15.]

[6] In order to eliminate the integrative function of money and, consequently, abolish the relative freedom of the economy *vis-à-vis* the political sphere, *communist authorities*

Liberalization of money prices and the integration of various uses of money quickly led to the restoration of the *internal convertibility of the domestic currency,* another key step in rehabilitating the market economy.[7] That is a major step in restoring both entrepreneurial and societal equality among citizens of the newly-emerging democratic polity, too. As it is both easy and popular, no surprise, therefore, that it was rather quickly achieved almost everywhere in the transition world.

One would expect that the freeing up of **employment and wages** should be considered as the logical corollary of the liberalization process. In a sense it is true; after all labor is by far the most important factor of production not only from economic but also from societal and political point of view.[8] However, in the absence of strong and effective entrepreneurial pressure to keep labor costs at an affordable level, embedded only in private ownership, *free wage bargaining and settlement can easily lead to uncontrollable inflationary pressures*. One should never forget that at

---

were always keen to decompose both interest rates and exchange rates meaning that interest rates and exchange rates were different not only for different products and services but also **according to the different status of the economic actors**. Multiple interest and exchange rates were applied depending not only on the specific type of the underlying transactions but also **on the economic and societal status of the economic subjects of these transactions**. *Multiple interest and exchange rates served as yet another way of overwhelming state control and led to a rigid, almost feudal stratification of society.* Thus, the unification of interest and exchange rates was in itself a major step in the reintegration of the economy and society by relieving enterprises and citizens from the paralyzing administrative control of the party-state.

7 Liberalization in transition does not require the immediate full external convertibility of the currency. *But some initial steps toward more convertibility are absolutely necessary.* If freedom of entrepreneurial activity includes not only domestic but also foreign trade, then importers need to have some limited access to hard currency. Likewise, freedom for people to travel abroad presupposes the right to purchase some foreign exchange. Finally, if a government is keen on attracting foreign investment, it needs to have a regime which allows for reimbursing foreign investors in case of dividend payments and divestiture. Therefore, even some elements of capital account convertibility might be necessary from the very start of transition.

8 Actually, free job selection was largely achieved even in the Soviet Union in the last period of the communist system. Therefore, it was no longer considered an important part of the liberalization process. Nevertheless, two aspects are of key importance. First, the communist system was inefficient in allocating and employing labor. It led to serious labor shortages, ironically strengthening the bargaining position of individuals when in search of jobs. *Second, it was an obligation to work not only morally but also legally.* Liberalization put an end to this more or less implicit obligation. People were no longer expected to work; they were now "free to be without a job" (of course, without necessarily being entitled to receive social transfers).

the beginning of transition all major, systemically important enterprises were still owned by the state as an inescapable legacy of the communist system. Governments alone, no matter how stable and powerful they might have been, could not constitute a strong enough counterweight to demands for higher wages.[9]

Finally, the new democracy clearly implied the final and full liberalization of consumer choices and preferences and quickly led to the **restoration of consumer autonomy**. Consumption was depoliticized and relegated back to where it naturally belongs in a true market economy and democratic polity: *the private sphere of existence.*[10]

The economic and, even more importantly, *the societal significance of liberalization* in transition can hardly be overestimated. In hindsight, many people regarded liberalization as premature or even harmful because a free market economy may produce excessive and seemingly irrational swings in prices especially when there is *still little or no supply-side adjustment.*[11] But the problem here was not what the newly-established mar-

[9] There was an inherent contradiction within the liberalization process in a former communist economy. Once prices were free and tended to increase, *there was more pressure and demand for the liberalization of wages* as well in order to prevent a sharp, seemingly inexplicable and politically unacceptable decline in living standards. In most transition countries, governments were not sufficiently enlightened and strong to resist the popular pressure and convince people that wage liberalization could lead to economic suicide. Most governments have fallen, typically, in one of the two following traps. Either they liberalized wages and then observed uncontrollable hyperinflation or reversed price liberalization, at least for basic consumer goods, which created new distortions (even shortages) in the transforming economy.

[10] Ironically, communist totalitarianism made people much more individualistic and much less responsible by seriously limiting consumer autonomy and at the same time destroying all independent social networks, institutions and preventing citizens to undertake even social initiatives independent from government and/or party control. The archetype of a new human being was created, indeed. But it was not an idealistically communitarian and proudly self-conscious Soviet human being. Rather, an inward-looking and mostly selfish individual incapacitated by the state to take care of oneself and fellow citizens let alone undertake responsible societal action. The lasting harmful consequences of this huge cultural and moral distortion and destruction can be easily detected even today. Often times, especially in the period of a deep economic and social crisis, people may vote *en masse* for proudly anti-liberal, populist and/or nationalist parties promising earthly paradise by strengthening and enlarging the state and making people, once again, more dependent on it.

[11] At one point even the most outstanding observer and analyst of contemporary events, János Kornai, contemplated a provisional dualization of the economy and suggested to apply liberalization only for the nascent private sector while keeping the still state-

ket economy may have created but what was still missing from it: **a critical mass of private businesses responding quickly to the fast changing structure of demand**. That was yet another inherent contradiction of the transition process which could be solved only over time. The reason for it was clear: *the temporal inconsistency between two distinct components of transition process, i.e. liberalization and privatization.* While liberalization could be implemented almost overnight, that was completely impossible in case of privatization. Moreover, as it was known from the outset, what mattered most was not just the privatization of existing state-owned enterprises but even more so the *proliferation of new ventures, large and small, foreign and domestic alike.*[12]

One of the most important functions of comprehensive liberalization in the early stages of transition was **to make explicit and visible the structure and degree of economic distortions caused by the constant and massive misallocation of resources in the communist system.** It was one of the minimum conditions necessary for avoiding further distortions.

As was already analyzed in much detail, the communist system in all its forms was always characterized by the *dictatorship it imposed over needs.*[13] From the reference point of a market economy, featuring freedom of choice, that is to be considered a serious constraint in terms of allocative efficiency. In the absence of officially acknowledged and sanctioned consumer autonomy, the whole structure of production in the communist system was deeply distorted by the **continuous misallocation of scarce resources**. These distortions were manifesting themselves on the macro

owned enterprises firmly under bureaucratic control. [See Kornai (1990).] In practice, his proposal quickly turned out to be unfeasible.

[12] As we will see in Chapter 2.4, privatization can hardly be advanced sufficiently and completed in one stroke, in a shock-therapic manner. Only formal privatization, i.e. the legal abolition of state ownership and a distribution of title by shares among the people could be achieved within a relatively short timeframe. That was the purpose of the so-called *mass privatization schemes* (voucher or coupon privatization). But it was an illusion to create real private ownership this way that would immediately show the true characteristics and dynamics of private businesses. Enterprises subject to mass privatization schemes kept behaving very much like former state-owned ones **because management incentives did not necessarily change with the formal distribution of ownership title.** *That is why it became so important to distinguish between formal (legal) and real (economic) privatization.*

[13] This was exactly the suggestive title of the groundbreaking book written by three outstanding Hungarian scholars, Ferenc Fehér, Ágnes Heller and György Márkus in 1983 when they were in exile in Australia. Dictatorship over needs was one of the most important characteristics of all variants of Soviet communism.

level either in *massive shortages* (in the classical Stalinist model), in growing reliance on *foreign borrowing* (in the modified Hungarian model) or in permanently high level of *inflation* (in the Yugoslav model).[14]

In either case, the new economy on the road of going private desperately needed *much more precise indications* as to where to channel its resources. But more precise signals can only emerge if (i) **consumer autonomy** is restored, (ii) **competition** can more or less easily work itself through the economic structure and can determine decisions in the new entrepreneurial environment and (iii) **price formation**, by and large, remains unhindered by distortionary bureaucratic regulation. Then, and only then, it is possible to separate the "stock problem" (the already existing legacy distortions) from the "flow problem" (new distortions which might emerge as a consequence of a still distorted economy and imprecise price and other signals).[15]

---

[14] In practice, of course, all three phenomena reflecting distortions were more or less present in almost all former communist countries. Nevertheless, it is possible to detect some systemic patterns in their presence. For example, by restoring the classical Stalinist model after the Warsaw pact intervention in August, 1968, the Czechoslovak leadership was deliberately suppressing inflation and refused to accumulate foreign debt. Hence, chronic shortages remained a dominant feature and kept demonstrating the inherent inefficiency of the communist economic management system in post-1968 Czechoslovakia. Romania, which had accepted foreign loans in the 1970s, decided to repay all of it in the 1980s. As a consequence, it became an extreme case of a neostalinist shortage economy. Poland was also relying heavily on foreign borrowing in the 1970s under the Gierek regime. When martial law was declared on December 13, 1981, to suppress the free trade union and societal movement of Solidarity, the Western powers were no longer willing to finance the Polish military regime with generous loans. As a result, Poland was forced to declare bankruptcy and its economy returned to the typical shortage mode of operation almost until the collapse of communism. Hungary, in contrast, was able to preserve its relative abundance and maintain its premature welfare state model which had been implemented with the NEM until the very end of the communist system despite *having accumulated by far the largest amount of per capita foreign debt in the Soviet communist world.*

[15] It goes without saying that comprehensive price liberalization does not necessarily require the complete freeing up of all prices in the economy. Utility fees, housing rent, even prices of a few basic foodstaples may continue to fall under administrative ceilings with periodic adjustments. But limitations to free price formation should be (1) only temporary; (2) reflect just narrow social considerations and, most importantly, (3) be applied almost exclusively in areas where competition would be very limited if not impossible even in case of full privatization of the assets involved. **Limitations on prices should clearly be the exception, not the rule**. Prices should reflect prevailing market conditions of demand and supply and be allowed to change according to these conditions. To achieve a more effective and efficient allocation of resources in the future, these are just minimum necessary, but far from sufficient conditions.

To get to know whether the new signals emerging from liberalization are precise or not was obviously impossible because of the continuing lack of meaningful supply-side adjustment. But that was less of a serious concern. The question was whether the *new signals were more precise and, hence, led to less waste and distortions than the previous, administratively set signals*. The issue was not whether the economy, having got rid of the administrative barriers, was capable of immediately achieving any equilibrium—that was something absolutely impossible at the very beginning. The objective was much more modest. It was for the **economy to start moving towards a more stable and sustainable dynamic equilibrium without total collapse and/or disintegration**. In this sense, liberalization was indispensable in pushing the economy towards a *modus operandi* whereby market signals could play a decisive role in the henceforth more effective and efficient allocation of scarce resources. Therefore, liberalization of entrepreneurial activity, or more precisely, the *emergence of a new, autonomous business sector* was undisputedly and absolutely necessary albeit far from sufficient condition for the establishment (or restoration) of a market economy.

Liberalization, pushed through in a highly distorted and inflexible economy dominated by hitherto administratively directed state-owned enterprises, was not without very serious negative consequences. Instead of chronic shortages which, in the light of black market prices could be viewed as hidden inflation, now *open inflation* and, not infrequently, *hyperinflation* emerged rather quickly. Moreover, in the absence of significant supply-side adjustment and/or full liberalization of foreign trade, hyperinflation was to become a relatively *permanent feature of transition* not just a short term one-off phenomenon. Serious market disequilibrium expressed by high level inflation was further exacerbated by the *collapse of output* in a significant number of large state firms which employed a big part of the workforce. **Inflation, output decline and the emergence of massive unemployment** were the three most important and closely interconnected new negative phenomena showing a deep structural crisis in all transition economies right after the establishment of political democracy.[16]

[16] "Although output has undoubtedly declined, it is important to note that the extent of this decline is uncertain. Fundamental measurement problems result from distorted price indices. Besides, how useful are such output comparisons in the light of past wasteful buildup of capital and inventories? Official statistics also largely fail to take into account the shadow economy whose growth is encouraged by new conditions where tax evasion may be a major source of income." Holzmann–Gács–Winckler (1995) 3.

Here comes the next major contradiction of transition: *a total confusion of cause and effect* when turning a command economy into a market based one. Transition from communism to capitalism proved to be not only a painful but also an obscure exercise. Instead of having been considered a legacy of communism, inflation, output decline and unemployment were frequently perceived *as a result of the liberalization process itself.* The longer these intricate and intertwined phenomena persisted, the more its true causes remained hidden. As a result, it took a huge effort and perseverance for governments to keep up momentum and block any attempt of reversal.

The history of liberalization in the early stages of transition shows a wide variety of patterns and scenarios. Some countries, first and foremost Estonia, Poland and Czechoslovakia, were able to maintain political momentum and avoid not only any major reversal of comprehensive liberalization but also to move forward with the next step: *macroeconomic stabilization.* That helped tremendously in taming inflation, moreover, in creating more favorable conditions to new entrepreneurial activity and, hence, triggering more supply-side adjustment and thus putting a floor under output decline. Other countries hesitated for too long and either postponed major components of liberalization—especially freeing up prices—or reversed it when the first negative signs of hyperinflation and mass unemployment materialized. Romania was a good example for the first, Bulgaria for the second case. But contrary to expectations, the negative consequences of economic distortions inherited from communism could not have been avoided this way. On the contrary: inflation became more persistent (in Romania throughout the 1990s) or lived parallel with serious shortages which led to the total collapse of the domestic economy (in Bulgaria in 1996). Output ultimately fell more in both countries relative to their northern peers and unemployment remained hidden and harder to tackle. These examples prove that the negative phenomena of hyperinflation, output decline and unemployment **were not caused but only made explicit by liberalization**. (In public policy it is a clear advantage because problems arising in an open and transparent manner can be addressed and eventually resolved more quickly and perhaps more efficiently.)

The confusion in societal conscience was a reflection of an underlying societal and cultural fact. **People in their capacity as consumers no longer wanted to buy the goods and services manufactured by themselves in their capacity as producers.**[17] But it never occurred to them

[17] "The fact that transition came with an often large initial decrease in output should be seen as a puzzle. After all, the previous economic system was characterized by myriad

that despite having no political and ethical responsibility for this unfortunate outcome, there was a strong disconnect between their producers' and consumers' self. At the same time many people genuinely felt that they deserved Western living standards immediately without achieving commensurate Western levels of productivity and efficiency in the first place. *The hypocrisy of the former communist nomenclature and the schizophrenic mindset of the Soviet man were revealed in full force.* And that is one of the most stubborn and tragic legacies of the communist system difficult to overcome even today.[18]

In any case, stubborn hyperinflation, persistent output decline and massive unemployment were clearly reflecting huge disequilibria in the economy no matter what people felt about the root causes of these negative phenomena. Therefore, there was tremendous political pressure to do something about them.

Here comes the fundamental question often asked by both Western and Eastern scholars: **is political liberalization compatible with economic transformation?**[19] Can emerging but still extremely fragile democratic governments undertake hugely unpopular measures to address hyperinflation, output decline and unemployment? And once they decide to do it, will they survive or succumb to populist backlash? Will democracy survive?[20] This is a powerful issue even today.

distortions. One might have expected that removing most of them would lead to a large increase, not a decrease, in output." Blanchard (1997). Frankly, in light of understanding the true nature of the command economy, it was just next to impossible to expect any increase of aggregate output overnight. The sharp output decline was by no means a puzzle. That was exactly what was to be expected.

[18] In the communist system people knew rather well that what they produced were, in the majority of cases, substandard products in terms of quality and appeal. (The comparison between, say, a Trabant and a Mercedes was a convenient source of a tremendous amount of popular jokes.) But they were convinced that it was the consequence of the system transmitting wrong incentives. Incentives were regarded as completely exogenous. People felt, rightly or wrongly, that they could do nothing about changing them. But perception was far from reality. *These motivations were largely internalized and distorted profoundly the psyche and the moral composition of human beings in the communist system.* That remains a hard and continuing constraint on policy even today.

[19] See Bartlett (1997) and the very first sentence in his book.

[20] It is absolutely true that "the introduction of a market economy in the post-socialist societies is a 'political' project, which has prospects of success only if it rests on a strong democratic legitimation. And it is possible that the majority of the population finds neither democracy nor a market economy a desirable perspective." Offe (1991) 881.

Democratic governments of the day in all transition countries could choose among various policy options. One alternative was to do nothing and wait for the slowly evolving incipient market economy to settle itself through spontaneous and uncoordinated initiatives of the various economic actors. But that was politically unfeasible.[21]

A more viable and frequently used option was to *reverse liberalization*. Unfortunately, politically and intellectually weak governments in several countries succumbed to popular pressure in this way.[22] But that was, as experience shows, only to prolong the agony of the economy, exacerbate the hardships of the people and ultimately increase the pain. The third option was the best: **to undertake comprehensive macroeconomic stabilization.**

2.3. Macroeconomic stabilization

Why stabilization? First and foremost because of hyperinflation and to tackle the underlying root causes of almost permanent inflationary pressure. Hyperinflation made rational economic calculation very hard, if not outright impossible, and provided a perverse incentive for economic actors to stop savings and investment.[23] Once having set in as an unavoid-

[21] Nevertheless, it happened in several countries with extremely weak post-communist governments. The best example is Bulgaria. As a consequence of crippling political and administrative inertia of the Socialist governments and the impossibility of raising Western credit, the Bulgarian economy soon entered a freefall and then collapsed completely in 1995–96. [See Crampton (1997), Chapter 9, Part I. "Incomplete transition 1989–1997."]

[22] This was a typical Balkan option as it came to characterize the erratic behavior of many governments in the South East European arena throughout the whole 1990s. Of course, price fixing and even the rationing of some basic necessities were acceptable and maybe even unavoidable in countries engulfed by war, as it was typical in all former member states of socialist federal Yugoslavia, with the exception of Slovenia. But interestingly, stop-go policies concerning liberalization of prices and foreign trade were observable in Romania in the first decade of transition and in Bulgaria at least up until the Kostov-stabilization in 1997.

[23] The communist shortage economy was always characterized by *directed investments supported mostly by forced savings*. Apart from the black market, ordinary people had limited or no access to a wide variety of consumer goods. In classical command economies, like the Soviet Union or Romania until the very end, it was a daily struggle to buy basic food staples. Longs hours were spent in queues without any guarantee to secure even daily necessities. Many big ticket items, like flats, cars and telephone lines, were available only after a decade or more spent on the waiting list even in Hungary, ostensi-

able malaise, **hyperinflation became a self-sustaining phenomenon, a self-fulfilling prophecy, reinforcing itself through several strong feedback loops**.[24] This devastating vicious circle had to be broken if supply-side adjustment and, ultimately, economic growth were to be restarted and then sustained.

The original and major sources of inflation in the immediate aftermath of communism were, above all else, *related to government behavior*, i.e. **large budget deficits financed by high-powered money issued by the central bank, still dependent on the government both legally and politically.** Therefore, it was not at all impossible for governments to tame inflation and inflationary expectations by implementing *macroeconomic stabilization,* provided there was adequate amount of sustained political will and power.

In an inflexible, half-paralyzed economy characterized by steep decline in output and immense shortages of successful entrepreneurial performance, demand usually exceeded supply to a large extent—hence hyperinflation. While in the long run the most important question was how to increase supply and adjust its structure to that of demand, *in the short run there was little alternative to curbing what was constituting itself as excess demand.* That was exactly the primordial task of short-term macroeconomic policy in an environment of hyperinflation.

As it is well-known, macroeconomic policy has three major components: *monetary, fiscal and income policy.* Successful stabilization in transition required the precise coordination among all the elements of macroeconomic policy, especially, because of the intrinsic interlinkages among them.[25]

Likewise, fundamental *institutional* and profound *regulatory* changes were required in all three areas of macroeconomic policy.

---

bly a country of consumer paradise. At the same time, huge unspent financial balances accumulated in retail savings accounts.

[24] Many of them are related to anticipation as a variety of learned rational expectations. [See Kornai (1990).]

[25] In the classical Stalinist command economy there was hardly any separate standing and significance of macroeconomic policy, let alone any meaningful distinction among the components of macroeconomic policy itself. Even the Hungarian modified and the Yugoslav model, although undeniably more market-oriented, did not create enough scope and depth to the effective use of sophisticated instruments of monetary, fiscal and income policy. It became increasingly obvious that public policies can work only in an environment where *autonomous market players find it in their interest to respond positively to the signals transmitted by macroeconomic policy.* [See Bokros (2011)] This is especially notable in the stabilization drive. [See Blejer–Škreb (1997).]

In the monetary sphere this process inevitably ought to have started with the establishment of an **independent (autonomous) central bank**[26] or the rejuvenation of central banking and the strict legal and consensus-based political prohibition of monetary financing of fiscal deficits, both fiscal and quasi-fiscal.[27]

Those countries which gained or regained independence after the collapse of communism had to start from scratch, i.e. to create a brand new institution to perform a task which was completely missing before. The majority of countries have fallen into this category in Central and Eastern Europe. Out of the 15 former member states of the Soviet Union, **14 were facing the task of issuing and managing a new currency**.[28] Slovakia and four of the six former Yugoslav republics (the exception was Montenegro, which never bothered creating its own currency) were also obliged to start a new life with a new currency and a new central bank.[29] But even the formerly formally independent countries—Poland, first Czechoslovakia then the Czech Republic after 1993, Hungary, Romania, Bulgaria and Albania—needed a comprehensive rejuvenation of central banking.

---

[26] Warsaw pact countries used to operate a *one-tier banking system whereby central banking and what was called lending was performed by the same money distribution center, subordinated to the ministry of finance, itself under the control of the central planning office.* The establishment of a two-tier banking system, i.e. the institutional separation of central and commercial banking, was a necessary first step in the process of recreating a strong and well-functioning monetary authority. (The GDR is a largely unimportant exceptional case for its wholesale takeover by what was formerly known as West Germany.)

[27] This requirement is particularly important in light of recent responses to the global economic and financial crisis. The most important and powerful public bastions of financial capitalism, like the American Federal Reserve System, the European Central Bank, the Bank of England and the Bank of Japan have all applied the most brutal Keynesian variant of monetary stimulus dubbed eloquently as quantitative easing. This is nothing else but an open and blatant **monetization of debt**, **in most cases public debt**. While there might be powerful and rational arguments to do this in an economic and financial crisis under truly exceptional circumstances, there can be no denial of the fact that this type of almost unlimited quantitative easing undermines one of the most fundamental pillars of market-based capitalism by *blurring the line between monetary and fiscal policy and obscuring the separate responsibility of governments and central banks*.

[28] Russia first kept the old Soviet rubel and later gradually replaced it with a new Russian one.

[29] Serbia retained the old Yugoslav dinar for a long time until the secession of Montenegro and then redenominated its currency as a new Serbian dinar.

An independent central bank and, more precisely, a monetary authority empowered to guide monetary regulation autonomously within well-defined legal limits, is an indispensable prerequisite of restoring and preserving macroeconomic stability in all cases. But it was even more important in an incipient market economy like the early transitional ones. At that time life savings quickly melted away by hyperinflation. People had little or no faith in the national currency as it never functioned as a convenient store of value. **Currency substitution**, i.e. the widespread use of Western hard currency, typically either the Deutsche mark (and, after the introduction of banknotes in 2001, the Euro) or the US dollar, became rampant in all former communist countries except the Visegrád countries (V4) and the Baltic states.[30]

The newly-independent central banks were expected to undertake three distinct new tasks: (i) to refrain from monetary financing of the fiscal sector, (ii) manage overall liquidity in the banking sector by refinancing the newly-established commercial banks and (iii) stabilize the price of domestic money in time and space by regulating interest rates and exchange rates. All these steps were of crucial importance in order to stop hyperinflation and restore (create) an adequate level of currency stability. It constituted the backbone of what was to become a separate monetary policy.[31]

At this point in the analysis a distinction may be made between what can be considered as *ideal and optimal* policies.[32] Ideally, a successful treatment of hyperinflation may have dictated an extreme **shock therapy**,[33] a sudden and drastic reversal or withdrawal of easy money, *a*

[30] The (re)creation of trust in the national currency was not an absolute necessity. States, old and new, may have opted openly for a **full currency substitution**, i.e. the official acceptance of a foreign currency as domestic legal tender. It was exactly what happened in Montenegro and Kosovo. But that was a rather late occurrence, and remained an exception. For reasons of sovereignty and prestige, all other newly-independent states decided to introduce their own currency and all states, which had formally existed before the start of transition, decided to keep theirs. As a consequence, *monetary stabilization became an absolute necessity.*

[31] A broad overview of monetary policy and a detailed analysis of the specific impact of 6 monetary policy instruments in the early stages of transition in 26 countries are provided by De Melo–Denizer (1999).

[32] Ideal policies, albeit they do not exist in reality, can be approximated by optimal ones. Optimal policies are the ones perhaps least constrained by politics, but still constrained.

[33] "If a country inherits hyperinflation, the safest approach is to introduce a *radical therapy*, as it is the most likely way to reduce inflamed inflationary expectations and thus to break the mechanism of self-fulfilling prophecy on which hyperinflation is based." Balcerowicz (1995) 180.

largely balanced budget and strictly conservative, prudent lending on the part of the new commercial banks. But a central bank alone, no matter how well-educated its leadership might be, could not bring about these changes without an equally disciplined approach *by the government and the banking system*.

Wherever early democratic governments were sufficiently determined and professionally well-prepared—like in Estonia, Poland and Czechoslovakia—a sea change in policy proved to be possible against almost all odds. If it was maintained for a period long enough to break inflationary pressures and expectations, it did induce a *significant change of attitude* beyond the commercial banks, including also that of private entrepreneurs and even managers of still state-owned firms.[34]

When implemented in parallel or in quick succession, **liberalization and stabilization could complement and reinforce each other successfully**. Were inflationary pressures and expectations gradually to subside, then, after a period of excessive volatility and seemingly irrational swings, prices tended to stabilize making rational calculations possible for entrepreneurs. Increasing predictability and transparency in market conditions could spark supply-side response from new entrepreneurs and even from old state firms. In a liberalized environment hitherto unavailable consumer goods could not only be imported but also produced at home. Had the exchange rate become not only realistic, but also relatively stable, then the new production was to be profitable. Reinvested profits could create further growth, jobs, maybe even taxes. **Incipient supply-side adjustment might result in making monetary and fiscal stabilization gradually less stringent and politically more sustainable.** *Thus, optimal policies could create a virtuous cycle.*[35]

---

[34] The most famous and clearly shock-therapic treatment of hyperinflation was the *Balcerowicz-plan* introduced on January 1, 1990 in Poland. With its consistent, crystallized, and rather well-communicated professional content it became a convenient reference point for all subsequent stabilization programs in the region. It was close to what can be regarded as an optimal plan for it rested on those three components which are the most important in breaking the vicious cycle of inflation: (1) applying a nominal anchor, i.e. first a fixed exchange rate then a crawling peg with a preannounced schedule of consecutive minidevalutations and, finally, crawling peg only; (2) stopping the monetization of the fiscal deficit after three years thus finally eliminating the most inflationary way of financing the budget deficit; (3) restricting money creation by the commercial banking system with relatively tight refinancing facilities (including high interest rates) offered by the central bank. [See Wellisz (1997).]

[35] That was certainly possible even in cases where shock-therapic liberalization proved to be unnecessary. Hungary, the home of the modified, more market-oriented model of

It implies a further indispensable element of macroeconomic stabilization to be firmly in place: **fiscal prudence**.

The autonomy of monetary policy and of the institution carrying it out was, if not always accepted, at least widely-known and discussed. Much less attention was dedicated to the equally important problem of how to establish *the autonomy of fiscal policy* and how to align the obviously not independent finance ministry at least as *primus inter pares* among ministries within the central governmental public administration.[36]

Since the legacy of communism was a subordinate role of finance in the macro-management of the command economy which, itself, had been incorporated into the political sphere, the emancipation of finance and, within that, **the emancipation of fiscality**, i.e., the **separate consideration of government (public) finances,** was a fundamental issue in transition.[37]

The legacy of all variations of communism constituted an extremely heavy burden on macroeconomic management, and not only from legal and political point of view. Fiscal balances deteriorated rapidly and sig-

---

goulash communism, a country where quite comprehensive liberalization had largely been achieved *before* the political changes of 1989–1990 and considerable amount of private investment took place between 1990 and 1995, incipient but markedly-felt supply-side adjustment was helping tremendously the success of a somewhat belated fiscal stabilization which—after much hesitation—was undertaken only in 1995–1996. [See Bokros (1998c).]

[36] The autonomy of fiscal policy and the primacy of fiscality in government affairs are not readily obvious even in Western economic thought, let alone in Western government practice. As the global financial crisis has eloquently shown, first and foremost in the eurozone but also in many new member states of the EU, **governments tend to disregard fiscality until public deficit and debt reach unsustainable proportions.** Even then, it is the international bond markets which serve as a brutal early warning system rather than the usually cumbersome, unpredictable and rather slow domestic political process. This characteristic feature of government behavior may change as a consequence of the global financial crisis and the strong cross-border spillover impact of fiscal problems in common currency areas. [See Roubini–Mihm (2010).]

[37] And that raised a whole host of new problems, because "many issues in public finance remain inherently controversial. To establish the economic case for the public sector is to delimit the sphere that can be left to the invisible hand and the rules of the market. The scope of existing externalities, the acceptability of a market-determined income distribution, the shape of the social welfare function, maintaining full resource utilization, the issues of inflation and growth, all these have powerful bearings on the appropriate size and activities of the public sector. So does the capability of public policy to apply appropriate corrections, with the scope of public policy failure matched against that of market failure. Given this array of problems and their linkages, ideological and value issues are never far away. Moreover, the tools of fiscal policy changes with changing fiscal institutions." Musgrave (1985) 53.

nificantly as a consequence of output collapse and fast rising unemployment as well. But to explain to the largely uneducated electorate of the newly-emerging democratic polity *why on earth fiscal prudence and the restoration of fiscal equilibrium matter* was, and has remained to this day, one of the toughest challenges of transition.[38]

The **drastic deterioration of both explicit and implicit fiscal balances** was another natural consequence of the enormous distortions inherited from the communist system.[39] This was caused by, and was the reflection of, several key factors:

1. *Tax revenues from the newly-liberalized enterprise sector collapsed.* Parallel with marked output decline in a large number of state-owned enterprises, tax revenues (including social security contributions) suffered a sharp drop. This was not and could not be compensated by increasing tax revenues from the incipient private sector. There were several reasons for this. First, private firms were emerging only gradually. Second, most of them did not pay taxes even if they could and made every effort to conceal revenue. **Widespread tax evasion and avoidance was, and has remained, a defining feature of the new capitalist order**, reflecting both the legacy of communism and the low level of public trust in the newly emerging system. Third, the hastily reorganized tax administration was unable and unprepared to collect tax revenues from thousands of newborn small firms.[40]

2. Fiscal expenditure was forced to rise as a consequence of new items in central and local budgets. **Unemployment benefits and social transfers**, either deemed unnecessary or expressly denied by the communist system, now appeared as a consequence of both economic necessity and democratic political response to various and ostensibly new societal phenomena: *massive unemployment and rampant poverty*.[41]

---

[38] See Győrffy (2007)

[39] Once again, it is important to emphasize that the large deficits were not caused but **only made explicit** by the transition process. Like output decline, hyperinflation and massive unemployment, emerging fiscal deficits were, first and foremost, reflections of the enormous distortions and inefficiencies created by the command economy which had had an almost complete disregard to consumer preferences.

[40] An important reform could have been an early introduction of a modern personal income tax system, hence collect tax revenues increasingly from physical persons. But that was a tall order and could not have happened at the time of output collapse, hyperinflation and massive unemployment mainly for political reasons. (Hungary was an exception: it introduced personal income tax and value-added tax in 1988.)

[41] **Unemployment and poverty**, while having existed in communism in a hidden and disguised form, were now considered not only new phenomena but, even more importantly,

3. **Political democratization and decentralization** naturally led to fiscal democratization and decentralization which, in turn, resulted in the creation of a wide variety of new institutions and a proliferation of new entities at the level of both elected bodies and public administration. A large number of new political parties were formed with offices, territorial network, bureaucracy. Democratic parliaments established extended administration. Presidencies of the new democratic republics required experts, bureaux, protocol and pomp. Constitutional courts, state audit offices, parliamentary ombudsmen, regional governorships and other prestigious institutions of newly-regained and redistributed sovereign power were created with generous salaries, entitlements in money and in kind, luxury car fleet and lavish fiscal support. Finally, governments were obliged to establish new departments of central public administration to deal with formerly nonexistent public functions such as *competition, financial sector regulation, public procurement, privatization, treasury management, environmental regulation and cleanup*, etc. While most of these new institutions served absolutely legitimate public policy purposes, their establishment, functioning and financing was usually quite intransparent, cumbersome, unstable and unwieldy, making an excessive burden to state finances on the top of an incipient and still less than fully dynamic market economy.[42]

4. Decentralization was even more comprehensive and visible at the level of *federative entities, regions, rayons, counties, districts and municipalities*. Subsovereign governments, albeit many of them had formally existed before the collapse of communism, developed further as they re-

---

new concepts. The communist system had explicitly denied and claimed to have eliminated both. Although it was untrue, it served as a *last refuge for a no longer attractive, persuasive and fast disintegrating ideology* which had previously declared economic and welfare superiority to market capitalism. When this latter proved to be untenable, communists still claimed that even if the communist system might not have (yet) proved its superiority to capitalism by surpassing levels of economic output and general welfare, it was an undeniable fact that it created *more equality in society by eliminating unemployment and poverty*, which are constant inalienable features of the capitalist system. It was considered as an ostensibly convenient second best explanation for the legitimacy of quasi socialist revolutions in the Third World, especially in Cuba and Africa.

[42] A normative study of how the new state should look like and what rules the newly autonomous fiscal sector should follow is offered by László (1994). A comprehensive overview of public finance reforms, including new institutional elements, is presented by many authors in the book edited by Bokros and Dethier (1998). The most important lessons and consequences of the first decade of transition in public finances are discussed by Tanzi and Tsibouris (2001). A comprehensive account of the extent and the cost of state-building in selected countries is provided by Fritz (2007).

gained as much local sovereignty as they could in name of democratization, decentralization and subsidiarity.[43] Furthermore, there was a tendency of *fragmentation of jurisdictions, especially at the lowest level.* Even though reforms of public administration did not start at the early stages of transition, *a proliferation of subsovereign government functions and entities* was clearly visible across the whole transition world. That required even more fiscal resources, leading to either an overstretch of government finance or an immediate hollowing out of the democratic content.[44] This tendency was further exacerbated by the fact that subsovereign governments did not have and, in the great majority of cases, *did not wish to acquire autonomous taxing power.* That would have implied the assumption of more political responsibility, which many of them largely detested. Instead, they expected *increasing amounts of transfers* arriving from higher levels of the government hierarchy.

While not well-understood, the whole issue of subsovereign government finance and administration was a hugely important area of both political and economic reform. *It was a cross-cutting issue affected by almost all other structural reforms in transition.* Even the so-called first-generation reforms, like liberalization, stabilization and privatization had regional and local aspects which gave rise to regional and local demands for inclusion and participation. It is both the burden of specific reforms, like prudent fiscal management, but also the spoils thereof, like regional

---

[43] That was made possible partly by the extreme weakness of central governments, other times it was genuinely encouraged by the central authorities. Remember Boris Yeltsin's famous remark: "provinces and autonomous republics should grab as much sovereignty as they can live with."

[44] "It is important to recognize that the theoretical efficiency gains from decentralization can be significantly undermined in practice by institutional constraints. First, the administrative capacity of subnational governments may be quite weak. Overstaffing, poor technical skills and training of employees, and the inability to formulate and implement effective spending programs to fully exploit potential financing sources characterize many regional and local jurisdictions in a number of countries worldwide. The incidence of corruption at the local level is not negligible, either. Second, subnational governments often have not been able to develop modern and transparent public expenditure management systems, including adequate mechanisms of financial control, reporting and accounting, and evaluation of expenditure programs. Third, the size of local jurisdictions (which is often the result of historical developments or political factors) is not always consistent with the full realization of potential efficiency gains from decentralization." Ter-Minassian (1997) 5–6.

All these factors have been present in an even more accentuated way in all countries in transition not only at the beginning but also well beyond. Many of them can be clearly observed even today.

and local ownership of state assets and privatization revenue that raised tremendous interest and became subject of ferocious political fight within the generally weak states having emerged from the ashes of communism.

Given the extreme fragility of the newly emerging government sector, fiscal stabilization seems to have been an almost hopeless exercise. Interestingly, there were some expenditure items which offered themselves for significant reduction, thus mitigating the impact of overspending on the budget balance.

1. *Direct subsidies to state-owned enterprises as well as consumer (price) subsidies* could have been, and in many cases were, substantially curtailed, sometimes abolished altogether. It was a logical extension of liberalization in terms of eliminating market distortions. Effective adjustment to prevailing consumer preferences can be had only if **preferences incorporate and reflect relative costs, i.e. the underlying value-for-money considerations in a fairly explicit manner**. That required a relatively free formation of *close-to-market-equilibrium* prices for tradables and *close-to-cost-covering* prices for non-tradables. The liberalization of prices in the competitive sector (should have) implied the elimination of most, if not all, producer and consumer subsidies while the establishment of close-to-cost-covering prices allowed for some significant reduction of subsidies in public utilities.[45]

2. *Inflation,* although having distorted pre-stabilization expectations, may have helped as it could have worked toward restoring fiscal equilibrium by grossing up tax revenues while at the same time many items of outlays remained fixed in absolute terms.[46] Once both forced and voluntary financial savings were wiped out by hyperinflation, there was no more fuel to the fire unless the state started to rely on monetary financing of budget deficits, allowed a significant accumulation of interenterprise arrears and

---

[45] "There are two basic purposes of the public regulation of prices: the curtailment of the exercise of monopoly power and the elimination of certain forms of price distortions." Stigler (1975) 64–65. If anything, policy makers of transition understood all too well the interplay of these distortionary forces. That is why strict regulation of public utility tariffs has largely been maintained all along transition.

[46] This is a typical trick of fiscal policy creating an illusion of healthier fiscal stance but it can easily become a trap if stakeholders realize that they might be cheated and, hence, request a periodic adjustment to the size of expenditure items dear to them taking into account anticipated, rather than actual, inflation. As a consequence, disinflation may, and should, acquire overriding importance in policy making. For the efforts to achieve disinflation and its results in the early stages of transition, see Cottarelli–Szapáry (1998) and Cottarelli–Doyle (2001).

wages were increased without consideration to gains in productivity. As it was already noted, in the absence of commensurate gains in productivity and efficiency, early wage liberalization could have led to even more inflation. That was something to be avoided at any rate. Fortunately, it was very clear to leading policy makers of early stabilizations that **income policy needed to remain restrictive** and that required not only the avoidance of any premature liberalization but even more so the break with previous automatic adjustment in wages to inflation.[47] Correction was made, inevitably, by substantially lowering the living standards of a large part of society. But stabilization was there to put a floor under the recession, thus output decline could finally bottom out. Obviously, restarting growth was a completely different task and required the presence of additional factors. *While stabilization can be successful in reducing and eliminating excess demand, sustainable growth could only be built on supply-side adjustment.*

All in all, financial stabilization was absolutely not a hopeless exercise. With adequate professional preparation and longer lasting political support, democratic governments were able to break the vicious cycle of inflation and create a reliable and predictable business environment for entrepreneurial initiative.

2.4. Competitive privatization

Twenty years ago privatization was a widely applied tool of public policy not only in the transforming countries but in the developed and developing part of the Western world as well. But the concept was not the same.

There are three important aspects in which a rather sharp distinction can and should be made between the so called "Western and Eastern" privatization. The first is *systemic-theoretical*, the second is *comparative-historical*, and the third is *practical-political*.

Privatization is understood differently depending on the specific context. In the context of transforming a command economy into a market-oriented one and a totalitarian one-party dictatorship into a democratic

[47] That is why the first democratic government of Poland, led by Tadeusz Mazowiecki, abolished wage indexation which had been introduced in July, 1989 by the last communist government headed by Mieczysław Rakowski and imposed severe tax on wage increases over and above a very low index ratio of price increases. [See Dąbrowski (1992) 300.]

polity, privatization means not only the privatization of a few, albeit large and dominant, state-owned enterprises. It includes the *organic development of new private firms,* which is far more important than the denationalization of existing state-owned ones, inherited from the previous communist system. It implies the **privatization of the whole national economy**. It is supposed to bring about a fundamental change in enterprise behavior and the incentive structure for managers at the helm of private and state-owned firms alike. Privatization of the national economy means, therefore, that *the profit motive and the creation of more and more market value for owners, as principal stakeholders, is now a concept and consideration of paramount importance.* Finally, privatization also involves the **separation of the private sphere of existence from the public domain**, i.e. the relative autonomy of private economic activity from politics, culture, law, religion, ethics, public finance and administration, etc. As a result, after privatization enterprises are supposed and expected to act, first and foremost, in the interest of their private owners and follow behavioral rules with clearly identifiable separate economic utility functions. From that moment onwards individual economic organizations no longer existed as mere administrative units of a single monstrous state entity; **they were reconstituted as enterprises**.[48]

These are perhaps the most relevant distinguishing characteristic features of post-communist privatization in its *systemic-theoretical* aspect. But no less important is the *comparative-historical* one.

Privatization as a powerful public policy tool to recharge the batteries of the market economy was quite fashionable in the Western, first and foremost in the Anglo-Saxon, world throughout the 1980s. After the first and second oil shocks (in 1973 and 1979, respectively) inflation became a permanent feature of the economy in developed industrial countries. As a consequence of excessive labor and product market rigidities, monetary accommodation and the dominance of state ownership, especially in the financial sector and public utilities, the adjustment of the economy resulted in less growth and more inflation. Hence the typical

[48] The most important and visible legal procedure by which state-owned production units were transformed into enterprises is called *corporatization*. The term is somewhat misleading because not all state enterprises were obliged to put on a corporate form of limited liability. At the same time many of the newborn private firms remained unincorporated from strictly legal point of view. But these sophisticated distinctions of legal minutiae were largely unimportant at the beginning of transition. Hence, the term *corporatization* will be used. [The problems of legal system transfer and rejuvenation is discussed eloquently by Ajani (1998).]

phenomenon of the 1970s and early 1980s: *stagflation*.[49] Since all important stakeholders, first and foremost privileged state employees and managers of large state-owned enterprises, fought to preserve their income and political position, fiscal deficits skyrocketed. There was an urgent need to address the *toxic combination of high inflation, stubborn unemployment and low growth with better supply-side adjustment* at that time in the Western market economy. A surprising parallelism with transition, indeed.[50]

Margaret Thatcher came to power in the United Kingdom on May 4, 1979. In her long decade of being prime minister, the British conservative government carried out a comprehensive program of sweeping privatization. More than 20 large enterprises were sold to private investors during the 1980s, most of them public utilities, i.e. natural monopolies, at least partially. That changed profoundly the British corporate landscape and contributed significantly to the comprehensive rejuvenation of the British economy after several decades of sclerosis and stagnation.[51]

It would be preposterous to compare the privatization in the UK to the privatization in the post-communist countries which started a decade later. First, no matter how much state ownership there had been before, the British economy, without doubt, had always remained a

[49] Haberler (1986) presented alternative explanations for stagflation, a "Keynesian," a "monetarist-rational expectation" position and a "traditional conservative" one. A comprehensive evaluation of stagflation was made by Bruno and Sachs (1985). A monetary perspective is offered by Barsky and Kilian (2000).

[50] The Anglo-Saxon privatization drive did make a tremendous impact on policymakers all over the world, including that of the transition countries. It is in sharp contrast with the so-called "Washington consensus" which is widely regarded as the dominant model blueprint for transition. [See Berend (2009) 42–49.] But despite the illusion of and belated rationalization of events by many scholars in this respect, reality was quite different. Most policymakers were completely ignorant even of the existence of this term, and in no way inclined to follow its policy prescriptions. [See Laar (2010) 171.]

[51] The British privatization drive was not only an economic but also a political success to be repeated in many parts of the world. When in France a conservative-liberal coalition came to power in March, 1986, it immediately started an even more ambitious program of privatization. The French approach to privatization was radical compared to that of the UK. In the UK each individual transaction required specific legislation. In France the parliament approved a general framework law on privatization as early as July, 1986, which gave a comprehensive authorization to the government to manage and carry out specific deals on its own. Privatization then came to the agenda of center-right or right-wing governments in the US, Canada, West Germany, Japan, Chile and Turkey. But it became fashionable even with Socialist governments in Spain, Australia and New Zealand. [See Letwin (1988).]

market economy. Second, denationalizing 20 large firms was much easier than to sell tens of thousands enterprises, large and small alike. In the UK there were thousands of domestic investors, wholesale and retail, financial and institutional, strategic and portfolio types, too. Large investable funds were abundantly available; after all, the City of London was a financial center of global importance. A vast army of legal firms, investment banks were available and eager to assist the government in carrying out specific transactions. In contrast, former communist countries did not possess any significant amount of domestic financial savings and whatever forced savings there might have been, were quickly wiped out by hyperinflation. Moreover, *potential domestic investors had little or no professional expertise to run these enterprises properly*. Finally, the absence of a well-established democratic polity and strong, clean governments with adequate administrative capacity as well as the lack of reliable advisory services to be provided by prestigious domestic firms made effective and efficient privatization almost impossible.

At the beginning of transition the British way of privatization was more of a political and, at times, an ideological beacon rather than a practical example to be followed *because it was concentrating on public utilities*, arguably the most complex type of transactions involving a fair amount of regulatory change well before any specific transaction could take place. Post-communist governments were keen to show some early success by implementing a **fire sale of small properties** (repair shops, retail outlets, restaurants, trucks, machinery, etc) which created a relatively large number of small entrepreneurs interested in the success of the very process rather quickly. (In many cases former employees were offered preferential access to these assets.) In addition, the first democratically elected governments had a *very shallow administrative capacity* hardly adequate to execute complex transactions. That is why a large number of relatively simple transactions were carried out in the area of competitive sectors. Complex transactions involving financial sector entities and public utilities had to wait for restructuring and re-regulation to take effect first.

Despite all these fundamental discrepancies, the British initiatives and the global decade of privatization in the 1980s made a profound impact on the hearts and minds of both the democratic political leaders and the society at large. Privatization became a political imperative and an economic necessity. It was rightly considered—on the one hand, positively—as the **embodiment of economic freedom**, and—on the other hand, negatively—as the **most important factor against any attempt to communist restoration**.[52]

The practical-political aspect of privatization is best represented by the overwhelming need of supply-side adjustment. Governments wanted to restart growth as quickly as possible. But growth could be fuelled only by productive investments which, in turn, required interested private owners.

As liberalization could realize its full positive potential if it was soon accompanied by stabilization, stabilization, in turn, could accomplish its goals in full only when it was followed by a critical mass of privatization.

Without proper stabilization, liberalization might have primarily, if not exclusively, led to hyperinflation, output decline and massive unemployment. Stabilization, although it may have brought down inflation at the beginning, in turn, could have ended up with even more output decline if not a total collapse of the national economy without supply-side adjustment and growth brought about by privatization.[53]

Methods of privatization were publicly debated at extreme length before, during and even after privatization for a long time. That was a fa-

---

[52] It is important to remember that transition did not start at the same time in Central and Eastern Europe, let alone in the former Soviet communist world. Political changes were out of sync: democratization started in Poland as early as in 1988 and the first democratic government facing the frightening transition agenda took power on August 24, 1989, *almost exactly two years before the coup d'état in Moscow* which could have changed the course of history for the worse by restoring communism by the force of Soviet arms. The government of Tadeusz Mazowiecki was well aware of the potential danger of reversibility and it was high on the mind of the Czechoslovak leaders as well. Privatization, therefore, became an indispensable political imperative in order to establish facts on the ground and make transition as much hard to reverse as possible.

[53] The matrix of structural reforms in transition expresses these intrinsic interlinkages absolutely clearly. All building blocks are linked with all the others; it is an obvious feature of this construct. But the strongest links can be detected in the individual lines. So much so that specific blocks in individual lines almost cannot be interpreted as having standalone importance. When governments concentrated only on some of these blocks and neglected all others, **no positive impact of these isolated measures was forthcoming**. Furthermore, *random selection of transition measures and their inconsistent application without putting them into the context of the big picture guaranteed failure almost immediately*. Liberalization without stabilization was the best way to discredit liberalization itself. Likewise, stabilization without privatization was the best recipe for turning it into a disaster by the total collapse of the economy. (As we will see in the next chapters, public utility privatization without proper restructuring and re-regulation of what was clearly a natural monopoly area was a well-paved road to *farce, mockery, political backlash and, finally, reversal.)*

vorite national pastime everywhere in the first enthusiastic period of transition.[54]

But modalities of privatization can be discussed in a constructive manner only if **the objectives of privatization** are clearly stated and, in the case of multiple and usually contradictory objectives, **an order of preference** is established among them.

From the viewpoint of progressively overcoming the dreadful "cul de sac de civilisation," represented by the communist system, the key question was to improve, first and foremost, **the material living standards of the people**. For that to happen, economic growth, and even more so, *rapid and sustained growth of national output* was clearly the number one prerequisite.

In addition to a consistent macroeconomic policy and favorable business environment supported by adequate institutions, rapid and sustained growth required large amounts of *new capital investment into the newly privatized enterprises which were supposed to be governed by efficient and prudent private owners*. In light of this simple line of reasoning, the crucial issue in privatization was, and has remained ever since, **the simultaneous prevalence of new investment and good corporate governance**.

Another frequently stated goal of privatization, at least when disposing of relatively sizeable state firms, was to *maximize the selling price and, hence, the privatization revenue to the national budget.* While an absolutely legitimate objective in itself, in most specific cases it was hard to reconcile with the primary interest of maximizing new investment channeled into the enterprise by high quality professional investors. Even the few valuable state-owned enterprises inherited from

[54] It is interesting to note that nowadays privatization is not on the agenda of many governments in transition countries in any meaningful way. Unfortunately, that is not a sign that transition is over by now. Rather, it is a powerful symptom of the negative connotations privatization have acquired along the way. Moreover, as a consequence of the global financial crisis, governments in Central and Eastern Europe are putting an emphasis on a *renewed and expanded role of the state, including in enterprise management*. Confusing the role of the state as a regulator and as an owner of productive assets, some countries are now falling victims to populist policies trying to restore a good part of the socialist economic policy agenda. That shows the highly cyclical nature of economic and societal development, the extreme fragility of the achievements of transition, the marked weakness of the democratic institutions and culture and, last but not least, the reversibility of the whole process. (A recent eloquent example is the wholesale expropriation of the mandatory private pension system and the partial renationalization of the oil and gas company MOL in Hungary in 2011.)

communism required a *large infusion of new technology, know-how, patents, machinery, organization, management, finances, accounting, supply chain, marketing, distribution, etc.* which could only be supplied by **first-class strategic investors**. That required **a dilution of state ownership** rather than an outright sale bringing about a change of title in the first place. Governments, privatization agencies, therefore, were clearly confronted with an immediate stark choice: *dilution or divestiture?* While the former was the best method of privatization from the viewpoint of the enterprise and, ultimately, that of the national economy as well, the latter might have been a more pressing objective in the short run given the often dire situation of government finances.

In practice, however, this contradiction could, and often was, solved by a **two-stage approach**, where the first stage was characterized by dilution and the second by divestiture. If and when governments could afford being patient in terms of not demanding much revenue out of privatization overnight, this method proved to be truly optimal because the value of the diluted state holding appreciated tremendously as a consequence of the capital infusion and good governance achieved already in the first phase.[55]

But to generate sizeable new investment and at the same time improve corporate governance for any firm to be privatized was a very tall order. The real tragedy and insurmountable legacy of the communist system was manifesting itself in the fact that the command economy and society prohibited the accumulation of both private capital and, in the great majority of countries, significant experience in private entrepreneurship, too. As a consequence, at the beginning of transition, *there were neither an adequate amount of investable funds, nor a sufficient number of educated, skilled and experienced individuals capable of acting as professional investors and managers in any meaningful manner.* Hence, not infrequently, the only way to overcome this

[55] One of the best examples of this multistage approach was used in case of the Hungarian Telecommmunications Company (formerly called MATÁV, now Magyar Telekom) which was privatized in *three stages*. In the first phase 30% of the shares of the state-owned telecom firm were sold to a foreign consortium owned by Ameritech and Deutsche Telekom in 1993. In addition to divestiture, the Hungarian state asked for a huge amount of new investment to be channeled into the company as well. As a consequence, the first transaction was already a hybrid one: dilution cum divestiture. (Part of the proceeds of the sale was also directly clawed back into the enterprise by the state itself.) The second phase was pure divestiture in 1995. The third step was the parallel listing of the company at the New York and the Budapest Stock Exchanges in 1997. [A detailed description of this specific transaction is given by Mihályi (2010) 688–702.]

serious limitation in the privatization drive was to invite **first-class, preferably foreign and primarily strategic (professional) investors**.

It has been extremely difficult for the proud nations of Mitteleuropa, the Baltic and the Balkan area and their fairly nationalistic political class and intelligentsia to accept the inevitable dominance of foreign investors in the privatization process even though that was also very much in the national interest, when soberly conceived. Well-connected people, members of the former nomenclature, small local entrepreneurs coming to daylight from the shadow or semi-official economy, did not want to share the riches even though they were, in the great majority of cases, unable to pay for the assets they wished to acquire. Weak governments in the early stages of transition quickly succumbed to the pressure of these hyperactive elements of society and devised various schemes to overcome the limitations constituted by the lack of domestic capital accumulation. At the same time the inability of most domestic investors to provide strong, effective and efficient governance to newly-acquired firms was simply ignored or denied in name of overflowing national pride.[56]

It might be shocking to claim today that more often than not by far **the best way to privatize large state enterprises was to sell their controlling stake to first-class, reputable, rich and strong foreign strategic investors**. Now, more than twenty years after transition started, it is time to realize that when other methods of privatization were used then usually one of the two *sine qua non* conditions of effective and efficient privatization were not met, i.e. *new investment and good governance.*[57]

Three different methods were designed and implemented to overcome the domestically almost insurmountable investment barrier: (i) **restitution** (reprivatization), (ii) **mass privatization** based on free distribution of assets (voucher or coupon privatization) and (iii) **directed lending** on highly preferential terms either to insiders (management and employee buyouts) or outsiders (share purchase programs).[58]

---

[56] The negative consequences of these sub-optimal methods of privatization are strongly felt even today as local oligarchs now try to cement their ill-received gains by pervasive corruption and state capture. As history shows, if the symbiotic requirements of investment and governance are ignored, it leads not only to a sub-optimal economic outcome, but even more tragically, a **serious distortion of the democratic polity.**

[57] A balanced overview of pro and con arguments in the first decade of privatization is given by Nellis (2001).

[58] Of course, these methods of privatization were not considered as inferior by most if not all policymakers at the beginning of transition. As privatization is an inherently political process, crude and crass economic and political interests were promoted as if it was

Restitution was much more a political imperative than a rational policy alternative. It was inherently inefficient, created huge problems in societal equity and, in most cases, lacked adequate administrative procedures. No coincidence, therefore, that in most countries restitution was largely limited to *real estate* (agricultural land and precious large scale housing property) and affected productive assets only in a limited manner, most of which was built up after the communist takeover anyway.[59]

In most cases the success of restitution was ultimately decided by the mundane factor of *administration* both in terms of discovering the proper proof of bygone era claims on property but also *managing cadastre, precise registration of title, share certificates, etc.* without much delay or corruption. No surprise, therefore, that restitution was more comprehensively advanced only in what used to be East Germany, in the five new Bundesländer.[60] This intrinsically cumbersome process was undoubtedly and significantly helped by German culture (Pünktlichkeit & Genauigkeit)[61] and huge West German administrative and political

about finding the best possible methods of privatization. Restitution, mass privatization schemes and creating new owners by lending were all considered legitimate. While their supporters wanted to enhance the scope of each of these methods, ultimately none of them gained exclusive prominence in the process of privatization. The reason for that was, once again, the brutal reality of state-owned enterprises: the overwhelming majority needed a huge amount of new investment and also much improved corporate governance. [See Frydman–Gray–Rapaczynski (1996).]

59 Some politicians and practicioners praised restitution as it was a rather speedy way to create facts on the ground and make still feared restoration of communist power more unlikely and potentially more difficult. It is no wonder that one of them is Mart Laar, who became prime minister of Estonia in late 1992 at the age of 32. Problems in the Baltic countries were immense and Soviet domination not at all a distant memory. In order to express and strengthen newly-regained national independence in a speedy way, restitution offered a convenient alternative. But, contrary to unsubstantiated claims made by Laar, it did not mean that reprivatization was a guarantee for a more efficient use or better upkeep of assets. [See Laar (2010) 175.]

60 An early synthesis of reprivatization in Central and Eastern Europe was given by a joint report of the Central and Eastern European Privatization Network (CEEPN) and the World Bank (1993).

61 Many citizens of East Germany—and by the same token, emigrated former citizens of East Germany living in the West—miraculously and meticulously preserved their written proof of former title to the assets they had possessed before the nationalization following the communist takeover. (Elsewhere in Central and Eastern Europe it was far less assured, except in cases involving the former landed aristocracy.) Was it also because the German people always felt the existence of the German Democratic Republic as a passing whim and whisper of history? We will probably never know…

support.[62] But even in Germany the inherent conflict between restitution and fast privatization was almost impossible to overcome.[63]

Mass privatization schemes were more prominent, quite fashionable and widespread at the beginning of transition. They were conceived as all-encompassing grand design schemes solving several problems of transition in one quick shot.[64] First, it acknowledged the politically very convenient fiction upheld by an otherwise obsolete communist ideology that *people in general were the owners of all productive assets in the national economy*. Second, it was conceived as a partial and symbolic compensation for the hardships and hopelessness endured in the command and shortage economy. Third, it was designed to create a well-balanced and equitable society of *people's capitalism* where everybody could become an owner without having had to pay for property. Fourth, it seems to have been a convenient and ostensibly elegant method to get around the problem created by the lack of financial savings and investments in the domestic economy and society.[65]

---

[62] In addition to administrative bottlenecks, in most countries other than East Germany restitution was highly unpractical. For it to advance properly there was a need for a *politically acceptable cut-off date:* who is the legitimate former private owner? Which one was to be restituted? That was an almost insurmountable problem in most places where valuable assets were confiscated and redistributed by violent methods several times and, quite often, in quick succession before, during and after World War II.

[63] See Pohl (1993)

[64] A still highly optimistic overview of mass privatization, its legal and institutional aspects, its impact on capital market development and corporate governance, as well as an analysis of 15 country experiences are given by Lieberman–Nestor–Desai (1997). However, one should not forget that this study was prepared before the Czech government and currency crisis of May, 1997 which changed not only the public but also the academic perception of mass privatization to the negative.

[65] The idea of mass privatization in Central and Eastern Europe is said to have been invented by Janusz Lewandowski and Jan Szomburg who wrote about the potential application of free (re)distribution of shares as a fundamental element of social and economic reform in transition. [Lewandowski–Szomburg (1989) 257–268.] The concept was quickly picked up by some Western scholars acting as advisors to the first democratic government of Poland. As it is typical, the idea was immediately presented as a panacea to most if not all difficulties which looked almost insurmountable at the start of transition. The line of reasoning went as follows: "One key point in our strategy is that much of the privatization should be accomplished through the free distribution of shares to various groups, including workers, pension funds, and mutual funds, rather than through the sale of shares in an initial public offering (IPO), which was standard practice in the well-known British privatizations. In Eastern Europe, *the free distribution of shares would help sidestep the difficult, costly and time consuming process of enterprise valuation, and recognizes the scarcity of financial capital in private hands*. [Lipton and Sachs

Mass privatization (also called voucher or coupon privatization) made it possible **to create millions of domestic owners** (shareholders) almost overnight. That was politically very important, perhaps even justifiable.[66] But it solved neither the issue of *additional investment* channeled into the formerly state-owned enterprises, nor the problem of effective and efficient *corporate governance*. On the contrary, most of the companies subject to mass privatization ended up being managed by the **former administrators** who could easily overrule the dispersed owners, the formal title holders. Even if the majority or the blocking minority stake of the shares ended up in the hand of newly-established privatization investment funds (PIFs) as intermediaries, that did not necessarily help solve the governance problem either. With the interjection of these seemingly more professional intermediaries the question was *who would control and govern the PIFs*. The latter were either under the control of *still state-owned banks* (like in Czechoslovakia) or under the supervision of the *state privatization agency* (like in Romania) or—if they managed to collect and concentrate citizens' vouchers by the initiative of well-connected individuals—they were under *unsupervised insider control*. This latter arrangement represented the worst case and led to tremendous abuse.[67]

Advocates of mass privatization were, by and large, aware of the most important weaknesses of the scheme: the absence of strong, if any, corporate governance and adequate incentives to undertake additional investments.[68] But they certainly felt it could and would be solved, over time, by a *fast reconcentration of the shares in the hand of intimately interested investors*, capable to provide effective and efficient ownership influence over the management of the firms.[69] That largely proved to be an illusion, too.

(1991) 45, italics mine.] As it turned out, enterprise valuation was not just a technical problem which could be easily sidestepped by the wunderwaffe of mass privatization.

In contrast to the justification given by foreign scholars, some practitioners promoted mass schemes exactly for their alleged advantage of redistributing wealth while enterprises still had some residual value. "…the true value of the privatized enterprise rapidly decreases due to its unavoidable privatization agony and to the absence of a real owner during the privatization process. Having understood that, we tried to look for privatization techniques that would be faster than the standard ones. For that reason we prepared and successfully implemented a nonstandard technique called voucher privatization." Klaus (1997) Chapter 12. "The Privatization Experience. The Czech Case," 72.

66 See Lewandowski (1997) and Klaus (1995) and (1997).

67 See Mlčoch–Manochin–Sojka (2000).

68 See Klaus (1995) and Lewandowski (1997).

69 Some scholars, like K. A. Soós (2010) refer to the process of ownership reconcentration as *secondary privatization* in contrast to the original transfer of ownership, which is con-

Directed lending to insiders and outsiders on highly preferential terms was widely used in case of what was later called "small privatization," i.e. the denationalization of small scale assets to private individuals who could act as **owners and managers of the acquired assets at the same time**. Compared to the other two methods, this was probably the most successful, because, despite largely pushing aside the investment problem, it created **real owners** who assumed *considerable risk* for the proper management of the assets purchased largely on loans. To repay even some symbolic amount with or without interest injected some necessary anxiety into the behavior of the new owners and stimulated at least a more effective and efficient use of the acquired assests even without making the case for new investments. Retail trade entities, small repair workshops, restaurants, consumer service outlets, agricultural land, livestock, farm tools, pieces of real estate, etc. were frequently privatized in all transition countries in this way after the dissolution of the large administrative umbrella organizations which had managed and overseen their operation before.[70]

sidered *primary privatization.* This terminology, used originally by Polish authors, seems to have been borrowed from capital market language, where there is a clear distinction between a primary sale of securities, an initial public offering (IPO) or auction, and their subsequent trading over the counter or on an established stock exchange. Unfortunately, *transposing the term to the privatization area is misleading and does not reflect the original use in practice which was prevalent at the beginning of transition.* Despite many justified reservations against mass schemes, there is no denial to the fact that voucher privatization represented denationalization by giving title of ownership to millions of citizens, or investment funds managed by private individuals at least in legal sense. As a consequence, *subsequent trading of either vouchers or shares which were already in the hands of non-state actors cannot and should not be called privatization.* Even more importantly, the term "secondary privatization" was very widely used for something else throughout the 1990s in the whole post-communist world: **a second phase of privatization of the same enterprise**. (See footnote 55.) Privatization transactions almost never implied the sale of 100% of the shares of any enterprise in one shot. In case of transactions with several tranches and executed over a protracted period of time, **secondary privatization was meant to be a second tranche of shares to be sold in a different period of time**, either to the counterparty of the first tranche or to different classes of potential owners.

The importance of *sequencing* in privatization can hardly be overestimated. The sequencing of individual transactions over time by *using different methods and approaching different classes of investors* was by far the most important way of harmonizing conflicting governmental objectives as well as societal interests.

[70] For a sweeping overview and detailed analysis of the problems and results of what was then called small privatization see Earle, et al. (1994) and EBRD (1999) Chapter 2.

Small privatization, however, was feasible only in case of a relatively small part of the economy wherever small scale and small value assets were better kept and managed within the framework of a small private enterprise. Large firms, especially if they were technologically integrated vertically, could not be sliced off and sold in small packages even if there was political will to do so. Rightly or wrongly, large firms were in most cases considered still valuable and important "flagships" of the otherwise fast disintegrating transition economies. There was every reason to denationalize them just on a **going concern basis after corporatization**.[71]

But the privatization of large scale enterprises involved new challenges not prevalent in small privatization. The most important among these was **the need of significant restructuring**, technical, organizational, financial and managerial alike. In most individual cases it was outright obvious that even the best performing or ostensibly best managed state enterprises needed a fair dose of additional "hard" capital (machinery, know-how, technology) and also "soft" capital (organization, accounting, marketing, management). The question was formulated in a straightforward way: was it necessary or at least better to undertake restructuring *before privatization* or was it advisable to leave it to the new owner to implement it *after privatization*?[72]

On the basis of popular and political emotions, if not wishful thinking, the answer would have been in the affirmative: yes, flagship companies should be restructured, reorganized, substantially improved first and then privatized *at a much higher price*.[73]

---

[71] See EBRD (1999) Chapter 2., Nellis (2001) and Mihályi (2010).

[72] This question was particularly relevant in the Visegrád countries (V4) and perhaps also in Slovenia and Croatia (V6) for the simple reason that these countries did have a few relatively modern state-owned enterprises which seemed to have been more capable of competing directly with Western firms and imports. Some of them were considered not to be in need of a major restructuring. Governments felt that by making a little additional investment in the capital stock and technology of these firms they may reap considerable benefits in a postponed privatization transaction. Unfortunately, the market loss for imports usually eliminated most of these expected returns. In small and open economies private sector development proved to be faster and more efficient than privatization in its narrow sense. [See Borish–Noel (1996).]

[73] The hypocrisy of the former communist nomenclature, discussed in Chapter 2.2, spilled over to the new elite and created strong illusions about the viability of still unreconstructed state-owned enterprises. Likewise, the schizophrenic mindset of the Soviet man proved to be infectious and found its way to the post-Soviet human being. Sizeable groups of workers were afraid a priori of the potential consequences of privatization and demanded instead continued government support and further public investments. It is an

There are two fundamental problems with this knee-jerk answer. First, if state-owned companies can be restructured, reorganized and their efficiency and profitability restored or significantly improved by the state, then why to privatize at all? Why to relinquish state ownership when it makes possible to reap the benefits of strenuous governmental efforts and investments? Second, and more importantly, if it is possible to restructure, reorganize and improve the efficiency and profitability of state-owned firms by conscious and direct government intervention why on earth had it not been happening throughout the dark long decades of the communist system? Why was it next to impossible to create and operate excellent, world class enterprises under central planning with so much sacrifice from the whole society and so huge investments carried out by the state?

The answer was as obvious then as it is now: *the state is, as it has always been, incapable of restructuring, reorganizing, improving and then running a large number of business enterprises in an effective and efficient way.*[74] The whole history of the communist system proved this lesson eloquently. It was also reinforced by the transition experience.[75] As a consequence, in case of the great majority of state enterprises the right way to go was to sell them without any significant governmental attempt for restructuring and, definitely, without any meaningful amount of addi-

unusually strong cultural legacy of the communist system, conveniently reinforced by populist parties even today at the aftermath of the global economic and financial crisis.

74 It is important to acknowledge that the above statement reflects a liberal value judgement. But the value judgement is based on historical facts: never in the history of capitalism was it possible for any state to run effectively and efficiently a **large number** of business enterprises, comprising a **significant part** of the national economy and creating a **dominant share** of the national output. State ownership in selected business ventures can only be effective and efficient if and when (i) the overwhelming majority of the economy is in private hands, (ii) state-owned firms are compelled to follow the market behavior of the dominant private enterprises, so that **they are behavior takers and not behavior makers** and (ii) all enterprises, state and private alike, are *kept at arms' length from the state in general and the government in particular*. [See Bokros (2005) and (2007).]

75 "To make a loss-making state enterprise more attractive for potential buyers, the state may undertake some pre-privatization restructuring. However, this approach has been problematic, especially when the state effectively left the restructuring to the incumbent management. General experience points toward deterioration of asset values under state ownership. Furthermore, major strategic decisions with high "sunk costs," such as the development or discontinuation of product lines, the closure of plants, and capital expenditure should ultimately be taken by a party that has a long-term profit interest. The state should therefore leave significant restructuring decisions to the eventual private owner." EBRD (1999) 175.

tional public investment. It was certainly true at least *in the competitive sector*, e.g. manufacturing industry, most of primary agriculture and food processing, construction, internal and external trade and a large chunk of business and consumer services. That is why privatization in all these areas can also be called, in retrospect, **competitive privatization**.

2.5. Public utility and financial sector privatization

In addition to the competitive sector, there is another major part of the economy where internal and external competition is always constrained by *some natural monopoly element*. This natural monopoly element in the production and distribution chain of particular products or services is present as a result of either some natural-physical-geological-biological conditions, like in mining, forestry or fishing, or *technological conditions*, like the finite number of frequencies used in mobile telephony, radio and television or finite capacity of pipelines, landlines, transmission networks and tracks as it is well-known in the transportation of oil and gas, electricity, water, sewage, telecommunication and rail transport. Most of these latter areas of economic activity are conveniently called **public utilities**.[76]

Elements of natural monopoly are not necessarily permanent. They may and do change over time, sometimes quite fast, especially as a consequence of *technological development*. The best example of it is the invention and fast spread of mobile telephony. By using frequencies in the airwaves the physical landline wire became largely obsolete and no longer represented an obstacle to the spatial usage of almost an infinite number of telephones. Nevertheless, the finite number and length of frequencies constitute now **another form of a natural monopoly**.

Last but not least, there is a very special part of the market economy which is not constrained by a natural monopoly but made particularly fragile and highly vulnerable by the existence of an *extremely delicate and controversial principal and agent problem*.[77] It is the **financial sector**,

---

[76] In case of utilities the "public" attributive does not mean that the firms offering utility services are either in state ownership or in the hands of the general public. It implies only that given the importance these services carry in everyday life, the **physical infrastructure operated by these enterprises should be open and accessible to all potential customers on an equal basis**. Because of the fixed network these utilities need in order to deliver services to the public, they can also be called *network utilities*. [See Newbery (1999).]

[77] See Stiglitz (1987) 966–977.

including banking, commercial and investment banking alike, insurance in both life and non-life varieties, investment and pension fund management, etc. In all institutions involved in what is conveniently called financial intermediation, the underlying fundamental societal and economic problem stems from the fact that financial intermediaries are playing with *other people's money.*[78]

In the communist system many of these areas of economic activity were particularly underdeveloped as a consequence of ideological stigmatization and/or practical neglect. The only significant exception was the **energy sector**, including coal mining, oil and gas extraction, electricity generation, etc. For a number of communist countries, first and foremost for the Soviet Union, but also for Poland and Romania, exportation of coal, oil and natural gas was a principal earner of much needed hard currency. In addition, forced industrialization with a significant bias towards heavy industry required an excessive amount of energy inputs. Last but not least, most sectors of heavy industry were characterized with a particularly wasteful usage of energy which increased further the importance of *primary energy production.*

While coal production and electricity generation were expanded and the ever growing physical output was celebrated as a sign and proof of the viability and ultimate superiority of the communist system,[79] electricity grids, both in their high and low voltage variants, had become increasingly obsolete and wasteful. Likewise, oil and gas extraction was pursued and promoted, especially in the Soviet Union, in a ferocious manner, but much less priority was given to transportation and distribution. Emphasis was always laid on primary production as it was politically visible and quite fitting into the myopic and skewed system of central planning for the most part based on physical targets. *Environmental degradation* and the *wholesale decapitalization* of the public utilities was simply the other side of the same coin: no such visible high growth of primary output could have been achieved if more resources had been diverted to secondary investments improving the efficiency of the physical infrastructure.[80]

---

[78] One important sign of the excessive risk inherent in any financial sector firm is shown by the relatively low level of share capital and other tiers of capital reserves compared to the balance sheet total, i.e. the low ratio of equity held by the shareholders compared to the total liabilities assumed by the financial enterprise.

[79] Never to forget Lenin's famous dictum: Soviet power plus electrification is communism.

[80] The profound neglect of physical infrastructure was even more prevalent and visible in the cities where the housing stock, roads, public transportation, electrical wires, gas pipelines, aqueducts and sewage, etc. all suffered from chronic disrepair and fell into

The financial sector was an even more neglected and underdeveloped area of the communist economy, even at the time of its decline and final collapse. It was a direct result of the stubborn and inflexible communist ideology which relegated money relations to a very subordinated place of existence. Hence, communist countries possessed a narrow, distorted and rudimentary financial sector.

First, *banking constituted the overwhelming majority of financial sector activity*. Apart from the banks, usually there was a single large insurance monopoly and literally nothing else. As money and capital markets were, by definition, non-existent, there were no savings instruments other than bank deposits allowed. Securities, either in debt or equity, were completely unheard of. As a result, there was no need for stock exchanges, securities trading, investment vehicles, fund management, etc. Second, the banking sector itself was of peculiar nature: it was a **one-tier system**[81] in which the central banking function was not separated from that of commercial banking, i.e. the issuance of money, and the regulation of its supply was not a component of macroeconomic policy and management clearly separate from the microeconomic task of credit allocation to enterprises. Third, all banks that existed were constituting **monopolies** in their respective sphere of activity: in all communist countries usually there was a bank specialized in foreign trade, another offering services to the household sector (typically called a savings bank) and a specific development bank concentrating its efforts and resources in financing long term investments. All these banks maintained dominant or even exclusive positions in their relations to clients because the latter typically had no choice but to deal with them in case they were engaged in foreign trade, retail services or investment finance, respectively. Thus the system, built up along strictly specialized and monopolistic lines, **excluded competition**.

decay. Overutilization of urban infrastructure at the expense of its capital stock (consumption out of amortization) was a general characteristic feature of the communist economic and societal management system. No wonder, therefore, that most cities of the communist commonwealth became less and less attractive over time. Ironically, it was compatible with the implicit policy of the authorities to neglect or even discourage tourism, especially with the West.

81 As it was already mentioned in Chapter 1.3, the only exception was Yugoslavia which maintained the two-tier banking system throughout the communist period. At the same time, the regulation of credit by the Yugoslav Central Bank was not only tight, but overwhelmingly based on *administrative measures* rather than an indirect regulation of the money supply. That made the two-tier structure of the Yugoslav banking system very formalistic and largely emptied out the autonomy of the commercial banks.

Under these circumstances *the rudimentary banking system was a subordinated mechanism, a vehicle of the command economy in the allocation of resources in financial form.*

This narrow, distorted and rudimentary state of financial services under communism has particular importance and direct relevance even today. As money played very little or no meaningful role in everyday life, it was obvious that sophisticated institutions involved in financial intermediation were largely superfluous as well. But in the absence of financial institutions, non-financial economic agents, i.e. enterprise managers and households, had almost no chance to learn even the rudimentary rules of finance. As a consequence, **financial education and culture could not develop** at all. This is yet another painful legacy of the communist system, which made transition economies and societies particularly vulnerable to external and internal shocks.[82]

By their very nature and the specific role they play in a market economy, the privatization of public utilities and banks constituted a much bigger challenge and represented a much more complex problem than the sale of any other productive assets in all other areas of the economy in transition. For one thing, competitive privatization could always end up not only in bankruptcy and/or liquidation,[83] but also *in the complete cessation of a particular activity in the domestic economy*. It might imply not only the sale of physical assets and the closure of former state-owned enterprises but the termination of a particular economic activity *without necessarily creating an unsurmountable gap in market supply*. In case of manufacturing, mining,

[82] Among the internal ones two are particularly worth mentioning. On the one hand, the particularly sinful and destructive **pyramid schemes** were spreading like wildfire in the early 1990s, especially in the Balkans. On the other hand, the excessive reliance on Swiss frank denominated mortgage loans, first and foremost in Hungary, Romania and Poland, are making hundreds of thousands of families bankrupt as a consequence of the more than 50% appreciation of the Swiss currency in the last three years. [See Hudecz (2012).]

[83] Actually, bankruptcy and liquidation were extremely important and useful methods of privatization by releasing assets which previously had been locked in non-viable operations and inefficient uses. Soviet ideology made the absence of enterprise failures and closures a symptom of the superiority of the communist system while in fact, that was a *clear sign of sclerosis and paralysis,* just another face of the lack of supply-side adjustment. Therefore, it was a major positive step in transition that the exit of enterprises was made possible almost automatically within the framework of liberalization. The problem, however, was, that orderly exit required a comprehensive legal framework; a detailed and balanced regulation aiming at harmonizing strongly conflicting interests of the stakeholders involved. As we will see in Chapter 2.10, that was very slow in coming. And it is still one of the weakest areas of judicial practice even today.

agriculture, fishing, forestry, etc., although highly unlikely in practice, it is always possible to import up to 100% of the goods consumed in almost any country. In theory, there is no absolute necessity to produce television sets, shoes, even food or drinks in the domestic economy. In the extreme, all these products can be imported from the world market without supply limit. That is absolutely impossible in case of public utilities and financial institutions. While all electricity consumed in the domestic economy can be imported, *there is always a need for a high and low voltage domestic electricity grid to bring the power to the customers.* In the financial sector it is just impossible that all intermediation of financial savings and investments should take place outside the country by non-resident banks. In addition, it is indispensable to operate a domestic payment system; therefore, *it is imperative for any economy to include at least some banks domiciled at home.* In case of public utilities, **it is exactly the subsector constituting the natural monopoly element in the production and distribution chain which should be domestic**, i.e. operating in the territory of the country.[84] In case of banks, the very essence of commercial banking, i.e. **lending, deposit taking and operating a payment system**, will inevitably require the existence of at least some domestic financial institutions. As a consequence, even if privatization of the existing state-owned enterprises leads to the abolition of all these organizations as going concerns, *new firms must appear on domestic soil.*

Furthermore, public utilities and banks—once again by their very nature—are *usually big firms,* in need of sizeable amount of capital and reserves. Both the initial and ongoing investment requirements emerging in these areas are typically huge. As a consequence, *entry of new players into the market is always restricted.* Moreover, especially in those specific areas where the natural monopoly element appears, there were already very large domestic enterprises at the start of transition, no matter how bad and inefficient they might have been. Last but not least, not only public utilities and banking were considered as "strategic sectors" of economic activity but even the huge state enterprises operating in these areas were always considered "strategic" from political point of view.[85] As a consequence, the idea of

[84] It is important to note that for an enterprise being domestic does not imply domestic ownership.

[85] To label any area of economic activity or any enterprise operating in any of these sectors as strategic is a very doubtful and dubious exercise from the viewpont of scientific considerations. However, it does not prevent governments even in the most open economies and liberal-minded environments to resort to the political weapon of blocking foreign companies to acquire control in some of these fields. (Remember the hostility of the US

privatizing public utilities and financial firms proved to be a tall order for many governments in most countries in transition.[86]

But there was a convincing case why to privatize legacy enterprises even if they were bad and inefficient. The reason why obsolete, wasteful and chronically undercapitalized public utilities and banks were ultimately so much sought after by new investors, especially foreign strategic partners, even in the most devastated former communist countries was that these *legacy firms had the markets*. When it came to the privatization of public utilities and banks what was at stake was not so much the net asset value of particular state-owned firms but **the future growth potential of the market captured by them**.[87]

---

to the takeover of some American seaports by Dubai World; the intervention of the federal government was justified by national security reasons.) In less than fully open economies and increasingly illiberal environments areas considered strategic are even defined by specific legislation, creating a situation where restrictions to entry or takeover no longer demand any economic rationale or explicit justification. (See for example "Lex MOL" in Hungary, approved by the Hungarian parliament in 2008, apparently with "national consensus.")

86 The dilemma was hard to solve for prospective new entrants to the area of operation of public utilities as well as to the financial sector. Was it better to start a greenfield investment and acquire market share by way of organic development or was it more advantageous to make a big leap by buying a controlling stake in one of the existing major players? Ironically, in many cases, the reluctance of governments to privatize "strategic" enterprises solved the problem for the outsiders; they had no choice but to start something anew. Nevertheless, if the new firms proved successful, the *dynamics of the power position changed quite rapidly*. Obsolete, inefficient state-owned enterprises, especially in the financial sector, lost market share and value very quickly and there was a growing fear that if they were not sold before long, then ultimately there would remain nothing to privatize any more. (On a personal note: that was exactly the argument I used when trying to convince my prime minister, Gyula Horn of Hungary in 1995 to sell all financial institutions which had still been in state hands at the time of my service as finance minister.) Obviously, that was much less relevant in case of those firms in the area of public utilities which captured the natural monopoly element (electricity grid, pipeline network, railway tracks, etc.). These old state monopolies were able to use and, not infrequently, abuse their position and suck out a good part of the profit of the new entrants by applying exorbitant charges for the use of their infrastructure.

87 Opponents of privatization quickly realized this phenomenon and turned it into a seemingly eloquent argument *against* privatization. Why privatize if private—and in most cases, foreign—"sharks" were interested, first and foremost, in capturing the domestic market? Curiously, this argument was taking hold not only before privatization but, not infrequently, even *after* that. When central and local governments made mistakes in preparing and carrying out the specific transactions, or the new regulatory regime was ineffective and the former state monopoly was simply turned into an equally

The importance of public utility privatization was further enhanced by the interest and participation of *subsovereign governments*. Local infrastructure of the natural monopoly element of public utilities, e.g. low voltage grid, low pressure gas pipes, communal water and sewage, etc. was typically, if only notionally, in the hands of local governments. In many countries, that was the only "valuable" asset they possessed even if these assets constituted more of a recurrent liability as a consequence of long-term neglect and decay. Nevertheless, the *constant and relatively reliable revenue stream* utilities and then local governments used to receive from the customers for providing these services made them a desirable and attractive target for potential investors, especially for large foreign strategic ones.[88]

Last but not least, it is never to forget that in many countries, especially in the Balkan area (but also in the Caucasus and Central Asia), **transition in terms of implementing structural reforms was frequently blocked and postponed considerably by interstate and/or civil war** which resulted in a significant physical destruction of productive assets and infrastructure.[89] That is important at least for two reasons. First,

inefficient private monopoly, this argument provided an excellent excuse for the eventual *renationalization* of the same asset.

[88] When it comes to the choices facing local governments, these were stark, indeed. Since most utilities providing community services were rudimentary, obsolete, undercapitalized, ineffective and inefficient, there was a tremendous demand and popular expectation that these service would significantly improve. However, it was impossible to make improvements without significant amount of new capital investment. But neither the central, nor local governments were in a position to invest any meaningful amount into these firms. As a result, despite having considered some of the utility companies as cash cows for their capacity to generate quite solid, stable and predictable revenue streams, the ever growing investment needs acquired overwhelming importance. There was little choice, therefore, but to contemplate at least a partial privatization of the public utilities almost in every transition country. [See e.g. Hungary (1995) Chapter IV.D. "Finalizing Enterprise Reform" 67–73.]

[89] In the Balkan area first and foremost Bosnia and Hercegovina, Kosovo and Serbia, but partially also Croatia suffered from a conflict within the country but also outside aggression and foreign intervention. Macedonia and Albania had a prolonged civil strife. Transition could start in Bosnia and Hercegovina only after the Dayton Accord signed in 1995, which created the minimum legal and institutional framework for a functioning conglomerate of interlocking states, at least on paper. Despite winning the Serbo-Croatian war in the same year, Croatia did not make any significant progress in structural reforms in the first decade of transition (until the death of nationalist strongman, Franjo Tuđman, in December 1999). Serbia was almost constantly at war until the collapse of the regime of its nationalist strongman, Slobodan Milošević in 2000.

physical destruction reduced significantly the stock of privatizable assets, the national inventory of real estate and movable property. Second, a good part of these assets were lost forever and there was no compelling reason to restore them either in legal or in physical sense. The most important areas where *physical reconstruction of certain assets of legally existing enterprises* made not only economic sense but was indispensable, were exactly the public utilities and at least some of the banks; a situation that brought into even a sharper relief marking the difference between competitive sectors on the one hand and public utilities and banks on the other.

That can be justified very easily. During and after a devastating war both the military and the civilian population would need many items just for sheer survival. A good part of them, like food, drinking water, basic toiletries, clothing, tents, utensils, etc. can all be provided by humanitarian aid brought in from abroad. But many other essentials, like electricity, gas, sewage and payment services can be had only if the *domestic networks,* providing these services, are restored to a *minimum capacity*. It is not absolutely necessary to reconstruct destroyed factories to produce food, drinks, clothing or shelter; new firms and capacities can be established and brought into operation much more quickly. But it is not a viable alternative in case of basic public utility and financial services. It is much easier, quicker and cheaper to eliminate the physical bottlenecks created by the war in the existing facilities which, in turn, **already belong to existing legal entities**. Moreover, in a post-conflict situation nobody would be willing to undertake the enormous amount of initial capital investment which would be absolutely necessary to create an *alternative infrastructure* for basic utility and financial services.[90]

It is no coincidence, therefore, that in the Balkan area the privatization of public utilities and banks came to the agenda much more forcefully than the privatization of any other sector in the economy. By the same token, it reinforced the view in the whole transition world that the privatization of utilities and banks should be carried out with utmost care and it needed *much more government involvement and enhanced administrative capacity*.

[90] Even if the physical destruction suffered by the previously operating utilities is so large that building up a new system from scratch would require no significantly larger investments, the natural monopoly element of the old utility is still there and it captures the market. People are hooked up to old legal entities which hold the license for the provision of a particular service in all specific geographic areas. Likewise, they may still have some deposits in the old, devastated banks and they may expect payment services from them.

2.6. Restructuring public utilities and financial institutions

From the viewpoint of their restructuring, public utilities and financial institutions were also different from enterprises operating in competitive sectors. While in case of enterprises belonging to competitive sectors it was advisable to leave their restructuring to the new owners after privatization, it was not an option in the area of public utilities and financial institutions. These latter demanded **fundamental and comprehensive restructuring before any specific transaction** could have taken place.[91]

At the beginning of transition restructuring of public utilities and financial firms was always a two-dimensional exercise. For one thing, restructuring had to be considered and applied at the level of the *whole sector*. For another, *individual enterprises* usually required tailor-made restructuring.

In fact, it is important to break down all sectors into various **subsectors**. Within public utilities at least the following subsectors should be considered separately: *electricity, oil and gas, water and sewage, telecommunications and transport*. In each subsector, further disaggregation can and has to take place. In electricity, distinction should be made among *generation, transmission and distribution*; within oil and gas among *extraction, long-distance transportation and local distribution*. Water utilities consist of *extraction, treatment and distribution*; sewage utilities *include collection, treatment and disposal*. Telecommunication can be broken down to *landline, mobile telephony and media broadcasting*. In transport, railways, shipping, air and road transport are to be separated. Within railways, distinction has to be made between the physical infrastructure (tracks, signaling, stations, etc.) and passenger and freight transport. In shipping and air transport the ports and airports are hugely different from the shipping companies and airliners.

All these subsectors can and should be disaggregated even further because the sub-sub sectors may require specific and different treatment.

[91] In light of what was written at the end of Chapter 2.4 on the role and capacity of the state in managing business enterprises owned by it, this is a shocking statement and seems like a contradiction. On second thought, it is not. No argument is intended to be made here in favor of the state keeping public utilities and financial firms in its ownership. Restructuring does not necessarily imply either that the state has to make large capital outlays in any specific subsector or enterprise in these areas. More often than not it is clearly unadvisable. The need for *ex ante* restructuring stems from the very nature of public utilities and financial institutions; that is to say that the former always includes a *natural monopoly element* while the latter is characterized by *extreme fragility stemming from its overarching nature and systemic importance*.

In the historical endeavour of recreating the capitalist market economy, one of the most important policy goals was to **promote competition.** In the areas of public utilities, that required the **separation and unbundling of the natural monopoly component,** the subsector where competition is severely limited by the existing technology, and at the same time establishing the conditions to allow and promote as much **competition** as it was possible everywhere else.[92]

In all areas of public utilities the natural monopoly element is always a **network-like component** which either excludes competition or at least puts very serious constraints on it.

In electricity, the natural monopoly element is the *high-voltage nationwide transmission grid*; that is the area where the chance for entry of new firms is close to nil. This network has to be taken out of the former integrated socialist behemoth and put into a standalone corporation. Generation and distribution can be organized and operated on a more competitive basis. In oil & gas the *long-distance pipeline network* constitutes the natural monopoly; that is what needs to be unbundled from the former single socialist sectoral firm and get an independent legal form of corporation. Extraction and distribution can be had with much more competition. In water and sewage, it is the *trunk pipeline network*, in landline telephony the *long-distance cables*, in media broadcasting the *terrestrial network and the access to satellites*, in railways, *the tracks*, in shipping and air transport *most of the ports and the airports* should be considered as natural monopolies. In all cases, it is extremely important to **identify very precisely what exactly the natural monopoly element is**; it has to be defined in the narrowest possible way and, once cut out from the former socialist mammoth, *organized into a separate legal entity.*

Restructuring of public utilities thus implied the separate *corporatization* of the natural monopoly element which usually required a highly *complex legal and financial* exercise. That was one of the most essential steps of the new public policy regarding the whole sector. High-voltage national grids, central switches, long-distance (in many cases, national segments of international) pipeline networks, landline intercity cables,

[92] Electricity, oil and gas, water and sewage, individual subsectors of telecom and transport can usually be considered as *single product natural monopolies*. "Two concepts are fundamental for our understanding of single product natural monopolies: decreasing average cost and subadditivity. The first is very familiar and simply means that all costs fall with increases in output. The second is less familiar but very important. A firm with rising unit costs is able to produce a given level of output at a lower total costs than multiple firms if its cost function is subadditive." Berg and Tschirhart (1988) 22.

railway tracks, ports and airports—these were the most typical assets to be carved out of the old state sectoral monopoly and put into a **newly-established corporate entity with adequate equity capital** and low debt.[93]

Other elements of public utilities, while requiring substantial government attention, much time and administrative capacity, were saleable somewhat easier. Power plants, oil and gas fields, more precisely, exploitation rights, downstream assets, like distribution centers, gas stations, fluvial and maritime shipping companies, airlines, etc. could be made part of the *competitive areas of business activity*. Nevertheless, these components also needed a **considerable amount of legal and financial restructuring**[94] before any specific privatization transaction could have taken place. For example, individual power plants were conveniently bundled together with the coal mines which were supplying them almost exclusively. Electricity distribution in the national arena was divided into companies of largely equal size and growth potential. Petrol stations were to be grouped together in such a way as to ensure maximum competition by the operation of several parallel nationwide networks. On the whole, it was very important to make sure that there was going to be a more or less **level playing field** among these newly-established firms with old but easily rejuvenated assets in terms of both technology and efficiency.

Creating a level playing field was important with or without the subsequent privatization of the assets involved. Even if some of the successor companies were not intended to be sold, their survival depended on their

---

[93] Adequate capitalization is key for the future viability, smooth functioning and eventual privatizability of the new corporate venture. Since most public utilites had been seriously decapitalized in the last period of the command economy, adequate level of capitalization of the natural monopoly frequently required some additional injection of equity into the new corporation. Financial restructuring meant, however, first and foremost, the **nationalization of a big part of the previously accumulated debt**. Takeover of debt by the state happened, obviously, with the expectation of recouping and recovering most of the costs by the higher price achievable as a result of a more advantageous privatization.

[94] "If any industry is broken into potentially competitive firms, then a great deal of additional work is required. The assets need to be identified and allocated, as do contracts, liabilities, employment, pension assets, and the like. The financial structure must be designed and tested for robustness, pro-forma accounts prepared, and a past history of accounts relating to the assets of the new firm created to convince financial analysts of the commercial viability of the each proposed firm. Even if the managers of the original monopoly are completely convinced of the desirability of the reform, these tasks are inevitably time-consuming." Newbery (1999) 390–391.

capacity to compete. It is also important to note, that in all these largely competitive areas the **entry of new private firms** (new power plants, new extraction sites, new service providers, etc.) based on *greenfield investments* was not only possible but also **highly desirable**. Privatization of the existing assets must not have been delayed much because of the threat new and potentially much more efficient companies represented for them.

The restructuring of public utilities in many cases also involved the *closure* of some of the existing productive plants and, ultimately, the *liquidation* of several state-owned non-corporate enterprises. These steps were not necessarily identical. Factories, workshops, product lines, machinery, auxiliary services, etc. could easily be taken out of any state firm without liquidating the legal entity. The primary objective was to ensure the **future viability of the remaining enterprises as going concerns** and for that to happen the cessation or carving out of the most obsolete and loss-making components was not only inevitable, but also hugely beneficial. If and when most assets bundled in a company were hopeless, then, of course, the liquidation of the whole firm made perfect economic sense.[95]

Last but not least, the non-monopoly areas of public utilities invited more competition by allowing the (i) entry of completely new legal entities with completely new assets, (ii) dilution of state ownership by the issue of new shares in state companies with old assets and a subsequent modernization of these assets with help of the capital infusion made by the new shareholder, (iii) the privatization of state companies and a subsequent rejuvenation of the old assets by additional investment injected by the new private owners. In the great majority of cases, these investments were undertaken by **foreign strategic investors** with great enthusiasm and success.

Nevertheless, foreign investment into "strategic" assets, i.e. large enterprises of national importance, was and, has remained, politically sensitive and controversial to this day. Despite a resounding success in attract-

[95] Bankruptcy and liquidation are, without doubt, among the most difficult areas of corporate restructuring. In order for bankruptcy and liquidation procedures to advance in a civilized way, it required the existence of a **sophisticated legal framework and a relatively well-trained, prudent and transparent judiciary**. That was a very tall order for most if not all transition economies. The sooner the respective governments undertook the painful task of creating an adequate institutional and regulatory framework, the better service they made to the business sectors of their countries and, ultimately, to the whole economy. (Regulation will be analyzed more in detail in the next chapter and the role of the judicial system in Chapter 2.10.)

ing an enormous amount of additional investment into public utilities and financial institutions (which, in the absence of foreign contribution, should have been undertaken either by the state or by domestic private investors) and improving substantially corporate governance, populist-nationalist-socialist parties and political movements has kept attacking foreign companies and their allegedly harmful behavior periodically. Whenever such backlash has gone beyond a certain threshold of "normal" intensity, it has damaged the investment climate and slowed down, sometimes even reversed, much needed inflow of foreign investment into transition economies. (Hungary today is the best case in point.)

The restructuring of the narrow, distorted and rudimentary financial sector was no less of a challenge to fragile governments of countries in transition. While the financial sector, mostly consisting of banks, was quite small, most of the newly-established large commercial banks were almost completely rotten and bankrupt. Banks were technically insolvent, i.e. they had negative equity capital. *There was absolutely no chance to privatize any of the state-owned commercial banks before restructuring.*

In fact, the very establishment of these commercial banks constituted already a comprehensive restructuring of the financial sector. The one-tier banking system, prevalent under the command economy, was inconsistent with the requirements of the market and excluded even the possibility of competition. The newly created commercial banks—carved out of the mainframe of the former central bank—usually had much more freedom to offer **overlapping ranges of services to overlapping ranges of customers**. Although retail banking usually required a separate license and was not granted automatically from the outset, *competition in financing business enterprises* emerged almost immediately. Then financial institutions were developing slowly into universal banks.[96]

Although it was quite obvious, governments in transition countries were extremely slow in realizing the deteriorating situation. When commercial banks had been carved out of the mainframe of the former monobank, the intention was to give them "adequate" amount of equity.[97]

---

96 That was not easy to achieve because of the initial conditions. The state-owned commercial banks were established either along sectoral or regional lines. The first was applied in the Baltic states, Czechoslovakia, Romania and Bulgaria, the second in Poland. Hungary had a combination of the two. [See Bonin et al. (1998) 19–21.] The names of the new banks clearly reflect the different solutions.

97 It is an evergreen debate, intensive even today, what constitutes an *adequate level of capitalization* for different types of banks. It is important to remember that the Basel-type concept of capital adequacy was still in its incipient stage at the beginning of transi-

But as it was discussed much in detail, liberalization made the inherent weaknesses and tremendous inefficiency of the command economy explicit rather quickly. *Hyperinflation, output decline and unemployment* attacked in full force. The deterioration of the economic situation and the rapid erosion of the value and financial capacity of thousands of enterprises were reflected immediately in the **fast deterioration of the quality of the loan portfolio** of the newly-established state commercial banks.

This could have been an excellent way of showing immediately the systemic importance of the commercial banking system to the uneducated and largely unaware public. Unfortunately, even governments struggled to understand the nature and enormity of the problem and failed to act in time to mitigate the negative consequences. On the contrary; ministers, members of the parliament put tremendous pressure on bank managers to keep financing available for loss-making enterprises which were politically important for these well-connected individuals. Many managers of the state-owned banks acted happily on these requests. As a consequence, the **stock problem**, i.e. the amount of non-performing loans inherited from socialism, was exacerbated by the **flow problem**, i.e. new lending to bad enterprises, increasing further the portfolio of bad loans.

The bankruptcy of the newly-established and still state-owned commercial banks was further deepened by the *lack of adequate governance structures*, otherwise so exceptionally important in case of financial intermediaries. In the whirlwind of transitional recession the *prudence and integrity* of managers, members of boards, etc. could have made a huge difference in terms of putting a solid floor under the losses and stopping the bleeding of these still socialist dinosaurs.[98]

tion. At that time, there was widespread overconfidence among Western scholars and practitioners in the capacity of banks to manage risk and maintain the quality of their asset portfolio. The impact of globalization on the structure, quality and fast pace of change in bank portfolios was not readily understood, either. [See Acharya et al. (2011) Prologue]

[98] Unfortunately, that did not occur. "Representatives of various state institutions sitting on boards and supervisory boards of state-owned banks were following either the narrow interest of their government department, at best, or their own personal interests, at worst. These representatives were replaced frequently and in many cases were sent to promote specific political interests of their own constituencies. There were no prudential rules guiding their activity either. Modern banking legislation was introduced late and changing frequently. Regulatory and supervisory agencies remained weak and overly politicized, even in the most advanced economies. In sum, the structure of both internal and external governance remained largely inadequate…" Bokros (2001) 15.

Governments finally realized the nature of the underlying difficulties when the *solvency problem*, experienced by the large state-owned bank, turned into a *liquidity problem.*[99] State-owned banks were unable to compete with new private banks, foreign and domestic alike, for funding. Corporate and retail deposits were slowly but steadily migrating to healthier financial institutions and the state banks were obliged *to rely increasingly on central bank refinancing*. That made their position untenable even before the government or the general public became aware of their insolvency.[100]

Given the fast changing degree of insolvency, the marked inability and reluctance of governments to face the problem in full, *bank rehabilitation and recapitalization took place in several stages in all transition economies*. Rehabilitation involved the carving out of bad assets in exchange of newly-issued government bonds. Recapitalization meant the outright provision of additional equity as the finance ministry bought the additional shares issued. In both cases, solvency was largely restored, but liquidity only if the central bank was willing either *to buy the newly-acquired long-term government securities or at least accept them as collateral.*[101] The difference between the two methods lay in the fact that while in the case of rehabilitation the banks were freed from the arduous task of working out the non-performing assets, with recapitalization they were still burdened by this difficult job.

[99] Solvency and liquidity are difficult concepts to understand even for bank managers and government officials, let alone for the general public. Financial institutions are expected to pursue and preserve both. Many problems arise from the fact that **these two objectives, not infrequently, can come into conflict**. Under such circumstances operations become extremely cumbersome and banks go bankrupt very quickly.

[100] Liberalization of entry and exit was sooner rather than later extended to the financial sector as well. Governments were keen to see the establishment of new banks and other financial intermediaries in name of fostering competition and provide better services to non-financial enterprises and the household sector. They considered the proliferation of new financial institutions also as a clear sign of success in transition. Unfortunately, many of the newly-established banks and other intermediaries proved to be no better than the existing state-owned ones. Their behavior and governance reflected the same legacy of imprudent behavior, bordering on reckless risk taking and abuse. [See Chekurova (2001) and Jotev (2001).]

[101] That was not easy to achieve when the central bank, sometimes very proud of its newly-won independence, was reluctant to provide liquidity to specific banks by purchasing illiquid government debt. Central banks usually buy and sell government paper for the purpose of managing liquidity in the financial sector as a whole but operations should be made in the open and based in market considerations. (It is not for nothing that the transactions of the FED, the US central bank, when managing the liquidity of the US banking system, are called open market operations…)

Bank rehabilitation and recapitalization proved to be a time consuming, painful, politically very controversial and costly exercise. Unfortunately, government-orchestrated rehabilitations turned out to be a quite inefficient vehicle for creating safe and sound, competitive banks. Many governments spent a fortune on rehabilitating banks yet had very little to show for it. They spent at least 10%, but sometimes up to 25%, of GDP on this exercise, exacerbating further the fiscal stance of the countries in transition.[102]

In addition to the fast-moving-target nature of insolvency, the marked incapacity and reluctance of governments to tackle the issue, the single most important reason for the need to repeating bank rehabilitation exercises was the fact that while rehabilitation and recapitalization of the large state-owned banks may have eliminated the *stock problem,* i.e. the existing portfolio of non-performing assets accumulated in the past, there was little or no change in the **incentive structure of corporate governance** in order to address the *flow problem*, i.e. to prevent the reappearance and reaccumulation of additional bad assets in the future. For that to happen, a *completely new culture of prudent internal governance and management* was necessary. For that to set in, the **privatization of the state-owned banks, immediately after their rehabilitation,** proved to be absolutely indispensable.[103]

Not all kinds of privatizations led, however, to a significant improvement in incentives and, hence, *behavior, performance, productivity and efficiency*. That was assured only if the new owners acquired the **controlling stake** and they themselves represented a **sea change in culture**. Un-

[102] "It was found that most of the initial comprehensive bank bailouts of the state-owned commercial banks in CEE (Central and Eastern Europe—LB) had several common characteristics: (i) they were very expensive; (ii) they paid attention mostly (sometimes almost exclusively) to solving the immediate systemic crisis; and (iii) they paid very little or no attention to the long-term consequences of those campaigns. Therefore, most of these initial bailout episodes have been suboptimal from the long-term point of view, and have demonstrated the need for repeated rescue actions in a relatively short period of time and increased the explicit national debt to a large extent." Bonin et al. (1998) 115.

[103] Privatization was only a necessary, but far from sufficient, condition for improving significantly the performance and behavior of the state banks. In addition to changing the internal governance structures, the composition of management, etc. institutions and procedures of *external governance* also needed to change for the better. One of the most important areas of external governance is **regulation and supervision,** a precious public good to be provided by the state. That will be analyzed more in detail in the next chapter.

fortunately, strong, well-capitalized domestic investors capable of meeting these criteria were hard, if not impossible, to find.[104] Once again, as it turned out to be the case with the privatization of almost any large enterprise, **foreign strategic investors,** i.e. first-class, reputable and rather large foreign banks were the ones able and willing to supply not only a *considerable amount of additional capital but also the technical improvements and the new culture* which were so indispensable to make sure that the repetition of another or several rounds of recapitalization by the state can be and would be avoided in the future.

The wisdom of this policy was finally and splendidly justified in the last three years, during the unfolding global economic and financial crisis. While some large banks in Western Europe required government-orchestrated recapitalization in their home markets, **no subsidiary of any reputable and prudent foreign bank in Central and Eastern Europe was in need of getting capital injection from governments in the host markets.** Subsidiaries of foreign banks, while obviously suffering from a marked increase of their non-performing loans, *never asked for rehabilitation from host country governments*. Although their profitability plummeted and some stopped paying taxes for a while, *they were relying on the assistance of their mother institutions* almost exclusively. That proved to be a blessing not so much in disguise for the countries in transition.[105]

It is important to recall what exactly **the substance of this new culture of internal governance** must be. More than a decade after concluding the privatization of the former big state-owned banks even in the most

[104] In the meantime, that was also proven by the failure of a good number of new banks founded by local businesspeople after the political changes which also led to an excessive liberalization of rules concerning the criteria of establishing banks. This was a very typical, if not dominant, feature of development in early Russian banking in the Yeltsin era. Well-connected entrepreneurs founded small banks and started to collect deposits in order to finance primarily their own non-financial ventures. This type of *connected and insider lending* brought down many banks when the financial crisis hit Russia, especially in August, 1998. Hence, the reputation of private individuals as owners of banks with a controlling state became severely tarnished. The experience of Central and Eastern Europe in oligarchic banking was not better, either.

[105] That is why it is so absurd that populist-nationalist governments imposed further burden on the banks by introducing new taxes on financial transactions. While these might have been justified in Western countries to partially recapture the enormous sum of taxpayer money spent on previous rounds of bank rehabilitation, in Eastern countries some of the exceptionally high and unpredictable predatory taxes on banking were intended for nothing else but to fill huge fiscal gaps. (Again, the Hungarian experience is a case in point.)

reluctant and latecomer transition economies,[106] foreign banks now *dominate the financial landscape in all countries* of Central and Eastern Europe without exception.[107] Their relative success stems from the fact that they usually implemented **strict internal rules** governing the behavior of their managers and staff in areas of *liquidity management, risk assessment, asset creation, credit allocation, loan classification, in-house supervision, portfolio diversification, funding, client relationship*, etc. These are the so-called soft powers all prudent banks need in addition to having modern information and banking technology. But the most important ingredient of prudent behavior is keeping various interest groups, especially the political class, the government and individual business interests at **arm's length**, i.e. not to succumb to any undue pressure which would bend or destroy the intrinsic rules of this prudent behavior. That is a tall order which can be met only if the shareholders are at least *as powerful as the main domestic business interest groups* and they use this strength to demonstrate a *more prudent and honest culture and behavior.* If foreign strategic investors do possess this culture as a consequence of accumulated experience in their home turf and they are not afraid of displaying it in the countries of their subsidiary investments, they seem to be particularly **fit and proper** in the "wild-east" environment. Experience shows that they usually represent a more modern, successful, efficient culture not only in technical, but also in ethical terms. Hence, their culture can be regarded as largely superior to the local one and their role in the transition world could be considered as civilizatory.[108]

---

[106] Serbia was the last country starting serious bank restructuring only after the fall of the Milošević regime in 2000. By that time four of the largest Serbian banks were so devastated that there was no good reason to rehabilitate them at all. As a leader of a World Bank delegation I convinced the new Serbian government that it would be cheaper and more effective to liquidate those banks and compensate depositors only. The government accepted my advice and the four banks were effectively closed by New Year's Eve of 2001.

[107] "Foreign banking groups have made significant inroads into the region, leading to unprecedented integration between the banking systems of mature (mainly Western European) market economies and those in the transition region. In Central Eastern Europe and the Baltic states (CEB) and parts of South-East Europe (SEE) foreign banks dominate the market, and their local affiliates are the main source of external finance for many households and firms." [EBRD (2006) 58.] See also Tanzi (1995).

[108] These days this unique culture is tested particularly severely by neophite and overzealous governments like the one in power in Hungary. Conveniently riding on the high tide of *anti-bank cum anti-foreign* sentiments, an exceptionally harsh crisis tax was introduced in 2010. While there might be some rationale for such a tax from a narrow fis-

More than a decade has passed since the privatization of public utilities and large commercial banks went ahead at a massive scale in Central and Eastern Europe. The local subsidiaries of foreign enterprises have invested a huge amount of additional capital into the formerly obsolete infrastructure of public utilities and banks in the whole transition world. None of them required any subsequent bailout by the state of the host country. They have constituted an *unprecedented, reliable, predictable and solid backbone* of the local economy and contributed considerably to overall growth of output and welfare.[109]

The resounding success of selling both public utilities and banks to first-class, reputable foreign strategic investors shows clearly that privatization and restructuring are very *closely connected* in the area of public utilities and financial firms. The relationship works both ways. It was not possible to privatize large state-owned behemoths without **prior restructuring** in these two important sectors of economic life. At the same time it was impossible to reap the benefits, consolidate the results of restructuring if privatization was not taking place **immediately** after a minimum degree of restructuring. As the second line in the matrix of structural reform in

cal point of view, *it is explicitly counterproductive in wide economic terms*. To add insult to injury, the Hungarian government initiated legislation in late 2011 to allow individual holders of mortgage loans denominated in foreign exchange to repay their outstanding debt in full at a hugely preferential exchange rate. It resulted in additional losses for several banks and cut deeply into their capital reserves. As a third step, the government legislated a completely new, exceptionally burdensome and predatory type of a financial transaction tax which is to be levied to all money transfers between banks and their non-bank customers, including retail ones as well. These measures can be considered as deliberate attempts of an anti-capitalist, largely xenophobic and populist government to offer *undeserved advantages to selected few affluent people at the expense of foreign banks*. (The government explicitly declared that Hungarian banks would be recapitalized by the state if need be.) These moves could not be justified by claims that bank rehabilitation had been costly to the Hungarian taxpayer. As it was already mentioned, foreign banks never asked for fiscal support from the Hungarian government during the financial crisis. Banks are not excessively profitable either, because they need to replenish their reserves after writing off considerable losses. The impact of the excessive tax, the mortgage loan repayments at preferential exchange rate and the new financial transaction tax would inevitably strengthen the **credit crunch** which had set in at the aftermath of the weakening of foreign funding. All in all, these steps led to a *marked deterioration of the business environment* seriously limiting the capacity of the Hungarian economy to restart sustainable, export-led growth. No wonder, therefore, that the Hungarian economy has plunged into recession in 2012 once again. The credit crunch has significantly contributed to it.

[109] EBRD (2010).

transition would express eloquently, there was a need for a **critical mass of reforms in both areas** for the market economy to take hold in a less reversible manner. After all, what was at stake is once again the prevalence of supply-side adjustment. As it was already demonstrated, there was no chance for stabilizing and enhancing the hard-won achievements of either liberalization or stabilization without supply-side adjustment which, in turn, could have never taken place without full fledged privatization of the whole national economy.[110]

2.7. Regulation and supervision of public utilities and financial institutions

Even if pre-privatization restructuring proved absolutely necessary, it was far from sufficient for lasting success. In addition to inside governance, the importance of *outside elements of overall governance* cannot be overemphasized. The key components of outside governance were, and still are, **state regulation and government supervision.** Consistent, predictable, transparent, equitable, enforceable, and, curiously, *comprehensive, strong* regulation and supervision were also indispensable for the success of restructuring and privatization of public utilities and financial institutions.

The **role of the state in the economic affairs of a market-based society** has always been a subject of fierce and intensive theoretical as well as policy debate. The situation was especially ambiguous after the collapse of the communist system in Europe. It was particularly confusing in light of the overwhelming need and push for *comprehensive liberalization*, which was one of the first, relatively easy and rather popular set of measures of structural reforms indispensable for the establishment of a market economy. Should liberalization include *all areas* of economic life? If not, *which sectors* require regulation? Is it a *different kind* of regulation that is needed in a market economy? *How strong* does regulation and, consequently, its state-managed supervision have to be? What should be the *exact scope and range* of regulation in individual areas? Shall the economy have *split regulation*, i.e. to rely partially on *self-regulation* of economic actors and their institutions? These and many others were hard questions not only at the outset, but even today.[111]

[110] Bokros (2005), (2007) and (2009a).

[111] The *economics of regulation* is a full-bodied and stand-alone science, fast changing and developing even today. Its glorious advancement started roughly 50 years ago. Some of

Realizing the need for proper regulation and supervision was significantly reinforced by the mistakes of some early democratic governments, first and foremost the Czechoslovak and then the Czech one, led by Václav Klaus.[112] Many enthusiastic proponents of mass privatization schemes, including himself, felt that there was basically no need to regulate the incipient capital market which had been resurrected immediately as an almost automatic byproduct of the issuance of vouchers to all adult-age citizens.[113] When the lack of proper regulation and supervision, especially in the fast evolving secondary capital markets, led to serious violations of minority rights and much abuse, the *need for establishing a modern regulatory and supervisory framework gained unstoppable traction.*[114]

Regulation and supervision exercised by the state demand **considerable amount of relatively sophisticated administrative capacity.** It includes the continuous analysis of the operation and performance of whole sectors and a large number of individual enterprises. State institutions empowered with these tasks need to communicate with the highest levels of parliament and government in order to assist relevant policy making. Regulatory and supervisory agencies, while maintaining their operational autonomy, have to *coordinate and collaborate* with each other rapidly and permanently.[115]

---

the most important contributions to the workout of the theoretical underpinning of modern regulation were provided by Stigler (1975), (1983) and (1984). As a neoclassical-liberal (in American parlance, conservative) author, who was both learning and teaching in Chicago, he realized and acknowledged early that the state has a very important role to play in regulating many areas and aspects of economic life.

Theoretical underpinnings and sociological arguments for state-orchestrated regulation in the economy can be traced back to Weber (1947) and Schumpeter (1942).

112 He himself was eager to provide an extensive ex-post rationalization of his approach in several books. [See Klaus (1995) and (1997).]

113 Early proposition for an almost completely unregulated capital market environment was given by Třiska and Jelinek-Francis (1991). Highly critical evaluations of the radical approach are provided by Mertlík (1995) and Mlčoch–Manochin–Sojka (2000). A more supportive account can be found in Rudlovčák (2001).

114 Theoreticians as well as practitioners, leaders of important regulatory agencies in the Czech Republic desperately tried to alert the public and the government that proper legal framework and prudential rules had to be established in order to prevent further abuses. [See Ježek (1997), Mlčoch (2001) and Bokros (2001b).]

115 This is no small feat even in well-established, advanced, highly developed capitalist economies with financial and human resources available in adequate quantity and quality. Even the best and seemingly most sophisticated regulatory and supervisory architectures can fail to provide proper protection against market failure—which then transforms itself into **governance failure** very quickly. The inability of the US financial market regulatory

Regulation and supervision of public utilities and financial institutions are no easy jobs even in good times. The enormity of the task can be highlighted by referring to three additional complications. First, transition was never to be considered "good times." On the contrary, especially in the first decade, it was a period of *deepening macro and micro crises* which required almost **permanent crisis management**. Second, except for a few skeleton bodies for government surveillance, most regulatory and supervisory institutions were to be built up *from scratch with no prior experience and culture whatsoever*. Third, while the pre-privatization restructuring and the denationalization of public utilities and financial institutions consumed much energy and attention, basically it was undertaken to solve only the *stock problem*, i.e. the legacy of the past. Agencies, government departments dealing with the truly cumbersome and arduous task of restructuring and privatization were not supposed to remain permanent components of central public administration. In contrast, regulatory and supervisory institutions had to be equipped with powers and capacities to address not only the stock but also the *flow problem*. Once established and operational, they were expected **to stay in the game forever.** On the basis of these characteristics, the conclusion is clear: to design, build up and then make sure that they function properly, the establishment of the regulatory and supervisory institutions was *one of the most complex, highly politicized, resource intensive and time-consuming structural reforms* in transition.

The difference between restructuring and regulation in this respect can also be grasped by considering the **different possibilities for outsourcing**. In theory, much of restructuring can be assigned to *provisional* institutions, even to advisors, both foreign and domestic. Once the necessary political decisions have been made and the parameters reflecting government priorities are set, the day-to-day task of restructuring can be delegated to legal firms, consultancies, investment banks, etc. with periodic government review. This option is not there in regulation and supervision. There is an absolute need for *local administrations with strong governance structures, well-trained and well-paid staff*. Of course, these latter can be permanently assisted by advisors, technical missions coming from intergovernmental agencies, international financial institutions and elsewhere, but the state has **undivided, unalienable and non-transferable responsibility** for the proper functioning and performance of public utilities and financial institu-

and supervisory system to foresee and prevent the subprime crisis, the global proliferation of toxic assets and the fall of Lehman Brothers and AIG—among others—is a case in point. See for example Roubini–Mihm (2010) and Acharya et al. (2011).

tions which would inevitably require a *home-based, strong, stable and permanent network of regulatory and supervisory agencies.*

Regulation of public utilities obviously had to *concentrate on the natural monopoly elements,* usually the network utilities. As they were separated out of the old socialist sectoral conglomerates and put into new, stand-alone companies, their regulation was to be, and could be, made well-targeted, more precise and effective.

In case of network utilities, the two most important aspects to be regulated are **prices and access**. Both have several components.

Price regulation does not necessarily mean rigid fixing of the output prices(s). It can be much more flexible and, hence, effective if only the *range and frequency of price changes* are to be regulated. For that to happen the regulatory agency has to look at *cost allocation* within the firms, it may wish to determine *allowable costs, depreciation schedules, a decent rate of return*, etc. Usually an *incentive to cost reduction* is also built into the formulae permitting price adjustments.[116]

Regulation of access to the services of network monopolies is an even more complex exercise. The principle of *open access* has to be upheld and it should prevail in practice to the maximum extent possible. That is not easy because all utility networks have a technical *capacity ceiling.* They are very much interested to offer practically unlimited access below that level but unable to do so above that ceiling without some kind of prioritization.[117]

To set up **various ranking orders** of access for different customers, which may change periodically, *allowing even new entrants to compete*, is already a function of regulatory intervention. Of course, that is to be exercised in *consultation and cooperation* with the regulated monopoly.[118]

---

[116] See Berg and Tschirhart (1988) Chapter 8. "Regulation in practice: Why and how are firms regulated?"

[117] This is one interpretation of subadditivity. **There can be no capacity increases in small increments**. For example, when a high-voltage power grid is utilized at the maximum of its technical capacity, there is no economic possibility to go beyond that ceiling with just a small amount of additional capital injection. After all possible technical improvements have been made in the existing grid, creating additional capacity requires a **large investment with enormous sunk-costs to be recaptured over a long period of time**. This investment might be undertaken either by the existing firm or new entrants only if the resulting significant capacity increment can be sold in a sufficiently profitable way. More often than not long-term profitability of new capacity would demand *long-term delivery contracts*. To achieve that in a fragmented market might also need the assistance of state regulation and coordination.

[118] "An open, transparent single-price pool is the critical element in introducing competition into generation. It allows entry at the choice of the new entrant, which puts downward

The need for regulating access reveals why the natural monopoly element was to be unbundled. If the network utility was operated by a corporation also involved in production and/or distribution, it would be just natural for the company to give priority to its own production and/or distribution in the utilization of the nationwide network.[119] It would create a *conflict of interest* outright. That would seriously harm competition and create *an artificial monopoly in addition to the natural one*. That must be avoided at any rate.

It follows from the above that regulation of public utilities should not be limited to the natural monopoly element but it has to be extended also to the *more competitive areas of each sector*. When it comes to power generation and distribution, extraction of minerals, water, disposal of wastewater, allocation of frequencies, etc. **licensing** is key—both its *award and possible revocation*. Some of these activities are so important—either lucrative, like auctioning of licenses for mobile telephony, or politically sensitive like the distribution of licenses for media channels—that governments, parliament committees and members might wish to get involved directly in the process. Experience shows that it has become almost everywhere the hotbed of **cronysm, collusion and "grand" or political corruption**.[120]

---

pressure on prices, contract terms, and undermines collusion between incumbent generators. It follows that the main criterion in designing a market for bulk electricity is to ensure **the efficient contestability of the market place**. Efficiency requires that the correct signals on location, fuel-type, reliability, and degree of excess capacity are transmitted to generators, and this places a heavy burden on the design of access and use-of-system pricing of the transmission system." (bolding mine) Newbery (1999) 279.

[119] That is exactly what is happening in case of Gazprom. It is not only a significant producer of natural gas in Russia but at the same time it owns most of the nationwide pipeline network. As it happens, individual producers have a hard time to get access to this network and they never have it on an equal basis. **This is a very effective tool to exclude new entrants even from the more competitive areas.** No new producer will invest into a remote field if there is no chance to transport the extracted minerals to the customers.

This problem is well-known by policy makers, government officials, regulators and the general public in Russia. Despite the growing awareness, there is no intention on the part of the government to unbundle the pipeline network and place it into a separate company. That tells a lot about the power of Gazprom and the oligarchic nature of the Russian state fully captured by interlocking special interests.

[120] This is a somewhat different "3C" than what is refered to on page 49, regarding the modus operandi of the Soviet system. Instead of crime, there is now regular collusion. (Not that collusion must not be considered a crime.) In addition to public procurement, granting of licenses for various business activities has proved to be the *main area of corruption in the whole transition world*. At the beginning, it might have been rela-

Corruption or not, competition was and, has remained, one of the most important ingredients of the new incentive structure to improve efficiency. It was then, as it is now, absolutely clear that privatization, albeit necessary, is not sufficient. Transforming an inefficient public monopoly into an equally inefficient private one is no solution. On the contrary, it can create a strong backlash in public sentiments against the whole privatization drive.

That happened almost everywhere in the transition world and in many cases stopped, sometimes even reversed, privatization. Of course, botched transactions occurred everywhere almost by necessity. The administrative capacity of governments to manage complex transactions was quite shallow. But more often than not it was not the privatization itself which created the problems but the lack of prior restructuring and **the absence of adequate, sophisticated rules, regulation and well-established, strong and independent regulatory and supervisory institutions behind them**. Privatization transactions, no matter how complex and difficult they might have been, proved to be much easier than the reform of the state.

Regulation is there not only to tame the natural monopoly element but also **to create competition,** *promote new entry* wherever possible and viable in economic terms, *reward cost savings* and their passing on to customers, *participate in risk sharing* when it comes to substantial new investments, especially in green energy, saving and securing both energy and water.[121]

The regulation and supervision of *financial institutions* was an equally complex, complicated and politically controversial task. The difficulties

tively rare. "However, with the passing of time, and with increasing frequency, some government officials would be approached by bribers and asked to bend the rules or even to break the laws to obtain a government benefit or to avoid a government-imposed cost. Some will respond and will get compensation from the bribers for their actions. Others may start emulating them. The process is likely to be cumulative over time and resemble the spreading of a contagious disease. Acts of corruption that might have appeared shocking earlier will begin to look less shocking, and may even begin to be tolerated." Tanzi (2002) 22–23.

121 "...introducing competition into previously monopolized and regulated network utilities is the key to achieving the full benefits of privatization. Privatization seems to be necessary but it is not sufficient. Regulation is inevitably inefficient, suggesting that it be confined to the core natural monopoly of the network. Provided that competition is effective, it can replace regulation for network services and thereby increase efficiency. But liberalization also redistributes rents and raises new regulatory problems in managing the interface between the regulated and competitive parts of the utility." Newbery (1999) 386.

were partially identical to those experienced in the case of public utilities. But since the financial sector was a systemically underdeveloped part of the economy in the communist system, regulation and supervision became hugely important in transition not only for the existing enterprises after restructuring and privatization but also for the recently established ones.

The most glamorous and glorious components of the financial sector were the **institutions of the reconstituted capital market**. That required first the appearance of *securities*. The initial step was the issuance of debt securities, corporate and municipal bonds as well as central government debentures. Shares, representing a title of (fractional) ownership, could emerge only as a consequence of ownership liberalization right after the political changes.

As was stated before, the communist system, even in its most market-oriented variants, could never tolerate the reappearance of any elements of the capital market because that would have led to the creation and then massive proliferation of private property. In some countries, interestingly, the Rubicon of capitalism was overstepped *before the political changes* when the communist authorities allowed first the issuance of corporate and municipal bonds to be purchased by other state companies and, gradually, by the people at large. **The intention was to increase domestic financial savings to finance corporate and municipal investments and reduce the need for foreign borrowing**. That was just a pragmatic consideration. But once securities were issued, i.e. the *primary market* was opened up, it was only a matter of time when the *secondary market*, i.e. the free trading of securities could emerge. Slovenia and Hungary were the first countries stepping cautiously on the road of capital market development as early as in 1987–1988.[122]

With the reappearance of securities which, by definition, carry the notion of *tradeability*, secondary markets emerged soon, almost automati-

[122] The gradual erosion of the last vestiges of an outdated ideology repudiating shares was quite obvious in Hungary. Working at the Financial Research Institute of the Hungarian Finance Ministry, together with two of my colleagues we wrote an article on financial sector reform intended to be published in a non-political journal. We decided to use the word “share” in the article. The then finance minister, late István Hetényi, a highly educated and exceptionally competent economist, read the manuscript before publication and commented only that using the word “share” was “premature.” Instead of trying to come up with any ideological argument, he said simply that he can imagine the usage of this word perhaps next year. That tells us a lot not only about the personality in question but also about the *zeitgeist,* the spirit of the age immediately before the collapse of communism in the model country of goulash communism.

cally. At the beginning of transition, that was very much supported politically as well. After the collapse of communism, in the early euphoric atmosphere of the *gründungszeit*, all newly-elected democratic parliaments and governments felt that the establishment of a **recognized securities exchange** was an *important symbol as well as a shining proof* of the successful restoration of market capitalism.

Ribbon cutting ceremonies for the opening of stock exchanges across the region were well-attended by government officials and foreign dignitaries. Although the symbolism was important, the content was usually shallow at the beginning. Spontaneous, unregulated secondary trading of securities was much more important than the transparent, well-regulated price discovery resulting from the concentrated manifestation of supply and demand in well-organized and regulated stock exchanges. In the capital market area the promoters of "wild east" capitalism were openly in conflict with those who wished to follow a more traditional institutional approach.

In many countries, securities trading was born out of the necessity of creating a secondary market for vouchers distributed within the framework of mass privatization. That did not mean that vouchers, and shares acquired in exchange of them, inevitably had to be traded in a spontaneous manner, as some influential proponents of the mass privatization schemes envisaged. This latter tendency was most strongly felt first in Czechoslovakia, then in the Czech Republic, where the more conservative and traditional Prague Stock Exchange struggled for supremacy with a technically more innovative but largely unregulated over-the-counter trading platform, called RM System, which was a simple extension of the original voucher registration and distribution infrastructure.[123] In contrast, the Warsaw Stock Exchange was in the epicenter of a strongly regulated and highly transparent market. It had almost a complete monopoly on institutionalized trading, operated a central securities depository, cooperated with an equally strong and prestigious securities commission, etc. thus providing very favorable environment for *domestic as well as foreign portfolio investment*.[124]

---

[123] Supported by Václav Klaus, prime minister, and Vladimír Dlouhý, the powerful industry and trade minister, the most visible and eloquent person promoting unfettered capital market development was Dušan Třiska, chairman of the RMS which operated the automated secondary market securities trading system. In his numerous writings, he always opposed what he labelled market killing or market distorting regulation.

[124] Wiesław Rozłucki, the first and long-time chairman of the Warsaw Stock Exchange, aptly called the interrelationship between mass privatization and capital markets a "difficult marriage." He compared the Polish and Czech experience in the following way:

No matter how important, developed and sophisticated the capital markets and its non-bank type intermediaries have become over time, the **banking system** was, and has remained ever since, the backbone of the financial sector in the whole transition world. No surprise, therefore, that banking regulation and supervision constituted always the *core interface* between the state and the financial sector.

The three most important pillars of prudent and efficient banking in any sophisticated market environment are: (i) **internal corporate governance,** to be provided ultimately by prudent, effective and efficient *shareholders* and to be carried out by competent management of high personal integrity, (ii) **strong and fair competition,** to be guaranteed by the *domestic structure and international openness* of the financial system and, finally, (iii) stable and strong, transparent and predictable, prudent

---

"The Polish approach was more conventional, if not orthodox. The desire was to follow, as much as possible, the patterns of regulation, organization, and practices of mature, developed securities markets. In building capital markets, Poland clearly preferred a tested solution and compliance with international standards. It was thought that regulation should precede trading practices. Trading was to be centralized to concentrate the initial low liquidity. In technical terms, electronic trading with dematerialized settlement and a depository was to be introduced. The licensing of brokers became obligatory, along with strict prospectus requirements for issuers of securities. The market was open to small investors, who were to be protected from the very beginning.

As a result, early in 1991 basic infrastructure for the capital market was established in Poland, consisting of a stock exchange, a central securities depository, licensed brokerage houses and a securities commission. The regulatory and functional structure was based on practices of modern securities markets…

The idea of voucher privatization has always been popular in Poland. It took rather long, however, to design and implement the mass privatization program, covering 500 enterprises and managed by 15 national investment funds. By the time the program was launched in 1995, the structure and organization of capital markets were completed. The mass privatization program was shaped to fit in the existing structures of capital markets as opposed to the other way around.

Clearly, developments in the Czech Republic followed a different philosophy and strategy. Absolute priority was given to voucher privatization. Transfer of ownership was the main goal, and capital markets were seen merely as a means to achieve this goal.

The authors of voucher privatization in the Czech Republic treated capital markets instrumentally and not as a **public good in their own right**. The infrastructure of voucher privatization was to be used later as a network leading to the concentration of ownership. The speed of this process was considered essential for market reform. Common features of modern securities markets such as the high level of regulation and transparency or minority protection were seen as premature and potentially conflicting with the concentration of ownership." (bolding mine) Rozłucki (2001) 140.

and efficient **regulation and supervision**, which can be also labeled as *external governance.*[125]

The most important reason why regulation and supervision is especially indispensable in *commercial banking*[126] stems from the fact that the *core stakeholders*, i.e. **the depositors**, who provide the bulk of the funding, **are typically not represented in any of the internal governance bodies.** Depositors, to whom most of banking liabilities belong as financial assets, bear the brunt of the risk in financial intermediation. At the same time they *have no direct influence and representation at the boards or supervisory boards of commercial banks*. That is a fundamental structural weakness of commercial banking which, not infrequently, leads to reckless behavior in lending, counterparty risk assessment and management, and asset allocation. Regulation and supervision are basically there to make up for these structural deficiencies.

Investment and development banks also demonstrate significant vulnerabilities—it is by no means the privilege of commercial banks. Nevertheless, these **risks are different** in nature. In case of investment banks, unbearable risks might be created by excessive reliance of *interbank funding and concentration of speculative assets* which might turn toxic rapidly. Hence, regulation should prevent, first and foremost, *contagion*. Development banks undertake policy lending, provide long-term loans and equity investment in areas where private investors are reluctant or unwilling. Regulation and supervision need to focus on *cozy, collusive, corrupt and intransparent relations with state organs* which might pursue stated policies recklessly, favoring special interest groups.

---

[125] The triangle or trinity of good banking is explained further in Bokros (2001c) and (2002).

[126] Within the banking sector, *commercial banks* have always represented the most important subgroup in each transition economy. Commercial banks, i.e. banks engaged in *lending, deposit taking and executing payments* (transfers from and to current accounts) typically serve both *corporate and retail* customers. It is a key structural characteristic of commercial banks that they rely on **household deposits for a significant part of their funding**. On the one hand, that makes the commercial banks particularly important not only in economic but also in societal life. On the other hand, that is exactly what makes commercial banks extremely vulnerable—they have a hugely important group of non-professional stakeholders who are not in a position to influence internal governance of the banks in any meaningful way. Someone else have to step in and represent their interest. **To provide strong external governance on behalf of the general public, protecting the interests of depositors at large;** that is exactly the most important role of state-orchestrated banking regulation and supervision. [The inherent structural fragility of banking is widely discussed in contemporary financial literature. See e.g. Rajan–Zingales (2003), Wolf (2008) and Roubini–Mihm (2010).]

The *role and professional content* of banking regulation and supervision was absolutely not obvious at the beginning of transition. There were several important reasons for that. First, liberalization, the easy and popular early reform in transition was sometimes wrongly interpreted as no rules at all. Many emerging entrepreneurs supported this heavily distorted approach.[127] Second, even if governments immediately recognized the specific nature of financial intermediation and the necessity of some state intervention in that sector, it was unclear *what kind of regulation it should be* and to what extent it had to be *different from the administrative rules* which had been prevalent under communism. The most fundamental distinction between the two types of regulation could be traced to the difference *between the command and the market economy*. In the classical communist system regulation was often *negative, always administrative type* and when it came to individual organizations, it was *very specific* to them. In a market economy, while authorities may issue ordinances affecting only a single company, that is the exception, not the rule. *Regulations, by nature, are more general*. Most regulations in a market economy apply at least to a *subsector* and, hence, to **all enterprises in the same way**. This feature of regulation is based on the fact that individual firms have much freedom to act within the confines of the established regulatory regime and usually they do not get orders for specific business decisions.

[127] Emerging entrepreneurs, would-be tycoons, future oligarchs were never true friends of any regulation. Having gained considerable wealth, they used their influence to repel or weaken any kind of state intervention. It was most visible in Russia, where many oligarchs were able to get new banking licenses even after it was clear that they had had primary responsibility for the collapse of their former banks which they had used or abused to finance their own empires. The fiscal, currency and banking crisis, which broke out on August 17, 1998 is a case in point. Instead of recapturing some value to compensate the depositors at least partially, deposits were lost completely in many banks where the oligarchs left only bad assets while at the same time they opened new banks and managed to concentrate the good assets in them. The Russian Central Bank, which performed also the function of prudential regulation for the banking system, was much weaker than the oligarchs. Dubinin, the head of the Russian Central Bank resigned after accepting defeat in September 7, 1998. [The specific case of SBS-Agro Bank owned by the tycoon Alexander Smolensky is described eloquently by Hoffman (2002) 434–441.] The brutal wild-east nature of Russian capitalism and the risks inherent—not only in banking but in the life of those who happened to work for regulatory agencies!—was tragically manifested by the killing of Andrei Kozlov, first deputy chairman of the Russian Central Bank, head of banking regulation and supervision, on September 14, 2006 by criminals contracted by a bank of which Kozlov had revoked the license in June, 2006.

Market freedom, however, **creates uncertainty,** which, in turn, gives rise to a wide variety of **commercial and counterparty risks**. No surprise, therefore, that financial intermediaries, serving a large segment of the national economy, typically face *even more risk of even higher intensity* than non-financial firms. As a consequence, the most important task of prudential regulation and supervision in banking and other areas of financial intermediation is *discovering, analyzing and, ultimately, mitigating* risks with general rules of behavior imposed on financial institutions by an independent regulatory and supervisory agency.[128]

Third, there was no universally acceptable model of banking regulation and supervision in the Western world to be taken over as a ready-made, off-the-shelf solution. When transition started there was still a marked difference between the Anglo-Saxon model of financial capitalism and the Rheinland model of universal banking. Some countries, like Poland and Hungary, opted originally for the Anglo-Saxon variant and separated commercial banking from brokerage and investments. As the famous second Glass–Steagall Act (Banking Act, approved in 1933) of the US was gradually eroding and finally repealed in 1999, transition economies also abandoned the organizational separation between commercial and investment banking.[129]

As far as the **institutional setting** of financial sector regulation and supervision is concerned, two structural aspects merit highlighting. First, this important state function was sometimes conveniently located within the mainframe of the central bank. That was explained not only with the

---

[128] In case of banking see more in detail Greuning and Brajović-Bratanović (2000).

[129] In light of recent developments, many scholars feel that dismantling the barriers between commercial banking and more risky financial businesses contributed considerably to the meltdown of Wall Street and subsequent global contagion. [See Roubini–Mihm (2010)] I happen to share these views and would support at least a partial restoration of the separation between commercial and investment banking along the following lines:

"A less draconian approach to limiting the scope of banking activity, as Glass–Steagall did, is to recognize that some financial activities should not be allowed within systemic multifunctional firms. Among these activities are:

- Management of in-house hedge funds.
- Creating off-balance-sheet affiliates having no commercial purpose and dedicated to evading regulatory constraints.
- Running large proprietary trading positions in cash securities and derivatives that are not integral to the core process for financial intermediation.
- Acting as principal investors in nonfinancial activities such as real estate and private equity." Acharya et al. (2011) 42–43.

obvious *interlinkages between the effectiveness of monetary policy and the stability of the banking sector*, again as the backbone of the whole financial system. Since all transition governments were struggling with the shallow capacity and rudimentary nature of their public administration, the efficiency, power and prestige of the regulatory and supervisory organization was expected to be significantly enhanced by being placed under the umbrella of the central bank. Second, when universal banking finally took hold and conquered the whole transition world after the first decade of transformation, there was a new tendency to *consolidate all financial sector regulatory and supervisory agencies in one institution* and, of course, now outside the central bank.[130]

In hindsight, these organizational changes can be considered less crucial. So long as the *close cooperation and coordination among the various institutions* could be guaranteed, the specific organizational arrangement proved to be less important, especially when compared to the real issue: the **autonomy of the regulatory and supervisory institutions within the state and the integrity of their operational behavior and culture**. For the regulatory and supervisory role of the state to be exercised properly, the institutions authorized with this important public function were in need to acquire broad autonomy *not only in implementing but also interpreting and, in well-defined cases, even change the relevant rules and regulations*. With these seemingly excessive but certainly significant

[130] As capital markets started to develop, first a separate securities commission was formed in all countries. It was empowered with the regulation and supervision of the securities market institutions, including the stock exchange, market participants like brokerages, investment banks and investment fund managers. Another office was providing the same services to the insurance sector. When pension reforms took place in several countries in the second half of the 1990s with the establishment of both mandatory and voluntary private pension funds, there was a need for an additional and separate regulatory and supervisory authority. (Had health care reforms taken place with the creation of private health insurance, yet another agency could have been brought to life.) The proliferation of regulatory and supervisory institutions led to the growing need of *cooperation and coordination* among them. Since the operation of several agencies proved to be quite **cumbersome and also increasingly expensive,** especially in small countries with small financial sectors, many governments decided to follow the British example and established a **consolidated financial sector regulatory and supervisory authority.** (The UK approved the *Financial Services and Markets Act in 2000* and the *Financial Services Authority* was given sweeping powers and comprehensive jurisdiction over all financial services. It is now the irony of history that the new British conservative-liberal coalition government would dismantle the unified super regulator and supervisor as a consequence of its real or perceived failure to act more aggressively before and during the latest global financial crisis.)

powers, the role of the state in regulating the financial sector has remained a controversial issue.[131]

In sum, the creation and effective and efficient operation of regulation and supervision of key areas of the national economy was an *extremely difficult, not particularly glamorous, not even convincingly popular, but absolutely indispensable part of structural reforms in transition.* It has demanded enormous amount of political attention, professional energy and government resources. Successful privatization of public utilities and financial institutions required not only substantial restructuring before any transaction could take place, but also *comprehensive regulation and continuous supervision.* That was already a **reform of the state**—to be followed by a whole host of additional reforms in order to transform the state *from a market-substituting and suppressing device in a market-supporting and strengthening one.*[132]

131 "Good government is then the foundation of any sophisticated financial system—the base on which the pyramid of promises ultimately stands. Good government is also more likely to be produced by a property-owning democracy. But what about the positive role of government? What policies does a sound government need to pursue to limit the defects inherent in any financial system—moral hazard, herding, and panic—without restricting its benefits to a small circle of well-connected insiders?

Suppose there were no lenders of last resort, no government deposit insurance, no government regulation of financial intermediaries, and no government bailouts. Would the financial world be more or less dangerous than it is? The answer to this question is not at all obvious. While the perils to which financial systems are vulnerable are genuine, it is far from clear that government intervention makes things any better. What is certain is that without any prospect of intervention, financial systems would look quite different: banks would be far better capitalized; maturity mismatches would be reduced, with greater reliance on securities or on long-term and more illiquid deposits in banks; and deposits would be better matched by highly liquid securities. Given the frequency of banking crises, this might be a big improvement. Whether one believes government intervention has improved things depends on how one balances the failings of the financial system against the defects of government intervention." Wolf (2008) 19–20.

132 "The economics of transition typically focuses on the economic factors that shape the process. How strong is the entrepreneurial response to liberalization? How rapidly do state and privatized firms restructure? How quickly is labor reallocated between activities? Yet this approach does not pay nearly enough attention to the basic element of transition: the transition of government from the communist police state to an institution supporting the market economy. This transition of government is as essential for the economic transformation as it is for the democratization of the societies escaping communism." Shleifer (1996) 6.

2.8. Public finance and administration

Reforming the state in countries emerging from the ruins of communism has been an *inherently and intensively political process*. Of course, there is no such thing as technocratic reforms pushed through in a political vacuum. The political environment always has a major impact on the **nature, size and scope** of these reforms. Dictatorial regimes as well as democratic ones may well be in urgent need to undertake comprehensive and fundamental reforms of government services, but *democracies have a clear advantage.*[133]

Initial conditions for state reform were broadly unfavorable in the whole transition world. By and large, the communist state was a totalitarian one until its demise, at least in Romania, Albania, and the Soviet Union.[134] The totalitarian state, as it was already discussed, had smashed whatever there might have been in terms of civil society before and replaced it with a political one.[135] Now the task was to *allow civil society to reconstruct itself and rebuild the state within the framework of democracy*. With a weak and fragmented civil society, the perspectives to build a solid, efficient but at the same time democratic state were dim. As a consequence, **the establishment and advancement of democracy** was, by itself, one of the most important aspects of state reform.[136] It was like a chicken-and-egg problem, indeed.

Dismantling a totalitarian state and building up a democratic one was a two-faceted process. On the one hand, certain institutions were *abolished.* On the other hand, new ones were *created.* This was true not only on the political side, but also in the area of *economic governance.*[137]

---

[133] "...good governance and democracy are not so easily separated. A good state institution is one that transparently and efficiently serves the needs of its clients—the citizens of the state. In areas like monetary policy, the goals of policy are relatively straightforward (that is price stability) and can be met by relatively detached technocrats. Hence central banks are constructed in ways that deliberately shield them from short-term democratic political pressure. In other sectors like primary and secondary education, the quality of the public agency's output greatly depends on the feedback it receives from the ultimate consumers of government services. It is hard to imagine technocrats working in isolation from people they serve doing a good job in these areas. Hence democracy, apart from its legitimating value, has a functional role in governance as well." Fukuyama (2004) 26–27.

[134] Friedrich–Brzezinski (1965).

[135] Fehér–Heller–Márkus (1983).

[136] Bokros (2007) and (2009b).

[137] "When the communist power collapsed, so did the communist government machines that supported it and controlled economic life. Yet the remnants of a large government

All structural reforms in transition can be interpreted in light of *institution building*.[138] All of them imply the abolition of some old institutions and the creation of new ones, consistent with the requirements of the modern market economy. They differ only *in nature, scope and degree*. Liberalization was more about dismantling obsolete and negative state functions; stabilization, in turn, demanded new ones discharged by brand new institutions. Privatization, as the term itself indicates, was eminently about transfering control over assets to non-state actors but at the same time required some very important new state skills.[139] Restructuring, first and foremost, was active and robust state intervention. Contrary to conventional wisdom and false interpretations of communist practice, regulation and supervision were new government functions necessitating considerable amount of institution building and a new culture.

Reforms of **public finance and administration** also fit into this picture. They imply the *demolition of old structures* (organizations, regulations, rules, norms, etc.) and the *creation of new ones*. They can be best analyzed if

often remained, ready to continue political control. A principal goal of the political transition… was to replace these remnants with institutions supportive of capitalism. Such transition of government entailed two steps: First, the economies needed to be depoliticized: control by market forces had to replace control by the government. That meant ridding the government of the levers and resources it could still rely on to control firms. But second, the transition also required the government to take on new functions, such as provision of laws and regulations to support a market economy. The state had to be weakened overall, yet strengthened in a few areas. Some muscles needed to atrophy, others to develop." Shleifer (1996) 8.

138 *Institution building, state building and even nation building* have become fashionable concepts of policy activism with the desire to reconstruct dysfunctional states around the world in the last thirty years. These terms were used not only to describe the transition process from communism to capitalism but in a much wider context to cover all efforts directed toward the reconstruction of failed states as well as helping capacity building in poor countries. [See World Bank (1996), (1997), (2000) and (2002)]

139 The privatization of state-owned enterprises is of course an appropriate goal of economic reform but it requires a substantial degree of institutional capacity to implement properly. Privatization inevitably creates huge information asymmetries, and it is the job of governments to correct them. Assets and ownership rights have to be properly identified, valued, and transferred transparently; the rights of new minority shareholders have to be protected to prevent asset-stripping, tunneling and other abuses. Thus, while privatization involves a reduction in the scope of state functions, it requires functioning markets, and a high degree of state capacity to implement. This capacity did not exist in Russia, with the result that many privatized assets did not end up in the hands of entrepreneurs who could make them productive. The stealing of public resources by the so-called oligarchs did much to delegitimate the post-communist Russian state. [Fukuyama (2004) 18–19.)]

distinction is made between the **scope and strength** of the role of the state. In this context, scope refers to the *extension* of state jurisdiction and action. Strength would describe the *intensity and efficacy* of state intervention.[140]

Following the distinction made by Fukuyama, it is important to recall that *the communist state was very large in scope but not necessarily strong in all areas of activity. Surprisingly, its implementation capacity was rather weak, particularly in the economy especially by the time of its demise and collapse.* As a result, major structural reforms in transition could also be interpreted as a top-down policy drive for **reducing the scope of the state** but at the same time building up or **strengthening its capacity in some areas,** old and new. It was necessary to withdraw the state from areas where it had previously been suppressing and substituting the markets. By the same token, it was absolutely indispensable to intensify its presence in others where it could *support and strengthen the capitalist market economy.*[141]

Public finance and administration constitute an immense area of economic and societal life. The two aspects can and should be discussed together because there is no state finance without corresponding administration and no administration without some revenue intake or expenditure. On the income side of fiscal accounts there are *taxes and transfers* coming from other levels of the government. On the expenditure side all items are supposed to target specific, well-identifiable economic and societal groups which imply the existence of *execution, transmission, control and monitoring* mechanisms. Government operation needs **effective**, that is to say, *rational, timely, stable and tight* (rather than wasteful) administration of all incomes and expenses; that is key for democratic legitimacy. Likewise **efficiency**, which means that the *impact of income generation and expense payments corresponds to the stated goals* to the maximum possible extent. These objectives can be best achieved and, consequently, democratic legitimacy best guaranteed if the **operation of the fiscal sector is fully transparent.**[142]

---

140 "It therefore makes sense to distinguish between the scope of state activities, which refers to the different functions and goals taken on by the government, and the strength of state power, or the ability of states to plan and execute policies and to enforce laws cleanly and transparently—what is now commonly referred to as state or institutional capacity. One of the confusions in our understanding of stateness is that the word *strength* is often used indifferently to refer both to what is here labeled *scope* as well as to *strength* or *capacity*." Fukuyama (2004) 7.

141 Kornai (1990), Balcerowicz (1995) and Shleifer (1996).

142 "Fiscal transparency is defined… as openness toward the public at large about government structure and functions, fiscal policy intentions, public sector accounts and projec-

One of the most important ingredients of public finances is *fiscal policy*. As was already discussed, the **vigorous rejuvenation of fiscal policy** was a prerequisite for macroeconomic stabilization at the beginning of transition. As time passed and the transforming economies have demonstrated more signs of successful supply-side adjustment, the importance of fiscal policy has grown further. The expanding private sector, including both enterprises and households, started to respond more quickly and precisely to fiscal signals. Governments were obliged to take into consideration the reactions of an increasingly autonomous private sector in fiscal policy making as well. Thus, a *strong and mutually reinforcing feedback loop* has gradually formed between fiscal policy and the behavior of non-state agents in the economy. In other words, **markets have started to constitute a welcome constraint to government policy.**

That this has been occurring has been good news. But since governing is a painful *learning process* at all levels of government, the feedback loop does not always represent a virtuous circle. At times and especially with governments poor in knowledge and experience but rich in high self-esteem and complacency, these feedback loops have turned into a vicious circle. **Fiscal profligacy and fiscal alcoholism** plagued the scene in many jurisdictions. In a sense, and quite unfortunately, lax fiscal policy started to resemble the "normal state of affairs" as it was observable in case of less than fully responsible governments, especially in Southern Europe.

---

tions. It involves ready access to reliable, comprehensive, timely, understandable, and internationally comparable information on government activities—whether undertaken inside or outside the government sector—so that the electorate and financial markets can accurately assess the government's financial position and the true costs and benefits of government activities, including their present and future economic and social implications.

Transparency in government operations has several dimensions. First, at an aggregate level, transparency requires the provision of reliable information on the government's fiscal policy intentions and forecasts. Second, detailed data and information are required on government operations, including the publication of comprehensive budget documents that contain properly classified accounts for the general government and estimates of quasi-fiscal activities conducted outside the government. The third dimension consists of mainly behavioral aspects, including clearly established conflict-of-interest rules for elected and appointed officials, freedom-of-information requirements, a transparent regulatory framework, open public procurement and employment practices, a code of conduct for tax officials, and published performance audits. In all three dimensions, fiscal transparency is closely associated with the successful implementation of good governance." Kopits–Craig (1998) 1.

In addition to policy, *institutions* started to matter more and more.[143] Not only in macroeconomic theory but, more importantly, in transition practice. In order to achieve long-term stability and sustainability of the fiscal stance, governments had to go well beyond initial and immediate macroeconomic stabilization measures. Furthermore, stability and sustainability of public finances was not only important to avoid fiscal collapse, but even more so to promote long-term *sustainable growth*. Fiscal policy gained more relevance by incorporating societal goals like equity and inclusion. These wide ranging objectives manifested themselves in all areas of institutional change.

Public finances extend to an extremely broad area of economic and social life where the government has a key role to play. Public finances cover *revenue generation* in the broad sense (including taxation, custom tariffs and various fees charged for government services) and all areas requiring public expenditure and transfers, like the pension system, health care, education, culture and sport, judiciary, public administration, law enforcement, military & police, subsovereign governments, fiscal borrowing, public asset and liability management, treasury operations, subsidies to churches and non-governmental organizations, etc.

Probably the best known and, without doubt, the most visible example for a complicated, complex and politically controversial reform is that of the **pension system**. Unlike health care or education, old-age income provision has been rather *comprehensively restructured in all transition economies*.

This does not mean that pension reforms have always been successful. In some countries, fundamental steps were taken several times in a stop-go manner. Almost every government had something to say about and wished to leave its mark on the pension system. Reforms advanced on a broad front, and then some of them were retracted or retrenched. In these latter cases governments of the day in the new democracies always found convenient reference points in Western Europe for hesitation and postponement. As the partial privatization of the pension provision has inevi-

[143] "The importance of institutions in fiscal performance is not at all surprising in light of the recent institutionalist turn in macroeconomics. Once institutions are controlled for, trade and geography, among the most widely believed determinants of growth, cannot explain divergence in economic performance. Now instead of asking whether they matter at all, the new question is how they matter and through what channels they affect economic performance. In order to understand the sources of institutional change and the potential endogeneity of institutions, first we need to understand what institutions do and how they affect human behavior." Győrffy (2007) 43.

tably created a **significant transitional deficit,** the trend today is more a freezing or a reversal of earlier reforms than a further advancement or fine-tuning.[144]

All communist countries in Mitteleuropa, the Baltic and the Balkan area used to operate a **pay-as-you-go** (PAYG) type pension system where benefits for retired people were financed by current contributions of the working populace.[145] The communist variant of this type of pension system had been made increasingly *universal*, i.e. covering most, if not the whole, society over time and *exclusive*, i.e. there had been no any alternative or additional method of providing old-age income support for the elderly.[146]

One of the most important reasons why pension reforms came to the agenda of many governments not only in the transition world but also in the developed and developing countries was the **adverse demographic trends** undermining the **financial sustainability** of the dominant state-sponsored pay-as-you-go pension systems.[147]

Adverse demographic trends mean *shrinking and ageing populations* all over Europe. Not sufficiently offset by immigration, graying and de-

---

[144] The recent history of pension reform reversals in Poland and the wholesale expropriation of the assets of the mandatory pension funds in Hungary are important cases in point.

[145] As it is well known, the PAYG pension system is not a communist invention. The first old-age and survivor defined benefit scheme based on social insurance was established in 1889 in Germany.

[146] "As in other parts of the social sectors, these arrangements made sense under the old economic order. Basing the system on formal employment in state-owned enterprises was logical, because formal employment was in effect the only employment, and there was virtually no unemployment. Almost everyone worked in state-owned enterprises, so this was a natural basis for organizing pension entitlement. Individual contribution records were not necessary because, with full employment, it was reasonable to assume that every worker had a full contribution record.

The generosity of the system was logical, given underlying premises. The low retirement age was a victory of socialism. Easy access to pension while continuing to work had two roots. Wages under central planning were low, hence not market clearing, reducing the supply of labor; separately, firms with soft budget constraints but hard output targets faced incentives to hoard labor, increasing the demand for labor. These mutually reinforcing factors led to persistent labor shortages. Generous provisions for combining pensions with work were one response to those labor shortages." Barr–Rutkowski (2005) 136.

[147] The classic primer in pension system analysis and justification of reform is a seminal book published by the World Bank Report, 1994. It was one of the first publications highlighting the fiscal unsustainability of the pay-as-you-go pension systems in the long run due to negative demographic changes.

clining populations represent a serious constraint on economic growth and bring about heightened tensions in the pension system in most of Western Europe. The transition world has been facing the same problem with accentuated force. Instead of immigration, many countries suffer from *emigration*. And it is the most dynamic working-age segment of the population which may leave in droves. Overall population decline might also be faster as a consequence of grave and grievous *environmental degradation and unhealthy lifestyles,* like excessive drinking, smoking, drug abuse and even suicide.[148]

As the pay-as-you-go state-orchestrated pension system had been tailored in such a way as to provide some flexibility for changing demographics, the first idea of governments to adjust old-age income provision to the observed negative trends was to *change the parameters* of the pension system.[149]

---

148 Several countries lost hundreds of thousands of people as a consequence of international and civil war in the Balkans, in the Caucasus and in Central Asia. That makes the trend of demographic decline especially steep for the countries located there. Some countries not affected by war suffered also very dramatic fall. For example, Bulgaria lost more than one million people in the last 20 years as ethnic Turks left the country. But the most tragic situation can be found in the heartland of the former Soviet Union, in Russia. Life expectancy for men actually declined after the collapse of the Soviet system. Despite significant immigration of mostly ethnic Russians from Central Asia, the population of the Russian Federation declined by almost 10 million in the last 20 years. According to UN estimates, the population of the largest country of the world in terms of territory may fall below one hundred million by 2050. [See UN (1998)]

149 "On closer inspection it is possible to see that two reform styles have emerged: a *parametric* style and a *paradigmatic* style. A parametric reform is an attempt to rationalize the pension system by seeking more revenues and reducing expenditures while expanding *voluntary* private pension provisions. A PAYG pillar is downsized by raising the retirement age, reducing pension indexation, and curtailing sector privileges and a development of voluntary pension funds beyond the mandatory social security system is promoted through tax advantages, organizational assistance, tripartite agreements, and other means of administrative and public information facilitation. These among other things are happening in Austria, the Czech Republic, France, Germany, Greece, and Slovenia.

Other countries decided to change the paradigm in which pension systems operate—that is, to move away from the monopoly of the PAYG pillar within the mandatory social security system. A paradigmatic reform is a deep change in the fundamentals of pension provision typically caused by the introduction of a mandatory funded pension pillar, along with seriously reformed PAYG pillar and the expansion of opportunities for voluntary retirement saving. Among other measures, this is what three-pillar Bulgaria, Croatia, Denmark, Hungary, Latvia, the Netherlands, Poland, Sweden, and the United Kingdom decided to do." Holzmann–MacKellar–Rutkowski (2003) 8–9.

As it is well known, the pay-as-you-go pension system working within the framework of nationwide social security is an **unfunded intergenerational income redistribution** scheme. Its financial position at any given moment depends on the following factors: (i) the *number of people working* in the official economy in registered jobs and, thus, paying pension contributions, (ii) the *payroll tax rate* for pension contribution, (iii) the *number of retired people*, and (iv) the *amount of income* they get as pension.

In a dynamic approach, financial equilibrium can be improved by the manipulation of system parameters which have a bearing on these factors. Governments undertaking parametric reforms can do some or all of the following: (i) increase the legal and effective *retirement ages*, (ii) increase the *rate of the payroll tax*, (ii) lower the *replacement ratio*, i.e. the proportion of the initial pension compared to the last, or lifetime, or average, etc. wage, (iv) change the *indexation*, i.e. the periodic valorization of payments for those who have already retired.[150] Last but not least, governments may be successful in bringing more employees in the official economy and, hence, *increase the number of contributors* to the system.

Parametric reforms, however, were implemented not only for adverse demographics. The economic, financial as well as the societal fragility and unsustainability of the pay-as-you-go system was exacerbated tremendously by the *transitional crisis*. The bankruptcy and liquidation of thousands of state-owned enterprises led to a sharp rise in unemployment. The number of state employees paying pension contributions to the social security system

---

150 "To assess financial sustainability (in particular of unfunded schemes) requires taking a long-term view and considering flows as well as stock. A short-term view of… unfunded schemes provides no assessment of financial sustainability. After its creation the system pays few or no benefits for many years, while levying contributions from an increasingly covered labor force. This resulting cash surplus is no indicator of financial sustainability, since the inflow and contributions create a liability that needs to be honored in the future as pension payment, often 40 years away and then for a period of 20, 30, and more years. For this reason, flows (expenditure, revenue and balance) need to be projected *for 75 years or more*.

In the same vein, an evaluation of the flows should be enhanced by a calculation and assessment of the stock of commitments and assets. The first is done through the implicit pension debt, operationally best defined as the accrued-to-date liability—that is, the present value of accrued pension rights to retirees and contributors. The second is done through a mark to market evaluation of accumulated reserves, if any. A large and rising implicit pension debt needs to be covered by future contributions and, together with low and stagnant assets, provides an early warning of financial lack of sustainability." (italics mine) Holzmann–Hinz (2005) 105.

declined drastically. Moreover, many of the laid-off workers were pushed into *early retirement* which led to a marked increase of beneficiaries.[151]

Parametric reforms were done in various stages of development in many post-communist countries. Nevertheless, the transition world in general and the pay-as-you-go pension system in particular have always been facing yet another grave problem which could not be addressed by parametric reforms. In addition to demographic decline and the negative effects of the transitional crisis, it was plagued by rampant **tax evasion and avoidance**.[152]

Social security contributions, including pension, health care and, in some jurisdictions also unemployment contributions, typically paid by employers and employees in a split way, are *mandatory burdens on labor* and rightfully *perceived as yet another tax*. Employers and employees are usually unhappy to pay this levy and, not infrequently, they collude to minimize it. There are many obvious ways to do so. The easiest way is to register employment at the minimum wage. Considerable part of the total salary remains unreported and unrecorded and the payment takes place in cash. This is one of the most typical methods of alleviating the tax burden on labor in East and West alike. Whenever a country is *short on solidarity but long on high formal tax rates*, there is a potent mix for widespread evasion and avoidance.[153]

Unfortunately, former communist countries demonstrated, and in many respects still keep showing, an almost **total lack of societal solidarity**.[154]

The destruction of solidarity under communism was the direct consequence of the complete demolition of civil society and its replacement

[151] "For humanitarian reasons and to ward off political pressures, responses to rising unemployment included policies to allow older workers to retire early to make room for younger workers, and easier access to disability pensions. The retirement age, already low, was further reduced in the early years of transition.

Inevitably, these forces exerted a downward pressure on the level of pension and upward pressure on already high contribution rates. The social security contribution grew from about 25 percent of payroll in the early 1990s to about 35 percent at the end of the decade." Barr–Rutkowski (2005) 138.

[152] It is a phenomenon which goes well beyond the tax system and affects almost all areas of economic and societal life in the new democracies. It is as much economic as cultural and even ethical. In transition countries most people are not even ashamed by not paying taxes or trying to minimize their tax burden.

[153] There is a clear distinction between *evasion and avoidance*. The former is *illegal,* i.e. implies the formal breaching of the law, while the latter is *legal*, it just involves the use of "innovative" solutions to exploit the loopholes in the tax regulation. While this distinction is important from the viewpoint of public policy action aiming at reducing the malaise, both express a serious cultural and ethical degradation of society.

[154] See Bokros (2001d), (2001e), (2001f), (2001g) and (2004).

with a highly political one where formal **solidarity was imposed upon the people by coercive measures**. While the heavily fragmented and atomized society was mostly capable of escaping the forced variant of solidarity (especially after the most repressive periods of Stalinism), the communist system always remained strong enough to prevent the development of a genuine, voluntary solidarity based on horizontal, autonomous civil society relationships. As a result, people became extremely *individualistic and cynical* about everything which seemed to have been an attempt by the state to enforce and assert whatever societal bonds and obligations might have emerged. That is perhaps the most tragic and long-lasting negative legacy of the communist system.[155]

The lack of societal solidarity had a particularly detrimental impact on pension provision because the pay-as-you-go system is based primarily on **intergenerational solidarity**. Despite trying to achieve a rough equilibrium between benefits and contributions at the macro level, there was just an *extremely weak link between future benefits and lifetime contributions on the level of the individual.* With little or no solidarity in society, retired people were interested in **maximizing benefits,** while actual employers and employees in **minimizing contributions** at the same time. The former was reinforced by the pervasive and perverse *entitlement culture,* the latter was strengthened by the widespread and destructive *free-rider behavior.* This obvious inconsistency in incentives put the operation and sustainability of the pay-as-you-go pension system in fatal jeopardy.[156]

---

[155] "The original underlying values of traditional solidarity were largely destroyed by the elimination of individual autonomy and a resulting fragmentation and atomization of society. Autocratic and communist regimes had much in common in this regard. As a result of their brutal abuses—rent-seeking, usurpation and corruption—both systems were particularly successful in distorting the public psyche of their people. Open tax evasion became an undeniable national sport, petty fraud and corruption was part of everyday life for the vast majority of the people. The privileged talked proudly about their "innovative" ways of cheating the state. Ironically, this was seen as a constructive form of civil disobedience. No one felt that, at the end of the day, the price was paid by the less-fortunate and poorer segments of society. At the same time, the prostituting impact of small "crimes" universalized the feeling of guilt, making it impossible to regain the moral momentum needed for systemic change. Despite the widespread perception of moral degradation, communism was not abolished because of its ethical unacceptability—but because it proved to be unable to satisfy the ever-growing and increasingly westernized material aspirations of the people as consumers." Bokros (1998) 537–538.

[156] "The distortionary nature of the system was not surprising... Marxist ideology largely ruled out incentives as a legitimate way of analyzing society. Thus, little attention was given to incentive structures. Although the proper relationship between contributions

It was possible to mitigate the impact of demographic decline and the transitional crisis by parametric reforms. It was impossible to correct and compensate for the absence of societal solidarity, tax evasion and avoidance, for widespread free-rider behavior. That required **paradigmatic changes.**

The most important paradigmatic reform undertaken in a post-communist environment so far has been the **establishment of mandatory, fully-funded and privately managed pension funds**. Interestingly, wherever this reform was implemented, mandatory private pension funds were introduced not as a substitute for but *in addition to* a reformed pay-as-you-go pension system.[157]

This is an extremely important characteristic feature of the new construct. While pay-as-you-go arrangements always embody, presuppose, represent and express some degree of societal solidarity, mandatory pension funds with individual accounts are based primarily on the **principle of self-care**.

The principle and practice of self-care are indispensable ingredients of the modern capitalist market economy and the autonomous civil society. *It is not the antithesis of solidarity but the antidote of etatism.* Free individuals cannot feel responsible for fellow citizens without taking responsibility for themselves. Every citizen has a civic duty to take care of oneself, then the family, relatives, neighborhood, nation, etc. It goes out in concentric circles but inevitably starts with one's self. Societal solidarity is based on genuine, **enlightened self-interest** and can be built up only voluntarily.[158]

Mandatory and also voluntary private pension funds built on the importance of enlightened self-care have several important consequences.

---

and benefits can be debated, in most of the communist countries they were unrelated, often with arbitrary variations across different groups of workers. On top of this, the entire contribution was paid by the employer. In the communist system, however, the soft budget constraints created an upward bias in benefit spending. Thus, pensions with a distortionary formula giving no incentive to contribute were just one of many examples of adverse incentives permeating all aspects of economic life." Barr–Rutkowski (2005) 137.

[157] Mandatory private pension funds were introduced in Hungary (1998), Poland (1999), Latvia (2001), Bulgaria, Croatia and Estonia (2002), Slovakia (2005) and Romania (2008). In all these countries the mandatory private pension funds were conceived and established as the **second pillar of a multipillar** arrangement, in which the first pillar always remained the social security based pay-as-you-go type defined benefit scheme. (Interestingly, the Czech Republic started a second pillar in 2012.)

[158] Tocqueville (1835), Fukuyama (1995) and (2011).

First, pension funds create a strong and visible *link between individual contributions and claims on future benefits,* thus establishing an unusually *intensive incentive for financial savings at the level of the individual.* Cheating and collusion make sense no longer. Second, the operation of private pension funds is based on the *capital markets,* tends to *stimulate overall financial savings* and, at least in an environment of prudent macroeconomic policy and honest government, *economic growth.*[159] Third, *the arrangement leads to financial equlibrium almost automatically*—both at the level of the individual pension funds but also at the level of the whole private pension fund system—because it *defines contributions only.* Annual and future lifetime benefits depend on individual contributions plus the degree of success with collective investments in the capital markets. As a result, the system of (both mandatory and voluntary) private pension funds is **financially sustainable.**[160]

In addition to financial sustainability, **social and political sustainability** do matter as well. Despite being a complex reform in need of extensive administrative preparation and intensive public awareness, the establishment of the second pillar proved to be a *relatively easy and popular move* almost everywhere. It is no coincidence that it spread quickly from one country to the next and within a decade mandatory private pension funds were created in nine former communist countries in Central and Eastern Europe. Its smooth advancement can also be explained by the fact that

159 "The bottom line is that a funded pension plan, if appropriately managed, has a strong saving and capital market advantage over pay-as-you-go. A credible funded plan may be an important part of national savings policy that includes fiscal discipline by the government and inducements against consumer borrowing or dissaving other accumulated assets. Under these conditions, a pension system with a large funded component may be part of a country's strategy for increasing capital accumulation and growth. Although increased saving may not be desirable everywhere and at all times, many analysts would argue that it would be growth-enhancing for most countries and for the world as a whole today. For these reasons, many capital-scarce countries are becoming increasingly interested in funded old-age security arrangements." World Bank Report, 1994, 93.

160 That does not mean that fully funded pension schemes are without risk. They carry just *different types of risks*. "When people save for their old age, as in personal saving plans, contributions are specified and ultimately determine future benefits. But there is considerable uncertainty about future rates of return, the duration of working and retirement periods, and therefore about future annual benefits. So, workers bear considerable investment, disability and longevity risk… For privately managed funds, the inability of workers to evaluate the competence of investment companies and the possibility of outright fraud further increase investment risk." Ibid., 83–84.

people living in transition countries usually had very *little trust in the long-term viability of the prevailing social security system* and the capacity of the state to provide adequate pension in a predictable and reliable manner.

In Hungary, the very first country to introduce the fully-funded mandatory (second) pension pillar in the transition world, many people, for whom it was not at all compulsory to join a private pension fund, did so nevertheless. Moreover, many people above the age 50, for whom it was clearly said to be disadvantageous to join, decided to participate as well. In order to reduce transitional fiscal deficit caused by the pension reform, joining the second pillar was made mandatory only for those young people who entered the official labor market for the first time in their lives. On that basis, only a few hundred thousands should have joined each year. The attractiveness of the new arrangement was shown by the fact that out of a total workforce of less than four million, more than three million registered employees decided to opt for the second pillar as well. That was a sweeping victory for the reform and a quite explicit vote of no confidence in state management of pensions.

Fifteen years after the start of this truly fundamental paradigmatic reform of regional importance, it is now safe to say that the biggest threat to the long-term adherence to the multipillar system was the **transitional deficit** it created in the fiscal accounts of the countries in transition.[161] When the reform started, the universal expectation was that governments of the new democracies would be wise enough to make room for the transitional deficit stemming from the establishment of the private pension funds by *reducing public spending by a commensurate amount elsewhere.*

[161] This book is not about the impact of EU-accession and its many benefits to the transition economies. However, as far as the pension reform was concerned, the intransigent and narrow-minded behavior of the European Commission (EC) was less than helpful. Allowing the transitional deficit stemming from the pension reform to be excluded from the application of the Maastricht criteria only until the end of 2007, the EC managed to trigger a **major backlash against the second pillar** exactly at the time of the unfolding global economic and financial crisis which engulfed the world in 2008. Transition economies struggled to balance their fiscal sector right at the time when transitional deficits were no longer accepted as legitimate sources of public deficit and debt. Hence, several governments decided to reduce the amount of payments citizens sent to the second pillar in order to reduce the overall fiscal deficit. As was already indicated, the most extreme reversal of the multipillar reform was made by the new Hungarian government which came to power in 2010. The *wholesale nationalization of the mandatory, fully funded private pension funds* in 2011 was exceptional even by regional standards.

No matter what the economic wisdom of this underlying political assumption might have been, the fact remains that few governments in the transition world were either willing or capable of making substantial cuts in fiscal deficits and debts during the "good times" of the first decade of the new century.[162]

The fragility of the pension reform establishing mandatory, fully funded and privately managed pension funds highlights three key characteristics of institution building in transition. First, *nothing is irreversible* in historical development; politics can build up and then destroy important institutions. Second, the *international environment* for the small, open and poor countries of Central and Eastern Europe played an extremely important role not only in the quick advancement and widespread application of the same approach, but also in its recent, and maybe temporary, retrenchment or reversal. Third, the *efficiency of government regulation and supervision* proved to be crucial in the success or failure of what can be also termed as **partial privatization** of the pension system.

Private pension funds, both in their mandatory and voluntary variants, require **comprehensive regulation and supervision by the state**. In this respect the private pension funds are just an integral part of the overall financial sector and they need regulation and supervision exactly for the same reason as other parts of the financial business: *private pension fund managers are playing with other people's money.*[163] On paper, most countries adopted a comprehensive, good and sophisticated regulation. That was usually imported directly from Western jurisdictions and adapted to suit local circumstances. Nevertheless, even though formal institutions, like laws, regulations, written norms and rules, organizational and operational arrangements can be imported and implemented without much difficulty, the **culture of regulation and supervision** consistent with the market economy **can only be homegrown**. That takes time and it is not without serious setbacks.

Despite all its intrinsic professional complexities in design and economic, legal and political difficulties in implementation, the pension reform proved to be a relatively easy area of institution building because it largely required the attention, efforts and resources of the **central governmental public administration** only. There were many other key com-

[162] Of course, not all countries were in need of doing so. Estonia, for example, joined the eurozone in 2011 with a public debt of less than 8% of GDP; that is by far the lowest figure in the whole European Union.

[163] Even more: they are playing with the life savings of the whole society.

ponents of public finance and state services provision where reforms could not take place without the permanent, massive and intensive involvement of **subsovereign governments**. *Health care and public education* constitute two of the most important areas where local government finance and public administration are inevitably affected and has an indispensable role to play.[164]

2.9. Subsovereign governments

Exactly the same way as with the central government and national power structures, the *democratization of subsovereign governments* was one of the first steps of state reform at the very beginning of transition.[165]

Surprisingly, the political reform of local power has proved more difficult than the democratic rebuilding of the central government. The most stubborn and intractable problem stemmed from the fact that after the centralizing tendencies of the communist past which had been driven by considerations of effective administrative control, the establishment of local and regional autonomy went hand in hand with an **excessive fragmentation and atomization** of the government structure. First, it was not obvious what the natural geographic and political unit of the lowest as well as the intermediate levels of subsovereign governments should be. Second, as a backlash to communist overcentralization, local communities usually wished to restore the *smallest possible* unit of political and legal jurisdiction which must have been justified by historical legitimacy. But more often

[164] Interestingly, that shows another matrix arrangement in public finance and administration because individual areas of public finance and state service provision have a cross-cutting dimension represented by the different territorial layers of public administration. No surprise, therefore, that most countries in transition undertook comprehensive reforms of their system of subsovereign governments, too.

[165] In the structure of the totalitarian communist state architecture, local, district and regional governments (councils=soviets, as the corresponding Russian word indicated) had no autonomy. They operated under **quadruple control**. They were submitted to (i) a state administration of higher territorial level, (ii) the sectoral arms of the central government, (iii) most importantly, the corresponding parallel organs of the communist party and, (iv) last but not least, the secret police. Subsovereign governments, like the trade unions, were considered a **transmission belt of official policy** rather than representatives of the people living in the area of their territorial jurisdiction. Despite having a formal separation between the elected body of officials and the appointed administration, all elements and levels of subsovereign governments performed administrative duties only and behaved like another bureaucratic institution.

than not, these new units were **not sufficiently large** to be able to provide even a minimum degree of public services at an acceptable level of quality. The essence and defining rationale of local self-government is to be able to **discharge public services**. The more important the public services local governments offer and the higher their quality, the more valuable and legitimate local autonomy will be perceived by the populace.[166]

Of course, it is a matter of democratic and well-informed public choice to determine what exactly the *role and function* of the various levels of local self-government should be—and then fixing the size and the precise boundaries of the political and administrative units can follow that decision. Alternatively, the institution building process in the area of subsovereign governments can take a *reverse course*. If the democratic polity feels that the historically predetermined units have huge emotional value and they seem to be indispensable for democratic legitimacy, most of the boundaries probably should remain as they are or be allowed to recapture their historical configuration. But then the **redistribution of functions and finance should reflect their true capacity.**[167]

Local and regional governments in the transition world were in dire straits at the early period after the systemic changes. The vestiges and negative impact of the transformational crisis, i.e. *output decline, hyperinflation, massive unemployment and rampant poverty*, left huge and ugly scars on the face of self-government, itself taking shape rather slowly. Public finance and administration of local governments went into a *crisis management mode*. Tasks and expenses multiplied while income transfers, coming either from the central government or from local enterprises, dried up. Democratic content and legitimacy of local autonomy was threatening to be emptied out right after its recapture.[168]

---

[166] But "the large number of jurisdictions providing public goods distinguishes local public economics from the rest of public economics. Because individuals are mobile and vary in tastes, the determination of optimal level of provision public goods among a series of jurisdictions is complex, as is the meaning of 'optimality' itself." Rubinfeld (1987) 574.

[167] Experience shows that there is no ideal size of lowest and intermediate levels of government. There might be a *minimum threshold* according to the minimum number of people living in a certain geographic area. According to some analysts and experts, that is *roughly five thousand.* [See Davey–Péteri (1998) 15.] But even this threshold depends on the functions the particular local governments are expected to perform. Symbolic display of local autonomy can be compatible with lower population numbers as well.

[168] Under the communist system, local governments received funding not only from the central budget but equally importantly from the *state-owned enterprises* operating in the same geographic area. Moreover, the state-owned enterprises, especially the larger ones, performed *many important social functions* themselves. Many of these enterprises

If there is an area of continuous changes in the name of structural reforms in transition, it is precisely subsovereign public finance and administration. Power politics has always influenced extremely strongly not only the almost permanent reorganization of the territorial extension and jurisdiction of local and regional self-governments, but also the regular redistribution of functions in public finance and administration within the general government. In this constant back-and-forth process the *quality of public services suffered* the most undermining—sometimes fatally—democratic accountability.

As a consequence, the results of structural reforms in this area of public life are quite dismal more than twenty years after the political changes. The **quality of local government services,** most importantly, in public education and health care, **have seriously deteriorated in many transition countries**.

This is a particularly disappointing outcome since public education (mandatory primary and secondary schooling) and primary and secondary health care (general practicioner service and outpatient specialized care) are widely considered to be some of the most important public services to be provided by autonomous subsovereign governments. The erosion of quality and the increasingly unequal access to these immensely important public services seriously **undermine the value, prestige and legitimacy of local governments** even if these latter make every effort to blame the central authorities for the lack of adequate funding in these areas.[169]

provided *housing*, at least primary *health and child care*, like factory physician, nursery and kindergarten. In a societal system where all able-bodied persons were supposed to work, this arrangement was not illogical (see footnote 146 for a similar judgement on pension provision). When state-owned enterprises went bankrupt, were liquidated and/or privatized, or simply had no choice but to cut back on non-core costs, they usually got rid of these social expenditures first. More often than not these enterprises transferred their welfare assets to local governments which, in turn, usually had no funds to make an adequate use of these assets. As a consequence, the quality of many welfare provisions, especially in their in-kind variety, deteriorated tremendously, contributing further to the spread of poverty and social deprivation. [See World Bank (2000b).]

[169] Marked deterioration in the quality of and equal access to these services may provide a good excuse and an excellent opportunity to overconfident and overzealous central governments to take control of the ownership and management of almost all institutions providing these services. This is what happened in Hungary in 2012 when the government reversed twenty years of decentralization by "nationalizing" almost all public schools and hospitals which had previously belonged to autonomous local governments. In this respect Hungary once again has broken the regional trend. Needless to

Primary and secondary health care provision have remained a central focus of attention and management of local governments even if most of the financing to cover at least their operating costs comes from nationwide social insurance, one of the largest centrally managed unfunded parts of the universally applicable social security system. Local governments usually have the right to auction off local practices for generalists, who may operate either as public employees of local governments or as private entrepreneurs. In both cases they receive most of their income from the central social insurance pot on the basis of *capitation*. Nevertheless, physicians working under the watchful eyes of local authorities have no choice but to play by the rules of *territorial service provision responsibility*. Out- and in-patient specialized care facilities are typically in the hands of higher levels of subsovereign governments; these latter appoint the general manager of the hospital, who in turn has overwhelming influence over hiring and firing. The same holds true for local schools as well. No surprise, therefore, that many of these health care or educational establishments became hotbeds of cronyism, clientelism and corruption leading to a further deterioration of quality and access. The democratic deficit is immense, indeed.

One of the basic reasons for the marked decline of service quality was, and still is, the huge and sometimes further growing **inconsistency** between the allocation of tasks for the provision of particular public services and the availability of locally disposable financial resources supporting them.[170]

Local and even regional governments in Central and Eastern Europe have kept relying excessively on **fiscal transfers from the central budget**. Local taxation is either nonexistent or provides insignificant amount of revenue, especially for small local governments, especially in underdeveloped areas. Taxing real estate, one of the most important sources of revenue for local governments in the Western world, has not gained much importance in the transition countries. The virtual absence of local sources of revenue further undermine democratic accountability and legitimacy and makes local and regional governments excessively dependent on, if not politically subservient to, the central authorities.

The **shallow administrative capacity** of lower level local governments represented another hindrance. Elected bodies may have insisted on carrying out a specific task even if they were fully aware of the limited capacity and inadequate quality of the local administration.

---

say, the administrative centralization of ownership and management is no recipe for the improvement of quality, access and cost efficiency.

[170] See Kopányi–Wetzel–Daher (2004).

One way to overcome the huge and not infrequently growing gap between what were considered primary tasks of local governments and their financial and administrative capacity was to form **local government associations.** In most cases, the creation of these associations was voluntary. Central governments offered *financial incentives to pool resources* in order to provide better services and/or achieve higher economies of scale. That could work rather well first and foremost in the areas of *human infrastructure*. Primary and secondary schools, vocational training facilities and outpatient specialized care providers could be best operated in this way even if it may involve the closure of some institutions in certain remote, poor, underdeveloped and sparsely populated areas. Although it may have required making some exceptionally painful public policy choices, the pooling of resources usually led to better welfare outcomes.

In case of *services of physical infrastructure,* like local transportation, street lighting, fire brigade, road and park maintenance, garbage collection, wastewater treatment and disposal, etc. the *optimal size* of the service provider and the *efficiency* of the service provision do not necessarily depend on the financial and administrative capacity of local governments. **Most of these services can be outsourced or privatized;** there is no absolute need to provide them by any level of government. Some control functions may have to be pooled but human and financial resources do not. Local governments may wish to form an association to exercise *strong quality and financial control over the service providers* but they do not have to provide these services themselves or even establish and run their own companies for the provision of these services.

Another way of trying to mitigate the tension between local expectations and limited capability and resources was transferring the task for specific service provision to a *higher level of subsovereign government.* Desperate local governments, unable to maintain their own schools or outpatient specialized care facilities were more than willing to relinquish ownership of these assets and transfer them to a county or regional level of government. Nevertheless, district, county, territorial or regional governments were usually reluctant or unwilling to assume these tasks without taking over the corresponding financial and human resources.[171]

[171] Local governments, squeezed either by the financial crisis or political pressure, might be prepared to transfer their schools to the church or other potential societal agents if and when these latter happen to be better endowed or better connected politically. This is exactly what is happening now in Hungary where public schools are being transferred to church denominations, recognized and supported by the state.

Finally one has to face the negative consequences of demographic decline and emigration in transition countries, **the slow but largely irreversible death of many small villages.** While this phenomenon is understandably perceived as a tragedy for those who happen to live there and even for many who attach strong emotional value to small, close-knit communities and their natural habitat, it is impossible to stop this process without enormous fiscal costs and huge, permanent losses in equal opportunities. Public policy faces exceptionally sharp dilemmas in this area. In most, if not all, countries children have the sacrosanct constitutional right to high quality education no matter where they live, who their parents and relatives are, how much revenue they earn, how valuable assets they may possess. *Equal opportunities in life always start with equal access to acceptable quality education.* Nevertheless, it is impossible to provide the same quality in a small school of a poor and remote village where the number of pupils may be less than the number of teachers. **Therefore, the consolidation of the excessively fragmented school system is an absolutely necessary, albeit far from sufficient, condition of providing adequate education.**

But the choice to be made here is truly stark: either to keep the low quality small local school open and hence exclude many of its pupils from the possibility to get access to high quality primary, then professional, secondary and tertiary education or, alternatively, close down the small and unviable schools, concentrate resources in a much larger and hopefully better establishment at a regional center and use school buses to transport pupils every day. While in the US the second option is fully accepted, in many regions of the transition world it gives rise to extremely strong negative emotions and reactions.

In any case, it is quite clear that the system of subsovereign governments represents an area of economic and societal life which is full of strongly **contradictory public policy objectives.** On the one hand, according to most constitutional arrangements, citizens of the state have the inalienable right to get access to the same high quality public services no matter where they happen to live and how much they earn or possess. Equal opportunities must be upheld and promoted by the state in all walks of economic and societal life. On the other hand, it is obvious that local governments, very different in size, financial and administrative capacity, are obviously unable to provide the same high quality services everywhere. There is a need for robust *redistributive mechanisms* to equilibrate the huge discrepancies in capacity to an extent possible. But the contradiction is stark here: the more actively and extensively the mechanisms of equalization and compensation are used, the more they infringe upon the political autonomy of the local governments. **Equal opportunities and democracy are in conflict here.**[172]

These conflicts and contradictions, nevertheless, should not necessarily lead to a breakdown of the democratic polity. National government powers based on nationwide democratic processes can and should be constrained in order to make room for sufficient amount of local self-government with *appreciable democratic content in public service*. Similarly, local autonomy has to be clearly defined and circumscribed so that irresponsible or reckless behavior of local authorities does not spill over to the national arena. That is a very delicate political balancing act, requiring constant public attention, adequate government resources and legal fine tuning.[173]

Perhaps the four most important areas where this delicate and dynamic balance should be found and regularly reconstructed are **taxation, transfers, borrowing and asset and liability management.** The way these complex issues are addressed in the transition world tells us a lot not only about the efficiency of the state but also about the advancement, or the absence, of democratic culture.

In case of **taxation,** two tendencies might lead to a marked improvement of outcomes. First, *local taxation of physical assets, especially real estate,* including both commercial and residential property, should be considered. The point here is not just local revenue raising; that might be well-achieved by a wide variety of other taxes. In addition to revenue, real

[172] Public policy is full of contradictory goals; that is why it is often called an art rather than a science. The important thing is that when objectives come in conflict, there should be legitimate democratic procedures to establish a **ranking** among them and attach **relative importance** to each and every public policy goal. Of course, the *interest conciliation process* may lead to different rankings at different times, but the authorities at various levels of government should have sufficient democratic legitimacy to pursue particular policies and implement measures reflecting a *specific ranking based on local preferences at a time*. Obviously, that can be revisited and changed from time to time. That is exactly what the democratic multiparty election process intends to achieve.

[173] The importance of the delicate political balance between central and subsovereign government powers is underlined by the fact that both can seriously undermine not only the efficiency of the other but destroy the financial viability of the general government as a whole. Reckless borrowing of subsovereign governments can result in the accumulation of unsustainable levels of public debt and may even lead to fiscal collapse. The history of Argentina, which went bankrupt in 2001, provides sufficient warning. The dire situation of Spanish public finances due to inconsistent fiscal federalism is another eloquent example of what can go wrong and why.

estate tax does provide a *strong, highly visible and appreciable local feedback loop* if the revenue raised by it is directly clawed back to the improvement of local physical infrastructure, like roads, sidewalks, pavements, street lighting, park maintenance, water and sewage pipeline networks, etc. The fact that a local tax leads to visible improvements in the quality and aesthetics of local public space may make it much more acceptable than any other alternative. Furthermore, if a real estate tax is based on close or at least approximate market value of the underlying asset, then a close link is established between **the environmental footprint of the property and the financial burden** it represents to its private owner. Equity and fairness are best served this way and over time this particular fiscal arrangement may also lead to a marked reduction of tax avoidance and evasion which are among the most tragic and deep-rooted infectious diseases in these incipient democracies.

Of course, local or regional real estate tax is no panacea for all problems facing subsovereign governments. All local taxes suffer from the general problem that municipalities and regions may have widely different income generating capacity as a consequence of widely dispersed and unequal wealth and income produced by the local economy or citizens living within the boundaries of their jurisdiction. It is important to bear in mind that *local taxation may reinforce these inequalities*. But this effect can be mitigated by grants from the central budget and income redistribution among localities (to be discussed later in this chapter).[174]

Local real estate taxes are desirable for two additional reasons: on the one hand, the *tax base is visible,* on the other hand, it is *immovable* by definition. These two important characteristics make it possible for local governments to apply even *different tax rates* at their discretion without having to fear too much about the disappearance of the existing stock of the tax base.[175]

Some income taxes, especially those levied on personal income, can either be *shared* between central and subsovereign levels of government or *assigned* to the latter altogether. Nevertheless, in case of income taxes the

---

[174] Sweden is providing a plausible example of how local taxation can be efficiently combined with rather comprehensive regional income redistribution without necessarily curtailing the positive impact of taxation on local self-government. [See Thakur et al. (2003).]

[175] Over time, however, an excessively high (marginal) rate of a real estate tax may lead to the destruction of value by the emigration of local dwellers and the drying up of new construction in the area. As a consequence, local governments are best advised to use their discretion at setting tax rates with care, taking into consideration its long-term impacts on the retention and attraction of inhabitants and businesses.

discretionary power of subsovereign governments in setting tax rates is *substantially diminished because of the lower visibility and much higher mobility* of the tax base. Local governments may get a larger share of the personal income tax revenue but they are not in a good position to alter the tax rate. They are even weaker when it comes to income taxes on business enterprises.[176]

Subsovereign governments may receive either a *predetermined share* of the personal income tax revenue which was collected in their territory or there might be a *redistribution* of the overall personal income tax revenue among subsovereign levels of government according to a formula prescribed by the law. More often than not, this formula leads to a **strong equalization** of tax revenue across local and regional jurisdictions. There is another public policy tradeoff here: regional disparities can be best addressed by allocating revenue on the basis of *capitation* but that would kill off any local incentive to enhance the revenue generating capacity of the local governments. Conversely, the more incentive is given to subsovereign governments to generate revenue locally, the less equalization can take place.

To generate sufficient interest in raising local revenue and implementing measures to enhace local welfare and at the same time to bring about strong equalization would require the wide application of **transfers** which may or may not be linked to shared and/or redistributed tax revenue. If they are not linked to shared or redistributed tax revenue, they can be called grants.[177]

Transfers are best analyzed in terms of their role in financing *expenditure*. From that perspective, distinction is made between *block transfers* (general purpose grants) and *assigned* ones (specific purpose grants).[178]

---

[176] "Since the mobility of individuals and households tends to be less than that of businesses, the personal income tax appears more suitable for partial assignment—through tax overlapping—to the subnational (especially state or provincial) level. However, to minimize distortions and tax-induced movements of labor and capital, it is preferable that the tax base be homogeneous throughout the country and also that the rate differentials among subnational jurisdictions be kept relatively small. Since this tax should be levied on the basis of the residence principle, including in the base income from out-of-state sources, its administration would be carried out most effectively by the central government." Ter–Minassian (1997) 9–10.

[177] "Intergovernmental transfer mechanisms can be broadly grouped into two main categories, revenue-sharing arrangements and grants." Ibid., 11.

[178] "Beside revenue sharing, the main mechanism for intergovernmental transfers are grants from higher (federal or state) to lower (state or local) levels. Grants can be grouped into the following categories:

- *General purpose grants*. These are unconditional transfers, aimed at addressing vertical and horizontal imbalances.

Block transfers are intended to achieve significant equalization of revenue and usually have few strings attached or none at all. Local governments have wide autonomy in spending but bear great responsibility in their decisions. Needless to say that not all local governments can live up to the highest expectations of democratic accountability. As a consequence, the use of block grants has remained limited in the transition world.[179]

Assigned transfers have become more frequently applied. Although they can be spent only on specific targets determined by the law and, hence, their widespread use and specific way of operation would *significantly limit the spending autonomy of subsovereign governments*, they have proved to be perhaps the most effective and efficient tools for making sure that certain *basic services are provided by all local or regional governments in a fairly equitable manner*. Such transfers seem to solve the problem stemming from the widely dispersed financing capacity of subsovereign entities. As a result, some *crucial services, like primary schooling, can be provided at a more or less adequate quality across the whole country*.

Assigned transfers show their importance **in time of crisis**. Basic services can survive even if a local government goes bankrupt. For example, if kindergartens and primary schools are financed primarily by *assigned transfers coming from the central budget on the basis of capitation*, then the basic functioning and provision of these especially important public

- *Specific purpose grants*. These grants carry more or less tight conditions regarding the use of funds and/or the performance achieved in the program or programs financed trough them. They may be open-ended or subject to a cap. They may or may not have matching requirements for the recipient government. Specific purpose grants may be of recurrent nature, if used to finance current expenditure, or of a once-off nature, if used to finance investment projects." Ibid., 13.

179 "…it is possible to compensate for the disparities and mismatches to which territorial fragmentation gives rise. But there are costs in terms of the classical instruments of local autonomy and accountability. Municipalities become less dependent on the resources directly levied on their local economy, more dependent on redistribution by the state and on transfers with a greater degree of specificity.

Moreover, there is a danger of encouraging fragmentation simply by compensating small municipalities for their size and excessive per capita overheads. Some grant systems include a basic lump sum element which, though small overall, can be significant for tiny authorities; others, as in Hungary and Slovakia, may include an equalization fund for villages in deficit. There are dangers in compensating unviable authorities for their self-inflicted penury. State budget support should be an incentive to the sharing of administrative and service costs, not to misguided efforts to go it alone." Davey–Péteri (1998) 17–18.

services can be guaranteed almost independently of the financial situation of the corresponding local government entity.

The immanent fragility of the local government structure of countries in transition can be best grasped by the **high frequency of illiquidity and insolvency in the subsovereign sector.** Local governments can and do go *bankrupt*[180] as a consequence of many factors: (i) some of them might be just too small to perform even the most rudimentary tasks assigned to them by the law, (ii) others may just overstretch their capacity to deliver and get into financial difficulties, (iii) borrowing can get out of hand and result in a mountain of unserviceable debt, (iv) cronyism, corruption, bribery and theft can empty out the cashier if internal and/or external controls are inadequate.

Unfortunately, in an environment of widespread imprudent behavior *general purpose block grants may open the floodgates to abuse.* Hence, they need to be used sparingly and with great care. But to apply more assigned grants is only a second best option. Instead of encouraging the pooling of resources among local governments in a horizontal way, they may just keep and stabilize the system in a suboptimal mode of operation by offering a rather **costly vertical safety valve** and thus absolving local governments from their responsibility to take action in order to improve operational effectiveness and efficiency.

The inherent and explicit *political nature of public finance and administration* should never be forgotten at the level of subsovereign governments either. Incipient democracies have many recurrent child diseases. One of them is the strongly **confrontational nature of politics** both at the national and local arenas. It is highly probable that central govern-

[180] It is important to make a clear-cut distinction between *bankruptcy and liquidation.* In corporate life both exist, in government life only bankruptcy can be had. Corporate bankruptcy involves the suspension of ownership rights, liquidation means their extinction. **Local and regional jurisdictions as legal and political entities cannot be abolished;** only specific persons can be absolved from office and the elected bodies consisting of particular individuals can be dissolved only to be replaced by others in a new election. In contrast, bankruptcy is not only possible but sometimes *unavoidable and quite useful*; it requires the appointment of *an administrator* by the central government who would temporarily exercise almost all rights and responsibilities of the local government while trying to restore its financial viability. This job is similar to that of a bankruptcy receiver in corporate life. The person appointed by the central government should try to make an agreement with the creditors, arrange for a debt reduction, achieve a rescheduling of debt, cut costs and, at the same time, ensure the functioning of the local government in a truncated form while *maintaining the provision of the most basic public services.*

ments happen to have different party composition than subnational ones. (The smaller the jurisdiction, the less impact nationwide party politics may get into the picture. Mayors of small villages are not infrequently independent people; they do not belong to any party at all.) *Politics do have a tremendous impact on policy making and execution.*

Borrowing by subsovereign governments has also proved to be a double-edged sword. On the one hand, the *right to borrow* is, and should remain, an inalienable part of local and regional jurisdiction. Moreover, it is an absolute practical necessity at least for short-term liquidity management purposes.[181] On the other hand, borrowing is inherently risky because in case of adverse market events, the costs of servicing the debt might increase significantly.[182] Furthermore, it constitutes inescapable *moral hazard* in light of the fact that subsovereign governments can never be liquidated. Hence, the **threat of bankruptcy should be sufficiently credible** to deter from excessive debt and fiscal profligacy. Better yet, national legislation is needed *to limit the borrowing capacity of subsovereign governments.*[183]

---

[181] One of the most important reasons for subsovereign borrowing would be *financing investment projects*. Larger entities, like big cities or counties and regions, can finance well-defined and well-designed projects by issuing **long-term project bonds**. These bonds are typically very attractive investment alternatives for institutional investors. Subsovereign bond markets in general and municipal bond markets in particular constitute important segments of securities markets in the Western world; it was fast developing in the transition world as well at least until the outbreak of the global economic and financial crisis in late 2008.

[182] In addition to households, larger cities also raised a huge amount of *Swiss-franc-denominated loans* in Hungary, Poland and Romania in the first decade of the new century. Since interest rates for domestic currency loans were high and Swiss frank rates much lower, it was perceived as the cheapest alternative for a long time. Exchange rate risk was considered to be low before the global economic and financial crisis. Nevertheless, since the start of the crisis the Swiss frank has appreciated by almost 50% compared to local currencies of these transition countries. As a consequence, *the burden of debt service has skyrocketed* and now many municipalities, in addition to hundreds of thousands of households, face payment difficulties. The *strong moral hazard* involved here is clearly manifesting itself by the desperate attempts of central governments to bail out not only citizens but municipalities as well. [See Hudecz (2012).]

[183] Limiting the borrowing capacity of subsovereign entities is a tricky issue. On the one hand, any blanket administrative ban would be not only unconstitutional but also unpractical and impracticable: flexibility in raising at least short-term loans for liquidity purposes in order to bridge incontrollable time-lags between income and expenses has to be preserved. On the other hand, there is a need for limiting subsovereign exposure to debt due to the implicit guarantee of central governments to bail-out subsovereign

Borrowing has become part of an even bigger issue: **asset and liability management.** Massive borrowing by the subsovereign sector in transition economies was encouraged not only by the fact that it had started from an insignificant level and, hence, much room seemed to have been available for its rapid growth, but also stimulated by the peculiar characteristic that many subsovereign entities were *asset rich and cash poor* at the start of transition. Subsovereign governments inherited a tremendous amount of non-financial assets from the communist system, like housing stock, municipal enterprises, large shares in nationwide network utilities, commercial real estate, even agricultural land, forests, physical infrastructure, etc. Although a good part of these assets represented liabilities rather than assets on a net basis,[184] most of it could be used as *collateral* for borrowing. Banks, rather unfamiliar with collateral valuation at the beginning of transition, were eager to lend to regional governments and municipalities even though these latter carried *significant counterparty and liquidity risk.* One of the most important reasons behind the rather fast privatization of subsovereign assets was precisely the need to raise more cash for debt service and/or getting rid of nonperforming assets representing in fact net liabilities.

In sum, public finance and administration at subsovereign levels have proved to be another hugely complex area of transition with *no model and no end* in sight even after more than twenty years. After the implementation of certain basic reforms, like restoration of autonomy in constitutional terms, definition and allocation of mandatory as well as voluntarily assumed tasks and resources, learning the basics of budget planning, execution and control, financial and human resource management, etc. the subsovereign sector of most transition countries is still subject to periodic reorganizations almost in every aspect of its institutional setting. It also

entities. An operable balance should be struck between the two extremes. That can be perhaps best done if **the law limits the share of subsovereign expenses which can be used for debt service in any particular moment**. [See Bokros (1998c).]

But there is no *wunderwaffe* to be deployed here. Political circumstances and imperatives of the day can easily superimpose themselves on the best legislation and regulation. *Democratic consensus* on how to balance tasks and responsibilities at the local, regional and national level is therefore absolutely key.

184 It is an accounting identity which has found its way to colloquial language for good reasons. When a particular asset does not produce either financial income and/or utility, or its maintenance would require constantly more spending than what it yields, then it is a *net burden on the shoulders of the asset holder*. Hence, its net asset value may be negative which in accounting terms is identical with a net liability.

reflects the slow motion of cultural change. Subsovereign governments are still considered more of a *key element of political power* rather than a vehicle to discharging first-class public services for the benefit of the consumers in geographical jurisdictions. Although subsovereign entities cannot and should not be singled out as the most important hotbeds of political corruption, they provide particularly fertile ground for *cronyism* in societies where well-paid jobs are few and far between.[185] Local and regional economies and societies in transition countries are particularly infested with "tribal" links based on kinship, rent seeking behavior and market capture by politically well-connected vested interests, sometimes even organized crime. Arms'-length relationship is nowhere to be seen. *Democratic culture is lagging far behind the formally democratic organizations.*

2.10. Legal and judicial reform

One of the most important reasons why democratic culture lags far behind the democratic organizations is the large and sometimes still growing *gap between prevailing legislation and judiciary practice.* While the countries in transition have made considerable advancement in enacting modern market enhancing legislation in most areas of economic life, their implementation and enforcement still have yet much to be desired. Progress and regress have been observed in the application of protecting fundamental ownership rights, minority shareholders' interests in corporate governance, creditors' interests in bankruptcy, liquidation and foreclosure procedures, depositors' interests in closing banks, investors' interests in insurance and pension funds, enforcing competition rules, breaking up cartels, collusion, clandestine market distorting agreements, etc. For modern market enhancing legislation to prevail in an adequate and acceptable manner

---

185 This problem has reached such high proportions that in some countries it is now discussed quite openly. For example, Traian Băsescu, the Romanian president, repeatedly castigated rampant cronyism at the level of subsovereign governments in his public speeches in 2011. It has become a major argument in justifying the latest proposal of the central government to reshuffle the whole subsovereign government architecture in Romania. Then it provided a convenient excuse for the new coalition government led by Victor Ponta to start a frontal attack against the incumbent president in 2012. (It is just an apt irony of linguistics that the verb "a căştiga" means exactly the opposite in the Romanian language—to earn, to acquire or to win.)

there is a need for what is frequently called a *law-abiding state*. A very tall order, indeed.[186]

Another important characteristic feature of transition countries is the fast **proliferation of litigation**. On the one hand, it is absolutely natural. In the communist system the overwhelming majority of enterprises were part of the state economy and it was considered strange if not wholly unacceptable for one state-owned enterprise to sue another. With privatization and the organic development of new enterprises, small and large, foreign and domestic, a *rapid pluralization of the economy* took place and led to the *explicit manifestation of conflicts of interests*. These conflicts needed to be resolved; one way of doing so was through the courts. On the other hand, there has been an *overreliance on litigation* as a consequence of the absence of less confrontational or more amicable, or at least more consensual interest harmonization mechanisms like *arbitration* and extrajudicial processes like *mediation*. In the communist system there was no culture and practice to use these alternatives either. As a result, during transition the courts always have been, and still they are, overburdened, judges are not always well-trained and prepared, usually have no time to keep up with fast evolving jurisprudence. In some countries their remuneration is still inadequate, exposing them more to attempts of bribery.[187] Of course, courts and judges are not working in a societal vacuum; not infrequently they are subjected to undue influence, either political or personal.[188] All these factors seriously

[186] "The idea of a democratic, law abiding state is manifested in a pattern of transformations in the legal sphere and the market economy (with its various shades) is manifested in the economic sphere. In order to bring about this transformation in the proper fashion, it should be affected while keeping in mind the concept of a law-abiding state." Wyrzykowski (1995) 10.

[187] "In their day-to-day professional life, judges within the EBRD's region—particularly in the early transition countries—are faced with numerous challenges. They must cope with complex and constantly changing rules and regulations, deal with market economy concepts that simply did not exist when they were appointed, sometimes resist attempted infringements of their integrity and independence, and in some instances make it to the end of the month on a poor salary. It is no wonder these judges struggle to fulfil their mission." EBRD (2005) 37.

[188] That is a crucial point. The integrity and independence of judges and clerks do not depend exclusively on their salaries. While remuneration plays an important role, the socio-political environment is much more decisive. For example in Hungary the new constitutional arrangement, which entered into force in 2012, together with the subsequent cardinal legislation has seriously undermined the integrity and independence of the whole judicial system. The Constitutional Court was castrated. The judiciary can no longer be regarded as a strong and integral part of the *checks and balances* indispensable for a well-functioning democratic polity.

contribute to the weakening of judicial practice, to the deterioration of the quality and consistency of decisions. Litigation in many transition countries is *lengthy and costly;* its outcome is *unpredictable,* the process is not always impartial. No wonder that society has so much doubt about the independence, effectiveness and efficiency of the judiciary. Hence, the prestige of the courts remains rather low.[189]

One of the most important and symptomatic areas of legal and judicial reform in the new democratic and market-oriented environment is the regulation and enforcement of **bankruptcy and liquidation.**[190] It can still be considered underdeveloped and weak for a variety of reasons.

---

[189] Transparency International (TI) has put together and published its *Corruption Perception Index* (CPI) since 1995. According to the latest ranking of 2010, there are only two countries from our research area which have a better place than 30 (Estonia 26 and Slovenia 27). All other new EU-member states are between 40 and 75: Poland 41, Lithuania 46, Hungary 50, the Czech Republic 53, Latvia and Slovakia 59, Romania 69 and Bulgaria 73. The two largest states of the Western Balkans have also less than favorable ranking: Croatia 62 and Serbia 78. [See Transparency International (2010)] While the CPI is a complex index showing the perception of corruption in many walks of life in an aggregate form, undoubtedly one of the most important areas of corruption perception must be the judiciary. [See also Ofer (2003).]

[190] Bankruptcy proceedings can also be called **rehabilitation** because the most important aim of this exercise is to *restore the financial viability of the firm as a going concern.* A rehabilitation process can be invoked *either by the creditors or the debtors.* But even if the rehabilitation procedure is commenced by the creditors, it might be important for the creditors themselves to buy the debtors into the process because "total displacement of the debtor from the management of the enterprise will eliminate the incentive for debtors to avail themselves of rehabilitation procedure at an early stage and may undermine the chances of successful rehabilitation. On the other hand, allowing the debtor to retain full control over the enterprise creates a number of risks, including that the assets of the debtor will be dissipated to the detriment of creditors. It is therefore preferable for the law to provide for an arrangement whereby the debtor continues to operate the enterprise on a day-to-day basis, but under the close supervision of an independent, court-appointed administrator. However, the court should have the authority to displace the debtor's management entirely when there is evidence of gross mismanagement or misappropriation of assets."

"To ensure that rehabilitation proceedings are not abused by the debtor, there must be provisions that allow for the conversion of rehabilitation proceedings into **liquidation proceedings.** Such provisions should include a mechanism that allows the court to immediately convert the proceedings on its own motion, or upon a recommendation by the administrator of the creditors, when it is clear that rehabilitation is not feasible or when there is evidence that the debtor is acting in bad faith. To strengthen such a conversion mechanism countries should also consider specifying in the law that rehabilitation proceedings may not, under any circumstances, exceed a specified period. Such time limits may be of particular importance in countries where the capacity of the judiciary is limited." (bolding mine) IMF (1999) 59–60.

First, this was *a new or at least a rediscovered area of jurisprudence and judicial practice* because the communist system explicitly denied the existence of enterprise failure in its ideology and excluded it completely from practice. Indeed, the alleged superiority of the communist system—among others—was "proven" by the established fact that state enterprises were never exposed to bankruptcy and liquidation because "conscious planning protected them from the irrational, anarchistic and wasteful tendencies" of the market. In reality, **the lack of meaningful competition** kept all state-owned enterprises alive.

Second, there has been little or no time to learn or relearn either the regulation or the enforcement of bankruptcy and liquidation in a gradual, trial and error basis because the transitional crisis, characterized by enormous output decline, *pushed a large number of state enterprises into insolvency almost immediately.*

Insolvency was not the privilege of state-owned enterprises at the very beginning of transition. Private entrepreneurs met their fate quite often as well. Many people, who lacked even the basics of entrepreneurial skills, had no choice but to start some businesses of their own and many of them, the so-called "coerced entrepreneurs" went bankrupt quite rapidly. Others, with much better entrepreneurial skills but no personal integrity, realized very quickly that the fast changing and imprecise rules of bankruptcy and liquidation with usually very weak enforcement gave rise to tremendous opportunities for ripping off innocent people.

Third, *mass privatization schemes* and the widespread practice of what came to be called *spontaneous privatization*[191] had led to tremendous abuse well before any sophisticated legal and regulatory rules for handling bankruptcy and liquidation could have been put in place.

Spontaneous privatization was the initiative of well-connected socialist enterprise managers to sell state-owned firms **as if it was their own**. When the control of the fast disintegrating communist state had been considerably weakened or disappeared in the year immediately preceding the democratic change, **powerful managers used and abused the opportu-**

[191] See Bokros (1991).

"The spontaneous privatization of state property became evident as managers were granted control over state assets (by leasing, creating enterprises from structural subdivisions of larger enterprises, creating various associations, and the like). As the system of state control over enterprises collapsed, while the legal basis of privatization was missing, new owners to a considerable degree secured their control over enterprises by force, using criminal structures and bribing state officials traditionally responsible for controlling enterprises." Radygin (2003) 413.

nity of ownership vacuum for their own personal benefits. Sometimes even the transitional but at least still notionally communist government helped them in this endeavor by enacting legislation which enabled the "red barons" to privatize the state enterprises managed by them in a perfectly legal manner. The best and most notorious example for that was the Hungarian "Transformation Act" of 1989[192] which made it possible for enterprise managers to sell their enterprises—totally or partially—without any control or interference by the state and, most ridiculously, by any revenue arriving to the state. Fortunately, this legal window of opportunity for the blatant abuse of the absence of effective public control in the midst of transitional turmoil was quickly closed next year when the first democratically elected government established the *State Property Agency* (SPA) and centralized all state-ownership rights at and their practical exercise by this new government institution.

Fourth, as bankruptcy and liquidation were painful learning processes while the complete overhaul of the economy was still under way and the tensions were still escalating, it was almost always possible for *insider debtors to escape with the most valuable assets* before creditors could take appropriate measures through the slow moving courts. Last but not least, bankruptcy and liquidation rules and procedures were not necessarily considered by society as *constructive mechanisms to facilitate financial and legal restructuring* but invariably seen as yet other avenues for shaky and shady property redistribution deals not necessarily more cultured or civilized than other violent and abusive methods of privatization.[193]

---

[192] Law VII of 1989 on the Transformation of Economic Organizations and Business Associations.

[193] "...in an environment of high levels of corruption and the continuing redistribution of ownership, alternative solutions envisioned by the law and procedures for their adoption become a convenient tool for manipulation and applying pressure in the interests of different participants of this process. Of importance here is the type of arbitration manager appointed, as well as the choice between liquidation and rehabilitation (reorganization).

...it is hardly possible today to regard the institution of bankruptcy in Russia as a stable and efficient external mechanism that improves the management and finances of a company. The increase in the number of bankruptcy petitions apparently does not indicate an enthusiastic response by creditors to the new legal avenues open to them. Rather, it seems simply to provide a trial run of new methods of privatization, protection of managers against hostile takeovers, or, conversely, a way to hostilely take over assets of interest. It is not accidental that this process co-occured with the general rise in ownership redistribution around the time of 1998 crisis." Radygin–Shmeleva (2003) 479–481.

Another key ingredient of market strengthening legislation is **competition law.** On the one hand, that is important almost in all areas of the market economy but particularly in sectors of *network utilities* where competition is seriously constrained by a natural monopoly element. The same holds true for the financial sector in its widest possible configuration as well.

Competition policy and regulation were also completely new areas of economic and societal management in the incipient market environ ment exactly the same way and precisely for the same reason as bankruptcy and liquidation. Given the fact that the communist system deliberately excluded competition for its allegedly harmful and wasteful consequences, there was *no legal tradition and practical policy experience inherited from the past system to recognize the truly positive and negative impacts of competition, to utilize its benefits and exclude its drawbacks*. But the most serious problem was that unfettered, unregulated competition was not easily distinguishable from market-enhancing, market-strengthening competition. Bad regulation, i.e. market distorting administrative intervention was not easily separated from good regulation, which aimed at **eliminating artificial and mitigating the negative impact of natural monopolies**.

While the professional content, transparency and stability of regulation do matter a lot, rules enforcement, i.e. *the behavior of the courts and the whole judicial system* matters hugely too. Since all transition countries of Mitteleuropa, the Baltic and the Balkan area can be regarded as having **small, open, underdeveloped and converging** economies, *competition is predominantly coming from abroad and its rules from the European Union.* Nevertheless, the internal application of these rules is of great significance.

2.11. Matrix reloaded

Obviously, there have been many other areas of economic and societal life which have called for, and received, a fair dose of structural reforms in the last twenty plus years of transition. On the economic front mention should be made of *labor market arrangements, agricultural and rural development, international trade policy, social and family support, education and health care,* etc. They are all critical areas having a direct impact not only on economic growth and convergence but also on social cohesion, including poverty alleviation. Nevertheless, most of these public policy areas easily fit into the matrix of structural reforms in transition as *additional aspects of already discussed issues* and show even more intensively the intrinsic interlinkages among the different rows and columns.

The matrix itself builds on the concept of the World Bank which in its early assessments of the progress in transition made a distinction among *first, second and third generation reforms.*[194] But the matrix constructed here is much more complex and, definitely, more nuanced. While liberalization and stabilization have always been considered as *closely interlinked first generation reforms* by almost every scholar and practitioner, privatization has never been cut into two distinct components before. That gave rise to enormous confusion as to whether privatization belongs to quick, first generation reforms which can be carried out in a shock therapic manner or to much slower and complicated second generation reforms which require enormous state capacity for restructuring and regulation. The matrix here solves this problem by distinguishing between what is called competitive privatization and the privatization of public utilities and financial intermediaries. As a consequence, it becomes sufficiently clear that privatization as such does not belong to reforms which can be implemented overnight. (Real privatization, i.e. privatization other than mass privatization resulting in a formal change of title, cannot be implemented in a shock therapic way and even the theoretical concept of privatization as a one-shot macropolicy device is false.) As the second component of privatization does require much restructuring as well as comprehensive regulation and supervision, all reforms highlighted in the second line of the matrix significantly overlap with state reforms. Hence, it makes little sense to distinguish between so-called second and third generation reforms as if the former would refer to the businesses and the latter to the government sector only.

Having analyzed all of the elements shown in the matrix in some detail in the second part of the book, there is a need to recapitulate briefly these **interlinkages**. There are four important general aspects worth mentioning.

The first is that although all elements in the matrix are closely interrelated, *some of the links are obviously stronger than the others*. That suggests an **optimal sequencing** of structural reforms. That is exactly how the matrix is constructed. The first line shows the *early and immediate reforms* which could largely have been implemented in a shock therapic way because they mostly include macroeconomic decisions which had a direct and almost immediate impact on the sclerotic, deeply distorted and

---

[194] World Bank (1996).

inflexible economy inherited from the communist command system. However, apart from comprehensive liberalization and macrofinancial stabilization, **there was no need and no possibility to implement anything else overnight**. In case of the other elements of the matrix, where complex structural reforms involved painstaking and lengthy processes of institution building, a shock therapic type of implementation was just impossible even in such cases when the new governments had all the intention, political strength and stamina to do so.

It is important to recall that liberalization and stabilization, while also in need of some institution building in the peculiar transition setting, could have been narrowly conceived and implemented as **macropolicy measures** requiring almost nothing else but a blueprint and strong government resolve. In this very narrow sense a quick elimination of administrative barriers and a powerful and sustained push for macrofinancial stabilization was not only possible but highly desirable and clearly beneficial to the national economy. Those governments which managed to gather the political will and broad societal support to implement liberalization and stabilization in this shock therapic manner made *an enormous service* to their countries the impact of which can be felt even today.[195]

Second, as micropolicy reforms affecting individual enterprises as well as public finance sectors and budgetary organizations can never be designed and implemented overnight, **sequencing became more a matter of choice based on political preferences** in the second phase of transition.[196] More precisely, many of these reforms were to be initiated parallel and at the same time in order to allow their impact to develop in a mutu-

[195] Shock therapy, as it characterized macroeconomic policy implementation first in Poland, then in Czechoslovakia and Estonia, made a huge difference in giving a much needed initial boost to transition in those countries and also made it irreversible. No wonder that these are exactly the countries which have been in the best position to weather the storm of the contemporary global economic and financial crisis as well.

[196] But the policy objectives should have been redefined and pursued with perseverance and vigor because the second phase of transition was no longer characterized by "extraordinary politics" as described by Balcerowicz (1994) and (1995). Often the mood of the general public turned into disillusionment and sometimes even despair as the unrealistically conceived miracle of instant paradise failed to materialize. The sobering truth was clear to the "technopols" [see Williamson (1994)] who put together sometimes deeply unpopular stabilization programs in the early stages of transition. Experience also shows that only those countries were capable of getting out of the transitional crisis rather quickly and step on the road of renewed and sustainable growth which were strong enough to swallow the pills of macroeconomic stabilization and then complement it with structural reforms bringing about supply-side adjustment.

ally reinforcing manner. For example, privatization of big manufacturing firms could easily go ahead together with the restructuring of public utilities and banks; there was no reason to delay one because of the other. The only real constraint here was the *political and administrative capacity* of the government.[197]

Third, specific **structural reforms could and did go ahead in stages;** especially those implying long *transitional arrangements*. For example the retirement age within the framework of parametric pension reforms could not and should not be drastically increased in one shot. A five-year increase in the legal retirement age needed at least a full decade to be fully implemented. That was not a problem *if the end target was constantly kept clearly in mind and in sight.* All intermediate steps of a long chain of individual reform steps should lead to the specific end result which must be well-understood by and well-communicated to the members of society.[198]

One of the most important problems in advancing long-term and multistep structural reforms was the rather *short life span* of individual governments. More often than not, governments, which introduced some of the long-term and complex reforms, lost the next election and disappeared well before they were able to reap some of the benefits of the reform initiated by them. If and when the next government decided to abolish, or at least significantly modify some of the components or parameters of these reforms, it became next to impossible to assess, let alone feel and possibly enjoy, the impact of the original construct.[199]

---

[197] While the administrative capacity of a government is a fairly clear concept for everyone who has tried to pursue structural reforms with the help of a government bureaucracy, political capacity is still an opaque variable. "A first lesson for economists from the political science literature is that a government is not a single, rational decision maker. Indeed use of the word 'government,' followed by a singular purposive verb, is normally misleading. There are always a number of influences on decisions, and they may be more or less important depending on the issue or issues at hand. To suggest that a dictator, for example, has no political constraints is highly misleading: even in dictatorships there must be groups supporting, or at least not actively opposing, the dictator. For that reason choices of certain policies will in normal circumstances be politically costly if they seriously undermine support of key groups." Krueger (1993) 60.

[198] See Hausner (2001).

[199] Sometimes disputes and political divergences stalled reforms within the same government as well if strong personalities disagreed with the official position of the government. The fate of the Polish pension reform is a good example. "In June 1994 the medium-term 'Strategy for Poland' program, presented by the new deputy prime minister and minister of finance (Grzegorz Kołodko) first advanced the idea of radically reforming the PAYG system. Although the government and the Parliament accepted this pro-

Last but not least, it is imperative to remember that for transition to go ahead in a successful manner countries were, and still are, always in need of **a critical mass of structural reforms**.[200] This concept has slowly gained traction in the professional policy discourse because it cuts through the nowadays rather obsolete debate about speed and sequencing. Moreover, in the absence of strong and decisive action to initiate and carry out several interlinked reforms which could potentially reinforce the positive cumulative impact of specific steps taken in individual areas of public policy, **structural reforms will remain on the agenda of each and every single government in the transition world for a very long time.**

Reform fatigue and reform reversals have convinced even some intellectually progressive governments that significant steps in public policy can only be made in a *stealth manner*, if not with *outright cheating*. This approach, however, can never produce lasting results and it tends to reinforce the vicious cycle of stop-go policies which are explicitly harmful in the areas of business and public sector reforms. There are several reasons for that. First, both the business sector and the government sector are quite *fragile and weak* in most, if not all, transition countries; therefore, excessive volatility and/or sudden reversals of government policy will destroy whatever precious little stability there might be in the institutions of these sectors. Second, politics is increasingly *confrontational* in many countries in transition; even small steps in structural reforms are immediately put into a sharply adversarial political context and fought fiercely on that basis.[201] Third, the prevailing culture is still very much based on *suspicion*, viewing the **whole government as an opponent**, if not an outright enemy, of the business and civic sectors of society as a whole. Sometimes

gram, no specific measures followed. The delay was due to a dispute between the minister of finance and the minister of labor (Leszek Miller) over a proposed change in the rules of indexing pension benefits from the existing wage-related system to a price-related one. This stalemate lasted until October 1996, when Miller was replaced. The new minister (Andrzej Baczkowski) supported the idea of fundamental reform and the establishment of a multipillar system. He put a great deal of effort into getting the proposal for indexation passed by the Parliament, which cleared the way for fundamental reform." Hausner (2001) 215.

200 See Bokros (2009a).

201 The confrontational nature of politics is increasing even in a number of Western democracies and not only as a consequence of the global economic and financial crisis. Extremist tendencies, including fascist and xenophobic, are gaining strength and, more importantly, legitimacy in hitherto peaceful and consensual jurisdictions. The erosion of liberal democracy in the West inevitably has an important negative spillover impact on the coarse democracies of the East.

governments reinforce that perception by their overconfident predatory behavior. Fourth, there is still very little to show for *a stable and cultured middle class, independent professionals and critical minded intelligentsia* in the transition world. The economic and political formation of these stabilizing elements of society is slowed down tremendously by the global and European economic, financial and societal crisis and by the gradual but marked erosion of the same strata of society in the West, too. Given the significant political constraints reinforced by now clearly established vested interest which result in blocking major steps of structural reforms almost everywhere, one can be almost absolutely sure that the critical mass of structural reforms will stay as a requirement for a very long time in the future.[202]

As a result, the matrix of structural reforms needs to be *reloaded* time and again. **All its elements may need serious revisiting, review and revision**. Even liberalization may come back to the agenda because anti-market and populist governments, but even market friendly ones in their quest to tame what is perceived as unfettered markets, may well have implemented some measures which in reality have proved to be an undesirable hindrance to economic growth, job creation, financial equilibrium and social cohesion.

In light of the still unfolding global and especially European economic and financial crisis, this is no longer a shocking conclusion. *Macroeconomic stabilization* returned to the top of the agenda in all transition countries, because the domestic impact of the crisis required substantial monetary and fiscal adjustments.[203] Although privatization has not (yet) come

---

[202] The best example for the lack of critical mass is the absence of meaningful reforms in health care. Except for Slovakia, no country in transition has introduced a multipillar system in financing health care, i.e. **mandatory, fully-funded and privately managed health insurance companies** which would compete for the business of the general public. Debates on the mandatory pillar of private health insurance have been usually stalled on the issue of how much leeway should be given to insurers in deciding about the fee charged to their clients. Opponents of the reform conveniently referred to *adverse selection* which is supposed to be the consequence of introducing the profit motive. However, nobody among the promoters of reform have ever advocated for free rate setting. On the contrary, most of them accepted the idea of a flat fee, established by the regulator, precisely in order to avoid adverse selection.

[203] These adjustments, however, were no longer identical since there had been much divergence in macroeconomic policy among transition countries before the outbreak of the global financial crisis. Some countries, like Estonia, Poland, the Czech Republic, Slovakia and Bulgaria were in a rather comfortable position because fiscal policy had been by and large prudent, fiscal deficits and debts had remained well under control and the

back for political reasons—at the moment there is no country in Central and Eastern Europe where the government of the day would openly declare privatization as an important ingredient of its program[204]—circumstances may change rather quickly in the future.[205]

In any case, **state reform**, including first and foremost *the restructuring and rejuvenation of regulation and supervision*, especially in the area of financial intermediation, has become absolutely key in fighting contagion and mitigating the negative impact of the crisis on growth, job creation and social exclusion. Last but not least the fragility of public finances in concert with the still generally observed and experienced shallowness and sometimes markedly deteriorating quality of essential public services, including public administration, the less-than-fully user friendly hierarchy of subsovereign governments and the still overpoliticized legal and judiciary environment constitute a constant source of embarrassment for the

---

economic structure of these countries showed growing flexibility throughout the whole first decade of the new century. In contrast, some other countries, first and foremost *Romania and Hungary had excelled in accumulating large fiscal deficits and public sector debts in the same period.* Procyclical fiscal policies were not only unnecessary but rather harmful in achieving the worst situation of **twin deficits** (i.e. fiscal and current account deficits) and **twin debts** (i.e. fiscal and national debt). No wonder, therefore, that both Hungary and Romania were obliged to go back under the protective umbrella of the IMF, the European Commission (EC) and the European Central Bank (ECB) at the very early stages of the international crisis. The same holds true for Latvia, which was suffering from the collapse of the only domestically owned bank which, for its sheer size, brought down macroeconomic stability pretty much the same way as it happened in Spain, Iceland and Ireland.

[204] Of course, that does not mean that there is absolutely no meaningful amount of privatizable asset in the hands of the state. The political enthusiasm for privatization ceased to exist much earlier than the inventory of saleable assets at various levels of the state was depleted. Some countries are struggling with huge public debt; one way to reduce the burden thereof would be through a renewed privatization drive. Likewise, new impetus to growth could be given by the fast improvement in efficiency as a consequence of privatization.

[205] As it has already been indicated, liberal economic policies, including privatization of state enterprises have become unfashionable in the second decade of transition. "Neoliberalism" has become a curse for many politicians. **Policies of liberal inspiration are now largely swept aside by unbridled populism.** Unfortunately, these sentiments are fuelled and reinforced by the desperate situation of millions of people who feel themselves as hopeless losers. In this respect it is also strange and unhelpful that some brilliant Western intellectuals of high moral standing lent their names to anti-market sentiments and thoughts. [See e.g. Judt (2010) who, in his bitterness and despair, wrote in a summary manner that the "years from 1989 and 2009 were consumed by locusts." Ibid., 138.]

societies in transition. When populist policies and politics get exhausted and prove eloquently their ineffective and inefficient nature, the mood of the general public may change quickly and there might be once again favorable conditions for market supporting and strengthening policies.

Logically, the question which springs into one's mind is the following: **is transition over by now?**

3. Transition for the Twenty-First Century

My answer to that question is, unsurprisingly, a *definitive no*. This short reply can be easily deducted from the principal narrative of this book. But the long response is almost equally obvious: without further profound **economic, societal, cultural, ethical and psychological transformation**, the dire negative legacy of the communist system cannot be overcome.

Let us recapitulate what exactly this terrible legacy of Soviet communism is which seems so incurable with the arduous economic, political and social reforms, indicated in the matrix. Several aspects of this soul-wrenching and integrity-destroying phenomenon have already been touched upon. The most important one is the *excessive fragmentation, atomization of society* which makes it virtually impossible to build a well-functioning market economy and stable, mature democratic polity in a short historical period of time. The totalitarian communist system has failed spectacularly in providing much desired consumer goods, services and much promised material welfare to its subordinates but it was quite effective and efficient in cutting human links in civil society. *It destroyed the civic texture of the social fabric*. It resulted, on the one hand, in an almost complete obliteration of trust, confidence and societal solidarity, on the other, in a **grotesque rejuvenation of populism and tribal nationalism**.[1]

[1] "In the intoxication of their newly-won independence, the new democracies dug themselves into the trenches of their own historical past and the ideologies shed by their own lords. They cannot see out of them. If somebody had deluded himself ten years ago that exercising political liberties would have dissolved the cultural and mental isolation of post-communist countries because the citizens would learn to talk to each other, exchange their opinion, form civil organizations, assert their interests and, as a conse-

The excessive and brutal fragmentation and atomization of civil society was not without serious consequences. One of the most important distortions stemming from the debilitation of society is the *emergence and idiosyncratic consolidation of the oligarchic order.*

When civil society has no organically developed autonomous institutions filled with meaningful collective action of highly conscious individuals who happen to be bonded together with strong links of mutual trust, political *democracy remains an empty shell* which can then be filled and captured very easily by powerful elements of the emerging economic and political elite. Less important it is who these newly influential people are and where they come from.[2] The key feature of their rule is that they

---

quence, the unpleasant linguistic inclusions of the dictatorship will be decomposed, he must realize now that it has not exactly been happening this way.

Nobody could have foreseen the implosion of critical inclination and sense of reality to such a great extent. The legacy of the dictatorships has left its mark on the mentality of the youngest generation even more heavily than how much strength and autonomy could have been generated in the first decade of liberty. The fascist and communist vocabulary of the dictatorship has passed into everyday language with pride and without control. The political language of the communist dictatorship, which was formerly living in the ghetto of the editorials of party newspapers, all of a sudden has become the language of the public political discourse and the nationalist and racist language, hitherto forced into illegality, came into the limelight with pride, too. What else could the institutions of democracy do in the absence of democratic language and mentality? They run dry and empty. The new democratic states have hitherto been unable to find common language with one another or with the great European democratic communities. Under the direction of their freely elected governments, they crawled back into comfortable and dangerous isolation despite having fought and protested against it for four decades. Sometimes clumsily, sometimes gloriously, sometimes with fear, sometimes with blood." Nádas (2006) 108–109. (My translation from Hungarian.)

[2] Many scholars have struggled to grasp the essence of this phenomenon and explain the *origin, nature, stratification of the new ruling class in post-communist societies.* One of the most original and interesting attempt has been offered by Eyal, Szelényi and Townsley. They have formulated several theses around the Bourdieu concept of cultural capital. According to them, "[p]ost communist society can be described as a unique social structure in which cultural capital is the main source of power, prestige and privilege. Possession of economic capital places actors only in the middle of the social hierarchy, and the conversion of former political capital into private wealth is more the exception than the rule. Indeed, the conversion of former communist privilege into a post-communist equivalent happens only when social actors possess the right kind of capital to make the transition. Thus, those who were at the top of the social hierarchy under state socialism can stay there only if they are capable of 'trajectory adjustment,' which at the current juncture means if they are well-endowed with cultural capital. By contrast, those who relied exclusively on now devalued political capital from the communist era are not

capture the fragile and inefficient democratic state[3] and shape it strongly to their own advantage. There is little or no distinction between economic and political power, no transparent arms' length relationship between the emerging political and the entrepreneurial class. On the contrary; political parties and most of the formally elected representatives, while claiming to represent the interests of the whole society, function as *conduits and transmission belts* for not-so-hidden special interests. Corruption is rife; politicians receive huge and illegal financial support from special interests without the slightest opportunity for public scrutiny. They return the favors by shaping legislation according to the wishes of these special interests. No matter how sharp the open political battles are or appear, there is a limit not to be overstepped by any of the major players. It is constituted by the widespread and unspoken consensus to keep the parasitic expropriation of resources in place.

Nevertheless, the maintenance and upkeep of an *oligarchic order with a democratic facade*[4] is not easy. For it to function properly, i.e. without serious challenge from possible counterbalances constituted by independent domestic entrepreneurs, inevitably spreading and better organized

able to convert this capital into anything valuable, and are likely to be downwardly mobile." Eyal–Szelényi–Townsley (1998) 6.

3 State capture is a key concept popularized by the World Bank during the Wolfensohn drive to address corruption as a hindrance to development. Now it is widely used by scholars, analysts and politicians alike. In most cases state capture denotes a situation whereby the state is captured by special interests which are more powerful than the state itself. In transition countries it is better to talk about **oligarchic structures.** Powerful leaders of coercive state organizations (army, police and secret service) may form a coalition with business interests and transform the state into a **predatory organization** not only to ensure the stable flow of expropriated income but to prevent the emergence of independent business interests and political forces which may escape from their control and put their benefits from the steady income flow into jeopardy.

4 "(1) One should not regard democracy, as some are accustomed to do now, as existing simply wherever the multitude has authority, since in oligarchies and indeed everywhere the major part has authority, nor oligarchy as existing wherever the few has authority over the regime. (2) For if [the male inhabitants of a city] were one thousand three hundred in all, and a thousand of these were wealthy and gave no share in ruling to the three hundred poor, though these were free persons and similar in other respects, no one would assert that they are under a democracy. (3) Similarly, if the poor were few, but superior to the majority of well-off persons, no one would describe this sort of thing as an oligarchy, if the others had no part in prerogatives although they were wealthy. It must rather be said, therefore, that [rule of] the people exists when [all] free persons have authority, and oligarchy when the wealthy have it; (4) but it turns out that the former are many and the latter few, for many are free but few wealthy." Aristotle by Lord (1984) 122.

foreign firms and, perhaps, the slowly emerging civil society itself, there is a need for considerable amount of resources to be expropriated permanently via **established and respectable channels without too much coercion.**

The experience of the Russian Federation gives an eloquent example, which is openly admired and cherished by several petty autocrats in Central and Eastern Europe. **As the archetype of communism was the Soviet Union, the archetype of modern post-communist oligarchy in the 21st century is the Russian Federation.** In that country the development and solidification of oligarchic order has been made possible by the *abundance of exportable natural resources*, first and foremost energy, which can be extracted by large, vertically integrated, capital intensive firms, controlled by a small number of closely knit, politically connected and economically interlinked people. Having expropriated most, if not all important natural resources in the first decade of post-communist anarchy characterized by a weak, crisis prone and intermittently collapsed state, **the oligarchs were interested in a strong state** which would protect their monopoly, exclude competition and guarantee the steady flow of income in the whole construct. That is why the rich Russian oligarchs have expropriated the state itself, completed the capture of the state, made a compromise with the disgruntled and disappointed *siloviki leaders*[5] and invested in a strongman, forever-president Vladimir Putin, who has, at least until today, proved to be spectacularly effective in excluding or eliminating contesting oligarchs who may have represented a threat to the very existence of the oligarchic order and kept the aspirations of society under close control in the name of *managed* or *directed* democracy.

There were several major attempts in the small transition countries to institute and institutionalize an oligarchic order. Slovakia between 1993 and 1998 proved to be a fertile ground for such an experiment under the populist rule of Vladimír Mečiar. In the nationalist fervor whipped up after the velvet separation from the Czech Republic, the newly emerging political class tried to create a **closed and interlocking coterie of wealthy businessmen** with strong nationalist credentials in order to secure a constant flow of income to purchase continuous political support to the ruling

[5] Leaders of the army, police, but first and foremost that of the secret service are called "strong people," those who are interested in a strong state, who are willing and capable of using organized state force in order to attain either legitimate or illegitimate goals. No wonder, the siloviki are not only intertwined with legitimate business interests but also with organized crime. [See e.g. Politkovskaya (2004) and (2008).]

party. The magic bullet was to be provided mainly by the **insider privatization**, i.e. the firesale of huge chunks of industrial assets to well-connected people, mostly incumbent managers of the old socialist behemoths at extremely preferential prices. Several transactions involving large heavy industrial enterprises inherited from socialism represent lucid examples of blatant privatization abuse. The sale of the controlling stake in the giant Košice steel mill in 1994 and that of the Slovnaft refinery at the outskirts of Bratislava to newly-established shell companies formed by the incumbent managers are perfect cases in point.[6] But as the cozy system of insider privatization was based on *directed lending* and the incumbent managers were incompetent in turning the easily acquired assets profitable, all large state banks became insolvent within a few years. *The insolvency of the banking system* dried up the flow of foreign credit almost overnight which, in turn, put an abrupt end to fiscal overspending. Macroeconomic disequilibrium created by the hugely inefficient system kept alive with massive foreign borrowing came to the light with full force. As a consequence, the increasingly angry and disappointed Slovak electorate voted the Mečiar-government out of office in the elections held in 1998.

The example of the Slovak experiment with oligarchy provides a forceful lesson: **no oligarchic order can be easily kept in power in an extremely small and open economy without relatively prudent macroeconomic policies and efficient enterprises or without an abundance of easily exploitable and exportable natural resources.**[7]

More prolonged, protracted and, for that matter, more successful attempts for the establishment of an oligarchic order happened in *Croatia and Serbia*, the two largest and economically most significant former

[6] See Marcinčin (2000) 304 and 309.

[7] In the specific Slovak case, geostrategic factors also played an important role in the collapse of the oligarchic experiment. Vladimír Mečiar desperately wanted Slovakia to become a member of NATO for fear of alleged Hungarian revanchism and because of the fast deteriorating bilateral relations with Hungary as a consequence of the unilateral decision to divert a good part of the waterflow of the River Danube to allow the controversial Slovak hydropower plant built at Gabčíkovo to come into use. When NATO decided about its first enlargement in July, 1997, only Poland, the Czech Republic and Hungary received an invitation to join. **Slovakia was excluded for its inadequate democratic credentials**. That was a huge slap in the face for the regime and a humiliation for the Slovak people. Poland, the Czech Republic and Hungary joined NATO in March, 1999 and Slovakia finally was able to follow them only in March, 2004, two months before the EU-accession of all four Visegrád countries. By that time Slovakia made up for all lost time and successfully finished its catching up on transition.

member states of the old socialist federal Yugoslavia.[8] The Balkans provided a particularly fertile ground for the emergence of a nationalist oligarchy which maintained a firm grip on the local society, expropriating most surplus value for its own benefit. This process was facilitated by the war which, in any circumstances, would require the extreme concentration of material and financial resources. Local strongmen, like Franjo Tuđman in Croatia and Slobodan Milošević in Serbia, were able to steal the whole first decade of transition in name of building a strong nationalist state where all important productive assets were in the hands of cronies, protected by the ruling party at the central as well as the regional and local levels of power. This cozy arrangement was greatly enhanced and facilitated by the armed struggle which engulfed the Balkans until the very end of the twentieth century.[9]

But no matter how favorable initial conditions might have been, oligarchy has run its course and went beyond its past due date in a relatively short historical period of time even in the Balkans. In extremely **small and open** economies, lacking easily exportable natural resources and in societies living under the intensive influence of the demonstrational impact of the European Union, thus, having an **overwhelming aspiration of convergence** to the West in material abundance and welfare, the oligarchic order may lose its legitimacy rather quickly. There are at least four important reasons for that. First, in the absence of constantly expropriable income streams arising from the export of natural resources, *the local economy has to be based on effective and efficient labor producing goods and services acceptable to foreign and domestic markets*. Second, given the extremely small size and openness of the economy, the *local labor force has to be competitive* by international standards. Third, as the sources of domestic capital accumulation are limited, there is no choice but to rely on *significant amount of for-*

[8] The blueprint was copied, with various degree of success, in all successor states of the former socialist Yugoslavia, except for Slovenia. All these newly independent states were born out of violent civil strife or open war which creates even more favorable conditions for the emergence of an oligarchic order.

[9] In case of Croatia, armed conflict lasted only until 1995 and ended victoriously with the recapture of the Krajina in the short summer war. Serbia was in constant armed struggle first with Croatia, then in Bosnia and finally in Kosovo until the very end of the decade. Physical destruction in Croatia was concentrated in the Krajina region and the southernmost tip of Dalmatia (with the long Serbian siege of Dubrovnik and its surroundings). Serbia itself suffered little physical damage until the selective precision bombing of military installations, transport and telecommunication lines by NATO aircraft as a consequence of the Kosovo crisis in 1999.

eign direct and portfolio investment which, in turn, always poses a formidable challenge to the oligarchic order. Last but not least, the most talented, best trained and most mobile (usually young) people has always *more choice* and can always *emigrate in droves*; leaving behind a *dangerously exhausted, increasingly uncompetitive society*, exacerbating further the domestic economic and social tensions and pushing the country further away from successful convergence.

While the Croatian and Serbian societies were finally able to rise against the suffocating oligarchic order and find the path to the competitive market economy and democracy by the end of the twentieth century, the war and the oligarchic order have left ugly scars on the face of these societies and, more importantly, some deep distortions in the social fabric as well. Pockets of resistance of the oligarchy might survive and even rejuvenate themselves as the political culture and ethical composition of society still has much to be desired. In addition, the so-called "Balkan ghosts," i.e. the historical animosities of the past, are far from being totally exhausted.[10]

The oligarchic order has not been defeated completely in the transition world. Indeed, probably it cannot be defeated once for all. **Economic and societal forces interested in recreating and solidifying oligarchic structures receive intermittent boost from both market and government failures.** *The still unfolding global economic and financial crisis and, especially, its eurozone variant seriously weakened the pull of Western Europe as a desirable model and target for convergence.* It created disillusionment for many people who feel themselves losers of capitalism in general and losers in the transition to a market economy in particular. They blame the allegedly unfettered market forces for their personal failure and tend to demand significantly more state intervention. They are longing for cradle-to-grave **state paternalism**. *They do not realize that bread cannot be guaranteed, or at least better provided, without freedom.* They are willing to sacrifice democracy for job security and (the illusion of) welfare.[11]

[10] See Kaplan (1994).

[11] The best example of a desperate attempt to create an oligarchic order today can be detected in Hungary. After excessive macroeconomic mismanagement, fiscal profligacy and widespread corruption shown by the seven-year rule (2002–2009) of a Socialist and self-styled liberal coalition, the Hungarian people voted overwhelmingly for a populist and nationalist party (Fidesz) which openly proclaimed its authoritarian intentions and is now making every effort to build up an oligarchic order. Having gained a comfortable two-thirds majority in the Hungarian parliament in 2010, the government have moved quickly to destroy most political checks and balances, e.g. the Constitutional Court, the Fiscal Council, the State Audit Office, the Media Council, the Public Prosecutors' Of-

In addition to the crisis itself, there are several important factors coming to play here. One is that some **countries, particularly in Southern Europe, have developed strong oligarchic structures over time,** which, in turn, seems to have exacerbated their misery in the present crisis and made it more difficult to adapt quickly to the fast changing circumstances of the world market. *Greece and Italy are cases in point.* That shows also that the emergence and spreading of an oligarchic economic and political structure is definitely not the exclusive privilege of transition countries which inherited a particularly fragmented and atomistic societal structure prone to degenerating into an oligarchic order characterized by **crime, cronyism and corruption.**

The good news, however, is that in the extremely short history of transition no country in Mitteleuropa, the Baltic and the Balkan area has ever been successful in improving the material welfare of its people on the basis of an oligarchic societal order. Small and open economies always require an **open society**[12] in order to close the still significant welfare gap with mature Western, industrial, increasingly service- and knowledge-based societies. *These societies have no choice but to be open to new ideas, foreign culture and strive for global competitiveness if they wish to catch up with the West in terms of material abundance, welfare and even social cohesion.* Deviations will certainly keep occurring, **development will remain cyclical**, but the trend is likely to be favorable if Western civilization stays largely on its broad course and will reestablish its positive appeal toward societies in transition.[13] Likewise, economic liberalism may slowly, but surely regain its attractiveness as the best theoretical underpinning of liberal democracy.[14]

---

fice, etc. and has replaced the previous, thoroughly democratic constitution with a strongly authoritarian design based on a baroque caricature of a seemingly glorious historical imitation. But as a consequence of its brutally unprofessional, inconsistent, incoherent and irrational economic policy and management, coupled with uncultured and violent language in public discourse (including vituperative attacks on various organs of the European Union), Hungary has now deviated considerably from the slow but steady advancement of the V4 or even V6 countries and sunk to the level of the weakest Balkan countries, falling behind, in many respects, Romania and Bulgaria.

[12] Popper (1950).

[13] It is, therefore, quite sure that the tragic and farcical attempt of Fidesz to establish an oligarchic society in Hungary will end in tears and tatters for the present government. Sadly, in the meantime, it is going to cause much harm to the Hungarian economy, society and culture.

[14] "The findings presented here cast doubt on the argument that there exists a fundamental tension—or any tension at all—between economic liberalism and democracy in the con-

Although it is highly likely that the market economy, open society and democratic polity will ultimately triumph in Mitteleuropa, the Baltic and, perhaps with some delay, in the Balkan area as well, there is no absolute guarantee for it to happen this way. Authoritarian alternatives based on oligarchic order may remain highly successful (as in China so far) or at least limp on (as in Russia) for a long time without serious challenge and gradual erosion from within. As it is painfully clear now after the collapse of Soviet communism, **history does not follow a unilinear and deterministic course.** The fundamental variability of social institutions and the inherent instability of social structures should never be forgotten.[15]

---

temporary world. They reveal a straightforward, positive, linear relationship. They call into question both the oft-rehearsed argument about the need to insulate economic reformers from popular pressures and the notion that 'neoliberalism' undermines popular rule. They also show that the post-communist region is entirely unexceptional; the same logic of affinity between economic liberalism and political openness that holds globally obtains in the post-communist world. The affinity holds in the formerly Second and Third Worlds; nothing about post-communism or underdevelopment makes economic liberalism incompatible with democracy. Neoliberalism does not breed voodoo politics—unless it regards popular rule as involving more incantation and make-believe than authoritarianism does. 'Technocracy' may sometimes be arrogant; indeed, it is probably always arrogant. ...however, technocracy is less able or disposed to hurl itself against democracy when it is promoting economic liberalism than when it is nurturing economic statism. More economic liberalism, more political openness." Fish (2003) 198.

[15] "Weber's whole treatment is dominated, as is all his work, by two deep underlying convictions which need to be brought out explicitly as they have much to do with the empirical fruitfulness of his analysis. Both contrast with the dominant tone of much of 'economic' thought.

The first is the conviction of the fundamental variability of social institutions. To him the institutional system of the modern Western World is not a 'natural order' which has come about by the mere process of removal of obstacles. It represents, in every fundamental respect, one of several possible lines of social development. Other radically different structures, such as those found in the great oriental civilizations, are not 'arrested stages' in a development leading in the same direction, but are simply different. It follows that, at least in many of its principal aspects, our own situation is not to be explained by the operation of the most general factors common to the situation of all men, but by quite specific combination of circumstances.

The second closely related conviction is that of the inherent instability of social structures. For Weber human society, and underlying that, the situation of human action and the character of humanly possible responses to that situation, are shot through with deep-seated tensions which make the maintenance of any given state of affairs precarious. This is particularly true of what for Weber would undoubtedly be among the 'higher' structures, those displaying a high level of rationalization. 'Traditionalism' represented for him by far the most stable social situation, but one which was undoubtedly thought of as 'primitive' or backward." Parsons (1947) 31–32.

As a result, *conscious societal action* is absolutely key in the advancement of freedom and democracy. Enlightened governments and civil society should promote the fundamental values of liberal democracy and contribute to the rejuvenation and reinvigoration of democratic political culture. Institutions and societal structures are still extremely fragile in the transition world and they need constant strengthening and nurturing in order to withstand either stealth attacks of illiberal democracy or highly visible assaults of populist-nationalist authoritarianism. The best way to make the economy and society resistant to illiberal and/or authoritarian backlash is to *revisit and restart market supporting and strengthening structural reforms*. All elements of the matrix of structural reforms should be reviewed periodically and the reform drive needs to gain new vigor. After several rounds of successful advancement of these reforms, there might be a chance for a **strong civic culture and morality** to emerge which, in turn, may make society mature enough as to avoid backward slippages. After a century of successful reforms, our part of the world may finally become no longer *accidentally occidental*.

References

Abraham, Florin. 2006. *România de la Comunism la Capitalism 1989–2004* (Romania from Communism to Capitalism). Bucharest: Tritonic.

Acharya et al. 2011. *Regulating Wall Street. The Dodd-Frank Act and the New Architecture of Global Finance.* New York: John Wiley & Sons, Inc.

Adam, Jan. 1995. *Why did the Socialist System Collapse in Central and Eastern Europe? The Case of Poland, the former Czechoslovakia and Hungary.* London: MacMillan Press.

Ajani, Gianmaria. 1998. "Transfer of Legal Systems from the Point of View of the Export Countries." In *Systemtransformation in Mittel und Osteuropa und ihre Folgen für Banken, Börsen und Kreditsicherheiten,* eds. Drobnig et al. Max-Planck-Institut, Mohr Siebeck.

Antal, László. 1985. *Gazdaságirányítási és pénzügyi rendszerünk a reform útján* (Our Economic Management and Financial System on Reform Course). Budapest: Közgazdasági és Jogi Könyvkiadó.

———. 2004. *Fenntartható-e a fenntartható növekedés?* (Is sustainable growth really sustainable?) Budapest: Közgazdasági Szemle Alapítvány.

Arendt, Hannah. 1958. *The Origins of Totalitarianism.* Cleveland, Ohio: A Meridian Book.

Aron, Raymond. 1965. *Démocratie et totalitarisme.* Paris: Gallimard.

Aristotle. 1984. *Aristotle: The Politics.* Translated and with an Introduction, Notes and Glossary by Carnes Lord. Chicago: The University of Chicago Press.

Auerbach, Alan J. and M. Feldstein, eds. 1987. *Handbook of Public Economics.* Amsterdam: North-Holland.

Balcerowicz, Leszek. 1994. "Poland." In *The Political Economy of Reform,* ed. John Williamson. Washington DC: Institute for International Economics.

———. 1995. *Socialism, Capitalism, Transformation.* Budapest: CEU Press.

Barr, Nicholas and M. Rutkowski. 2005. "Pensions." In *Labor Markets and Social Policy in Central and Eastern Europe,* ed. Nicholas Barr. Washington, DC: The World Bank.

Barr, Nicholas and P. Diamond. 2008. *Reforming Pensions: Principles and Policy Choices.* Oxford: Oxford University Press.

Barsky, Robert B and L. Kilian. 2000. *A Monetary Explanation of the Great Stagflation of the 1970s.* Ann Arbor: University of Michigan.

Bartlett, David L. 1997. *The Political Economy of Dual Transformations. Market Reform and Democratization in Hungary.* Ann Arbor: The University of Michigan Press.

Begović, Boris and B. Mijatović, eds. 2005. *Tschetiri godine tranzicije u Srbiji* (Four Years of Transition in Serbia). Belgrade: Centar za liberalno-demokratske studije.

Berend, T. Iván. 2009. *From the Soviet Bloc to the European Union. The Economic and Social Transformation of Central and Eastern Europe since 1973.* Cambridge: Cambridge University Press.

Berg, Sanford and J. Tschirhart. 1988. *Natural monopoly regulation. Principles and practice.* Cambridge: Cambridge University Press.

Billington, James H. 1966. *The Icon and the Axe. An Interpretive History of Russian Culture.* New York: Alfred A. Knopf.

Blanchard, Olivier. 1997. *The Economics of Post-Communist Transition.* Oxford: Clarendon Press.

Blanchard, Olivier, K.A. Froot and J.D. Sachs. 1994. *The Transition in Eastern Europe.* Chicago: The University of Chicago Press.

Blejer, Mario and M. Škreb. 1997. "Stabilization after Five Years of Reform: Issues and Experiences in Macroeconomic Stabilization." In *Transition Economies*, eds. Blejer, Mario and M. Škreb. Cambridge: Cambridge University Press.

Blommenstein, Hans and M. Marrese. 1991. *Transformation of Planned Economies: Property Rights Reform and Macroeconomic Stability.* Paris: OECD Centre for Cooperation with European Economies in Transition.

Bokros, Lajos. 1991. "Privatization in Hungary." In *Privatization in Eastern Europe: Current Implementation Issues*, eds. Böhm and Kreačič. Ljubljana: International Center for Public Enterprises.

———. 1998a. "The Unfinished Agenda." In *Public Finance Reform during the Transition,* ed. Bokros and Dethier. Washington, DC.: The World Bank.

———. 1998b. "Problems of the Reconstruction of the Banking System in Hungary" in *Systemtransformation in Mittel- und Osteuropa und ihre Folgen für Banken, Börsen und Kreditsicherheiten*, eds. Drobnig et al. Tübingen: Mohr Siebeck.

———. 1998c. "Stabilization without Recession. The Success of a Long-Awaited Financial Adjustment in Hungary." In *Financial Crisis Management in Regional Blocks*, ed. Scheherazade S. Rehman. Boston: Kluwer Academic Publishers.

———. 2001a. "A Perspective on Financial Sector Development in Central and Eastern Europe." In *Financial Transition in Europe and Central Asia*, ed. Bokros, Flemming and Votava. Washington, DC: The World Bank.

———. 2001b. "Rozdílné cesty visegradských dvojčat k relativní prosperitě—Povorábí procesu transformace v CR a Maďarsku." (Visegrad twins different path to relative prosperity—The transition process in the Czech Republic and Hungary). *Finance a Úver,* 4. Praha.

———. 2001c. "Banking Sector Reform in Central and Eastern Europe." In *A Decade of Transition: Achievements and Challenges*, eds. Oleh Havrylyshyn and Saleh M. Nsouli. Washington, DC: IMF.

———. 2001d . "A társadalmi szolidaritás és annak hiánya" (Societal solidarity and the lack thereof). *Élet és Irodalom*, June 6. Budapest.

———. 2001e. "A társadalmi szolidaritás és annak kényszere" (Societal solidarity and the compulsion thereof). *Élet és Irodalom*, August 31. Budapest.

———. 2001f. "A társadalmi szolidaritás és a nyugdíjrendszer" (Societal solidarity and the pension system). *Élet és Irodalom*, October 12. Budapest.

———. 2001g. "A társadalmi szolidaritás és a gyógyulás intézményei" (Societal solidarity and the institutions of health care). *Élet és Irodalom*, December 7. Budapest.

———. 2002. "Financial Sector Development in Central and Eastern Europe." In *Banking and Monetary Policy in Eastern Europe. The First Ten Years*, ed. Adalbert Winkler. New York: Palgrave.

______. 2004. "Competition and Solidarity." *Comparative Economic Studies,* 46.

______. 2005. *The Fight between Oligarchy and Democracy in Transitional Societies.* Budapest: The Analyst. September, Budapest.

______. 2007. "Az állam alkati torzulásainak eredete az átmeneti társadalmakban" (The Origins of State Distortions in Transition Societies). In *Fecseg a felszín és hallgat a mély* (The surface chattering, the depth keeping quiet). Budapest: Akadémiai Kiadó.

______. 2009a. "A reformok kritikus tömege" (The critical mass of reforms). *Élet és Irodalom,* January 23. Budapest.

______. 2009b. "Az intézményes demokrácia újjáépítése a populizmus romjain" (The reconstruction of institutional democracy on the ruins of populism). *Élet és Irodalom,* August 19. Budapest.

Bokros, Lajos and J.J. Dethier, eds. 1998. *Public Finance Reform during Transition. The Experience of Hungary.* Washington, DC: The World Bank.

Bonin et al. 1998. *Banking in Transition Economies. Developing Market Oriented Banking Sectors in Eastern Europe.* Edward Elgar.

Borish, Michael S. and M. Noel. 1996. *Private Sector Development During Transition. The Visegrad Countries.* Washington, DC: World Bank Discussion Papers 318.

Braudel, Fernand. 1973. *Capitalism and Material Life.* New York: Harper & Row Publishers,

———. 1995. *A History of Civilizations.* New York: Penguin Books.

Brown, Archie. 2009. *The Rise & Fall of Communism.* London: Vintage Books.

Bruno, Michael. 1985. *Economics of worldwide stagflation.* Cambridge, Mass.: Harvard University Press.

Brus, Włodzimierz. 1972. *The Market in a Socialist Economy.* London: Routledge & Kegan Paul.

Brus, Włodzimierz. 1981. "Economic Reforms as an Issue in Soviet-East European Relations." In *Soviet-East European Dilemmas, Coercion, Competition and Consent.* London: Holmers & Meier.

Brzezinski, Zbigniew. 1967. *The Soviet Bloc: Unity and Conflict.* Cambridge, Mass.: Harvard University Press.

———. 1989. *The Grand Failure. The Birth and Death of Communism in the Twentieth Century.* New York: Collier Books, MacMillan Publishing.

———. 1997. *The Grand Chessboard. American Primacy and Its Geostrategic Imperatives.* New York: Basic Books, HarperCollins.

Buchanan, James M. 1975. *The Limits of Liberty. Between Anarchy and Leviathan.* Chicago: University of Chicago Press.

Chekurova, Marina. 2001. "Restructuring the Russian Banking System." In *Financial Transition in Europe and Central Asia,* eds. Bokros–Flemming–Votava. Washington, DC: The World Bank

Cottarelli, Carlo and Gy. Szapáry, eds. 1998. *Moderate Inflation.* IMF and National Bank of Hungary.

Cottarelli, Carlo and P. Doyle. 2001. "Disinflation in transition." In *A Decade of Transition: Achievements and Challenges,* eds. Havrylyshyn and Nsouli. Washington, DC: IMF.

Crampton, R.J. 1997. *A Concise History of Bulgaria.* Cambridge: Cambridge University Press.

Dąbrowski, Marek. 1992. "The Polish Stabilization 1990–1991." *Journal of International and Comparative Economics*, 1.

Davey, Kenneth and G. Péteri. 1998. *Local Government Finances: Options for Reform.* Nagykovácsi: Pontes Ltd.

Davies, Norman. 2005. *God's Playground. A History of Poland.* Oxford: Oxford University Press.

Davies, R.W. 1998. *Soviet economic development from Lenin to Khrushchev.* Cambridge: Cambridge University Press.

Davies, R.W. 1989a. *The Industrialisation of Soviet Russia 1: The Socialist Offensive: The Collectivisation of Soviet Agriculture, 1929–1930.* London: The Macmillan Press.

Davies, R.W. 1989b. *The Industrialisation of Soviet Russia 2: The Soviet Collective Farm, 1929–1930.* London: The MacMillan Press.

Davies, R.W. 1989c. *The Industrialisation of Soviet Russia 3: The Soviet Economy in Turmoil, 1929–1930.* London: The MacMillan Press.

De Melo, Martha and C. Denizer. 1999. "Monetary Policy during Transition: An Overview." In *Financial Sector Transformation. Lessons for Economies in Transition*, eds. Blejer and Škreb. Cambridge: Cambridge University Press.

Deutscher, Isaac. 1949. *Stalin: A Political Biography.* New York and London: Oxford University Press.

Đilas, Milovan. 1972. *Conversations with Stalin.* New York: Harcourt Brace Jovanovich.

———. 1983. *The New Class. An Analysis of the Communist System.* New York: Harcourt Brace Jovanovich.

Earle et al. 1994. *Small Privatization. The Transformation of Retail Trade and Consumer Services in the Czech Republic, Hungary and Poland.* Budapest: CEU Press.

Engels, Friedrich. 1894. *Herr Eugen Dühring's Revolution In Science (Anti-Dühring).* London: Martin Lawrence Ltd.

EBRD. 1999. *Transition Report 1999. Ten Years of Transition.* London: European Bank for Reconstruction and Development.

EBRD. 2000. *Law in transition. Insolvency law and practice. Rebuilding through rescue or liquidation.* London: European Bank for Reconstruction and Development.

EBRD. 2005. *Law in transition. Courts and Judges.* London: European Bank for Reconstruction and Development.

EBRD. 2006. *Transition Report 2006. Finance in Transition.* London: European Bank for Reconstruction and Development.

EBRD. 2010. *Law in transition. Debt enforcement in times of uncertainty.* London: European Bank for Reconstruction and Development.

EBRD. 2011. *Towards better courts.* London: European Bank for Reconstruction and Development.

Eyal, Gil. 2003. *The Origins of Post-communist Elites. From Prague Spring to the Breakup of Czechoslovakia.* Minneapolis and London: University of Minnesota Press.

Eyal, Gil, I. Szelényi and E. Townsley. 1998. *Making Capitalism without Capitalists. The New Ruling Elites in Eastern Europe.* London and New York: Verso.

Fehér, F., Á. Heller and Gy. Márkus. 1983. *Dictatorship over Needs.* Oxford: Basil Blackwell.

Fejtő, François. 1971. *A History of the People's Democracies: Eastern Europe since Stalin.* New York: Praeger Publishers.

Fish, Steven. 2003. "Economic Policy Doctrine and Political Regime." In *Political Economy of Transition and Development*, eds. Campos and Fidrmuc. London: Kluwer Academic Publishers.

Friedman, Milton and Rose Friedman. 1980. *Free to Choose.* New York: Harcourt Brace Jovanovich.

Friedrich, Carl J. and Z. Brzezinski. 1965. *Totalitarian Dictatorship and Autocracy.* Cambridge, MA: Harvard University Press.

Friss, István, ed. 1971. *Reform of the Economic Mechanism In Hungary.* Budapest: Akadémiai Kiadó.

Fritz, Verena. 2007. *State-building. A Comparative Study of Ukraine, Lithuania, Belarus and Russia.* Budapest: CEU Press.

Frydman, Roman, C. Gray and A. Rapaczynski. 1996. *Corporate Governance in Central Europe and Russia.* Budapest: CEU Press.

Fukuyama, Francis. 1992. *The End of History and the Last Man.* New York: Free Press.

———. 1995. *Trust: The Social Virtues and the Creation of Prosperity.* New York: Free Press.

———. 2004. *State Building. Governance and World Order in the 21st century.* Ithaca: Cornell University Press.

———. 2011. *The Origins of Political Order from Prehuman Times to the French Revolution.* New York: Farrar, Straus and Giroux.

Gabrisch, Hubert and J. Hölscher. 2006. *The Successes and Failures of Economic Transition: The European Experience.* New York: Palgrave Macmillan.

Gat, Azar. 2007. "The Return of Authoritarian Great Powers." *Foreign Affairs,* July/August.

Gati, Charles. 2006. *Lost Illusions. Moscow, Washington, Budapest and the 1956 Hungarian Revolution.* Woodrow Wilson Center Press and Stanford University Press.

Gerschenkron, Alexander. 1962. *Economic Backwardness in Historical Perspective.* Cambridge, Mass.: The Belknap Press of Harvard University Press.

Greuning, Hennie van, S. Brajović-Bratanović. 1999. *Analyzing Banking Risk.* Washington, DC: The World Bank.

Győrffy, Dóra. 2007. *Democracy and Deficits. The New Political Economy of Fiscal Management Reforms in the European Union.* Budapest: Akadémiai Kiadó.

Haberler, Gottfried. 1986. "The Slowdown of the World Economy and the Problem of Stagflation." In *Stagflation, Savings and the State,* eds. Deepak Lal and M. Wolf. Published for the World Bank by Oxford University Press.

Haggard, Stephan and Robert R. Kaufman. 2001. "Introduction." In *Reforming the State,* eds. Kornai, Haggard and Kaufman. New York: Cambridge University Press.

Hall, Robert E. and A. Rabushka. 1995. *The Flat Tax.* Stanford: The Hoover Institution Press.

Hausner, Jerzy. 2001. "Security through Diversity: Conditions for Successful Reform of the Pension System in Poland." In *Reforming the State*, eds. Kornai, Haggard and Kaufman. New York: Cambridge University Press.

Hayek, Friendrich. 1944. *The Road to Serfdom.* London: Routledge & Kegan Paul.

———. 1948. "The Use of Knowledge in Society." In *Individualism and Economic Order.* Chicago: The University of Chicago Press, Midway Reprint.

Herman, Arthur. 1997. *The Idea of Western Decline in Western History.* New York: Free Press.

Hoffman, David E. 2002. *The Oligarchs. Wealth and Power in the New Russia.* New York: Public Affairs.

Holzmann, Robert, J. Gács and G. Winckler, eds. 1995. *Output Decline in Eastern Europe: Unavoidable, External Influence or Homemade?* Dordrecht: Kluwer Academic Publishers.

Holzmann, Robert, L. MacKellar and M. Rutkowski. 2003. "Accelerating the European Pension Reform Agenda: Need, Progress, and Conceptual Underpinnings." In *Pension Reforms in Europe: Process and Progress,* eds. Holzmann–Orenstein–Rutkowski. Washington, DC: The World Bank.

Holzmann, Robert and R. Hinz. 2005. *Old Age Income Support in the 21st century. An International Perspective on Pension Systems and Reform.* Washington, DC: The World Bank.

Hudecz, András. 2012. "Párhuzamos történetek. A lakossági devizahitelezés kialakulása és kezelése Lengyelországban, Romániában és Magyarországon." (Paralel stories. Evolution and management of hard currency retail lending in Poland, Romania and Hungary). *Közgazdasági Szemle* 4.

Hungary. Structural Reforms for Sustainable Growth. 1995. A World Bank Country Study, Washington.

IMF. Orderly & Effective Insolvency Procedures. Key Issues. 1999. Washington, DC: Legal Department, IMF.

Jedrzejczak, Gregory T. 1991. "Privatization in Poland." In *Privatization in Eastern Europe,* eds., Böhm and Kreacic. Ljubljana: International Center for Public Enterprises.

Ježek, Tomáš. 1997. "The Czechoslovak Experience with Privatization." *Journal of International Affairs* 2.

Johnson, Paul. 1991. *Modern Times.* New York: Harper Perennial.

Jotev, Petar. 2001. "Financial Sector Restructuring in Bulgaria 1997–2001." In *Financial Transition in Europe and Central Asia,* eds. Bokros–Flemming–Votava. Washington, DC: The World Bank.

Judt, Tony. 2005. *Postwar. A History of Europe since 1945.* New York: Penguin Books.

———. 2010. *Ill Fares The Land.* New York: Penguin Books.

Kaplan, Robert D. 1994. *Balkan Ghosts. A Journey through History.* New York: Vintage Books.

Kennan, George F. (published under the name "X"). 1947. "The Sources of Soviet Conduct." *Foreign Affairs* 25 (July).

Kennedy, Paul. 1988. *Rise and Fall of the Great Powers.* New York: Random House.

Kis, János. 1987. "The Restoration of 1956–57 from Thirty Years Perspective" (Az 1956-57-es restauráció harminc év távlatából) in *A forradalom előzményei és utóélete* (Paris-New Jersey: Magyar Füzetek.

Klaus, Václav. 1991. *Dismantling Socialism. A Preliminary Report.* The Center for Independent Studies, Occasional Papers 35.

———. 1995. *Ekonomická teorie a realita transformacních Procesu.* (Economic theory and the reality of the transition process) Prague: Management Press.

———. 1997. *Renaissance. The Rebirth of Liberty in the Heart of Europe.* Washington, DC: Cato Institute.

Koestler, Arthur. 1940. *Darkness at Noon.* London: Jonathan Cape.

Kohl, Helmut. 2009. *Vom Mauerfall zur Wiedervereinigung. Meine Erinnerungen* (From the fall of the Wall to reunification. My memoires). Munich: Knaur Taschenbuch Verlag.

Kontler, László. 1999. *Millenium in Central Europe. A History of Hungary.* Budapest: Atlantisz Publishing House.

Kopányi, Mihály, D. Wetzel and S.E. Daher. 2004. *Intergovernmental Finance in Hungary. A Decade of Experience, 1990–2000.* Washington, DC: The World Bank.

Kopits, George and J. Craig. 1998. *Transparency in Government Operations.* IMF Occasional Paper No. 158.

Kornai, János. 1959. *Overcentralization in Economic Administration.* Oxford: Oxford University Press.

———. 1980. *Economics of Shortage.* Amsterdam: North-Holland.

———. 1990. *The Road to a Free Economy. Shifting from a Socialist System: The Example of Hungary.* New York: W.W. Norton.

———. 1992. *The Socialist System. The Political Economy of Communism.* Oxford: Oxford University Press.

———. 2008. *From Socialism to Capitalism.* Budapest: CEU Press.

Korže, Uroš and M. Simoneti. 1991 "Privatization in Yugoslavia." In *Privatization in Eastern Europe,* eds., Böhm and Kreačič. Ljubljana: International Center for Public Enterprises.

Krueger, Anne. 1974. "The Political Economy of the Rent-Seeking Society." *American Economic Review,* 64 (June).

———. 1993. *Political Economy of Policy Reform in Developing Countries.* Cambridge, Mass.: The MIT Press.

Laar, Mart. 2010. *The Power of Freedom. Central and Eastern Europe After 1945.* Brussels: Centre for European Studies.

Lange, Oskar. 1936–37. "On the Economic Theory of Socialism, 1-2." *Review of Economic Studies,* 4 (October 1936, February 1937).

László, Csaba. 1994. *Tépett vitorlák.* (Torn sails). Budapest: Aula.

Lendvai, Paul. 2010. *Mein verspieltes Land. Ungarn in Umbruch* (My forfeited country. Hungary in change). Salzburg: Ecowin Verlag.

Lenin, V.I. 1964–1972. *Left-wing Communism, an Infantile Disorder.* Collected Works, Volume 31. Moscow: Progress.

Letwin, Oliver. 1988. *Privatizing the World. A Study of International Privatization in Theory and Practice.* London: Cassell Educational Ltd.

Lewandowski J. and J. Szomburg. 1993. "Property Reform as a Basis for Social and Economic Reform." *Communist Economies,* 3.

Lewandowski J. 1997. "The Political Context of Mass Privatization in Poland." In *Between State and Market,* eds. I. W. Lieberman, S. S. Nestor and R. N. Desai. World Bank Studies of Economies in Transition.

Lieberman, Ira W., S.S. Nestor and R. M. Desai, eds. 1997. *Between State and Market. Mass Privatization in Transition Economies.* The World Bank & OECD.

Lieven, Anatol. 1993. *The Baltic Revolution. Estonia, Latvia, Lithuania and the Path to Independence.* New York: Yale University Press.

Lieven, Dominic. 2003. *Empire. The Russian Empire and its Rivals From the Sixteenth Century to the Present.* London: Pimlico.

Lindbeck, Assar. 1998. *Lessons from Sweden for Post-Socialist Countries.* Discussion Paper No. 50. Budapest: Institute for Advanced Studies.

Lipton, David and J. Sachs. 1991. "Privatization in Eastern Europe: The Case of Poland." In *Privatization in Eastern Europe,* eds. Böhm and Kreačič. Ljubljana: International Center for Public Enterprises.

Lukacs, John. 1976. *The Last European War.* London and Henley: Routledge & Kegan Paul.

———. 1993. *The End of the Twentieth Century and the End of the Modern Age.* New York: Ticknor & Fields.

———. 2005. *Democracy and Populism. Fear and Hatred.* New Haven and London: Yale University Press.

Lukowski, Jerzy and H. Zawadzki. 2001. *A Concise History of Poland.* Cambridge: Cambridge University Press.

Marcinčin, Anton. 2000. "Privatization." In *Economic Policy in Slovakia 1990–1999,* eds. Marcinčin and Beblavý. Bratislava: SFPA, CPS and INEKO.

Mazower, Mark. 1999. *Dark Continent.* London: Penguin Books.

McFaul, Michael. 2001. *Russia's Unfinished Revolution. Political Change from Gorbachev to Putin.* Ithaca and London: Cornell University Press.

Mertlík, Pavel. 1995. "Czech Privatization: From Public Ownership to Public Ownership in Five Years?" *Prague Economic Papers,* 4.

Medvedev, Roy. 1989. *Let History Judge. The Origins and Consequences of Stalinism.* New York: Columbia University Press.

Mihályi, Péter. 1998. *A magyar privatizáció krónikája 1989–1997* (The chronicle of Hungarian privatization, 1989–1997). Budapest: Közgazdasági és Jogi Könyvkiadó.

———. 2010. *A magyar privatizáció enciklopédiája* (The Encyclopedia of Hungarian Privatization). Budapest: Pannon Egyetem, Veszprém–MTA KTI.

Milanovic, Branko. 2001. "Inequality During the Transition: Why did it increase?" In *A Decade of Transition: Achievements and Results,* eds. Oleh Havrylyshyn and S. M. Nsouli. Washington, DC: IMF.

Mishkin, Frederic S. 2006. *The Next Great Globalization: How Disadvantaged Nations can Harness their Financial Systems to get Rich.* Princeton: Princeton University Press.

Mitra, Pradeep. 2008. *Innovation, Inclusion and Integration. From Transition to Convergence in Eastern Europe and the Former Soviet Union.* Washington DC: The World Bank.

Mlčoch, Lubomír, P. Manochin and M. Sojka. 2000. *Economic and Social Changes in Czech Society After 1989. An Alternative View.* Prague: Charles University in Prague, The Karolinum Press.

Mlčoch, Lubomír. 2001. "Deset lekcí z deseti let ceské transformace" (Ten lessons from ten years of the "Czech Way"). *Finance a Úver,* 4.

Molnár, Miklós. 2001. *A Concise History of Hungary.* Cambridge: Cambridge University Press.

Musgrave, Robert A. 1985. "A Brief History of Fiscal Doctrine." In *Handbook of Public Economics,* eds. Alan J. Auerbach and M. Feldstein. Amsterdam: North-Holland.

Nádas, Péter. 2006. *Hátországi napló* (Hinterland diary). Pécs: Jelenkor Kiadó.

Nazi Conspiracy and Aggression. 1946. Office of the United States Chief of Counsel for the Prosecution of Axis Criminality. Washington, DC: US Government.

Nellis, John. 2001. "Time to Rethink Privatization in Transition Economies?" In *A Decade of Transition: Achievements and Challenges,* eds. Havrylyshyn and Nsouli. Washington, DC: IMF.

Nelson, Joan M. 2001. "The Politics of Pension and Health Care Reform in Hungary and Poland." In *Reforming the State,* eds. Kornai, Haggard and Kaufman. Cambridge: Cambridge University Press.

Neumann, Friedrich. 1915. *Mitteleuropa.* Berlin: Druck und Verlag von Goerg Kreme.

Newbery, David M. 1999. *Privatization, Restructuring and Regulation of Network Utilities.* The Walras-Pareto Lectures. Cambridge, MA: The MIT Press.

Nove, Alec. 1961. *The Soviet Economy.* Glasgow: Minerva.

———. 1969. *An Economic History of the USSR.* London: The Penguin Press.

Ofer, Gur. 2003. "Transition and Developing Economies: Comparing the Quality of Governments" in *Political Economy of Transition and Development. Institutions, Politics and Policies*, eds. Campos and Fidrmuc. London: Kluwer Academic Publishers.

Offe, Claus. 1991. "Capitalism by Democratic Design? Democratic Theory Facing the Triple Transition in East Central Europe." *Social Research* 58, no. 4.

Olson, Mancur. 1965. *The Logic of Collective Action.* Cambridge: Harvard University Press.

———. 2000. *Power and Prosperity. Outgrowing Communist and Capitalist Dictatorships*. New York: Basic Books.

Ormos, Mária. 1994. *Hitler.* Budapest: T-Twins.

Orwell, George. 1949. *1984.* London: Secker and Warburg.

Parsons, Talcott. 1947. "Introduction." In *Max Weber, The Theory Of Social and Economic Organization.* New York: The Free Press.

Péteri, Gábor and T. M. Horváth. 2001. *Regulation and Competition in Local Utilities in Central and Eastern Europe.* Local Government and Public Service Reform Initiative. Budapest: Open Society Institute.

Pirie, Madsen. 1988. *Privatization. Theory, Practice and Choice.* Aldershot: The Adam Smith Institute, Wildwood House.

Pohl, Gerhard. 1993. "Property Restitution in East Germany." In *Reprivatization in Central and Eastern Europe.* Ljubljana: CEEPN and World Bank Report.

Polanyi, Karl. 1946. *The Great Transformation. Origins of our Time.* London: Victor Gollanz Ltd.

Politkovskaya, Anna. 2004. *Putin's Russia.* London: The Harwill Press.

———. 2008. *A Russian Diary.* London: Vintage Books.

Popper, Karl R. 1950. *The Open Society and Its Enemies.* Princeton: Princeton University Press.

Radygin, Alexander. 2003. "Privatization, Ownership Redistribution, and Formation of the Institutional Basis For Economic Reforms." In *The Economics of Russian Transition,* ed. Yegor Gaidar. Cambridge, MA: The MIT Press.

Radygin, Alexander and N. Shmeleva. 2003. "Main Corporate Governance Mechanisms and Their Specific Features in Russia." In *The Economics of Russian Transition,* ed. Yegor Gaidar. Cambridge, MA: The MIT Press.

Rajan, Raghuram and L. Zingales. 2003. *Saving Capitalism from the Capitalists: Unleashing the Power of Financial Markets to Create Wealth and Spread Opportunity.* New York: Crown.

Rose, Susan-Ackerman. 1997. *Corruption and Development.* Annual Bank Conference for Development Economics. Washington, DC: The World Bank.

Roubini, Nouriel and S. Mihm. 2010. *Crisis Economics. A Crash Course in the Future of Finance.* New York: Penguin Press and Allen Lane.

Rozłucki, Wieslaw. 2001. "Emerging Stock Markets in Central Europe: Where do we stand?" In *Financial Transition in Europe and Central Asia,* eds. Bokros, Flemming and Votava. Washington, DC: The World Bank.

Rubinfeld, Daniel L. 1987. "The Economics of the Local Public Sector." In *Handbook of Public Economics,* eds. Auerbach and Feldstein. Amsterdam: North-Holland.

Rudlovčák, Vladimír. 2001. "Czech Capital Markets: Illusions and Disillusions." In *Financial Transition in Europe and Central Asia,* eds. Bokros, Flemming and Votava. Washington, DC: The World Bank.

Rybakov, Anatoliy. 1987. *Djeti Arbata* (The Children of Arbat). Moscow: Druzhba Narodov.

Schumpeter, Joseph. 1942. *Capitalism, Socialism, Democracy.* London: Allen and Unwin.

Sen, Amartya. 2000. *Development as Freedom.* New York: First Anchor Books Edition.

Shleifer, Andrei. 1996. *Government in Transition.* Harvard Institute of Economic Resesarch, Occasional Discussion Paper Number 1783. Cambridge, MA.

Šik, Ota. 1966. *Economic Planning and Management in Czechoslovakia.* Prague: Orbis.

Soós, Károly Attila. 1986. *Terv, kampány, pénz* (Plan, campaign, money). Budapest: Közgazdasági és Jogi Könyvkiadó–Kossuth Könyvkiadó.

———. 2010. *Politics and Policies in Post-Communist Transition.* Budapest: CEU Press.

Spengler, Oswald. 1928. *The Decline of the West.* An Abridged Edition. Oxford: Oxford University Press.

Solzhenitsyn, Aleksandr. 1973. *The Gulag Archipelago.* New York: Harper and Row.

Stoica, Stan. 2007. *România după 1989. O istorie cronologică* (Romania after 1989. A chronologic history). Bucharest: Meronia.

Stigler, George J. 1975. *The Citizen and the State. Essays on Regulation.* Chicago: The University of Chicago Press.

———. 1983. *The Organization of Industry.* Chicago: The University of Chicago Press.

———. 1984. *The Intellectual and the Marketplace.* Cambridge: Harvard University Press,

Stiglitz, Joseph E. 1987. *Principal and agent, The New Palgrave: A Dictionary of Economics,* Volume 3. London: Macmillan.

Szamuely, László. 1971. *Az első szocialista gazdasági mechanizmusok. Elvek és elméletek.* (The first socialist economic mechanisms. Principles and theories) Budapest: Közgazdasági és Jogi Könyvkiadó.

Szűcs, Jenő. 1983. *Vázlat Európa három történeti régiójáról* (An outline on the three historical regions of Europe). Budapest: Magvető.

Tanzi, Vito. 1995. "Corruption: arms's length relationships and markets." In *Economics of Organized Crime,* eds. Gianluca Fiorentini and S. Peltzman. Cambridge: Cambridge University Press.

———. 2001. "Creating Effective Tax Addministrations: The Experience of Russia and Georgia." In *Reforming the State,* eds. Kornai, Haggard and Kaufman. New York: Cambridge University Press.

———. 2002. "Corruption around the World: Causes, Consequences, Scope, and Cures." In *Governance, Corruption, and Economic Performance*, eds. Abed and Gupta. Washington DC: IMF.

Tanzi, Vito and G. Tsibouris. 2001. "Transition and the Changing Role of Government." In *A Decade of Transition: Achievements and Challenges*, eds. Oleh Havrylyshin and S. M. Nsouli. Washington, DC: IMF.

Tardos, Márton. 1981. "The Role of Money: Economic Relations between State Enterprises in Hungary." *Acta Oeconomica* 25.

Ter-Minassian, Teresa. 1997. "Intergovernmental Fiscal Relations in Macroeconomic Perspective: An Overview." In *Fiscal Federalism in Theory and Practice.* Washington, DC: IMF.

Thakur et al. 2003. *Sweden's Welfare State. Can the Bumblebee Keep Flying?* Washington, DC: IMF.

Tocqueville, Alexis de. 2000. *Democracy in America.* The Complete and Unabridged Reprint of the 1835 Original Bantam Classic Books. New York.

Todd, Emmanuel. 1979. *The Final Fall (La chute finale). An Essay on the Decomposition of the Soviet Sphere.* New York: Karz Publishers.

Toynbee, Arnold. 1948. *Civilization on Trial.* London: Oxford University Press.

Transparency International (2010): www.transparency.org/policy_research/ surveys_indices

Třiska, Dušan and C. Jelinek-Francis. 1991. "A Study of Privatization in the Czech and Slovak Federal Republic." In *Privatization in Eastern Europe*, eds. Böhm and Kreačič. Ljubljana: International Center for Public Enterprises.

United Nations. World Population Prospects: The 1998 Revision. 1998. New York: United Nations.

Varga, István. 1957. "A Közgazdasági Szakértő Bizottság elgondolásai" (Thoughts of the Economic Expert Committee). *Közgazdasági Szemle* (October–December).

Weber, Max. 1947. *The Theory of Social and Economic Organization.* New York: The Free Press.

Wellisz, Stanisław. 1997. "Inflation and Stabilization in Poland, 1990–1995." In *Macroeconomic Stabilization in Transition Economies,* eds. Mario Blejer and M. Škreb. Cambridge: Cambridge University Press.

Williamson, John ed. 1993. *Economic Consequences of Soviet Disintegration.* Washington, DC: Institute for International Economics.

———. ed. 1994. *In Search of a Manual for Technopols: The Political Economy of Reform.* Washington, DC: Institute for International Economics.

Wilson, Edmund. 1972. *To the Finland Station.* New York: Farrar, Straus and Giroux.

Wolf, Martin. 2008. *Fixing Global Finance.* Baltimore: The Johns Hopkins University Press.

World Bank. Governance: The World Bank's Experience. 1994. Washington, DC.

World Bank. Averting The Old Age Crisis. Policies to Protect the Old and Promote Growth. A World Bank Policy Research Report. 1994. Washington, DC.

World Bank. From Plan to Market. World Bank Development Report. 1996. Oxford: Oxford University Press.

World Bank. The State in a Changing World. World Bank Development Report. 1997. Oxford: Oxford University Press.

World Bank. Reforming Public Institutions and Strengthening Governance. 2000a. Washington, DC.

World Bank. Making Transition Work for Everyone. Poverty and Inequality in Europe and Central Asia. 2000b. Washington, DC.

World Bank. Building Institutions for Markets. World Bank Development Report. 2002. Oxford: Oxford University Press.

Wyrzykowski, Mirosław. 1995. "Selected Problems of System Transformation" In *Rechtsfragen der Transformation in Polen,* eds. Aregger, Poczobut and Wyrzykowski. Warsaw.

Zecchini, Salvatore. 1997. *Lessons from the Economic Transition. Central and Eastern Europe in the 1990s.* Dordrecht: Kluwer Academic Publishers.

Index

accidental occidental 2n1, 176
administrative capacity 59, 78n44, 83, 101, 104, 114, 118, 144–46, 162n197
asset and liability management 131, 147, 153
assigned transfers 150

Baczkowski, Andrzej 163n199
Bakarić, Vladimir 31n53
banking
  commercial banking 4, 46, 72n26, 74n34, 96, 98, 107, 122, 124n129
  investment banking 95, 124
bankruptcy and liquidation 97n83, 105n95, 134, 151n180, 156, 157–59
Beria, Lavrentiy 38
Bierut, Bolesław 38n70
block transfers 149, 150
borrowing 42n80, 66, 119, 131, 138n159, 147, 151–53, 171
Brezhnev, Leonid 41n78, 43n84, 49,
Bulganin, Nikolai 38

capital market 44, 46n91, 89n64, 91n69, 96, 114, 119–21, 125n130, 138
Carter, Jimmy 52n100
Ceauşescu, Nicolae 1
central governmental public administration 75, 140
Chernenko, Konstantin Ustinovich 4n6, 53
civic culture and morality 176
collectivization 23n34, 24, 26, 32, 35
command economy 5, 9–12, 14–15, 17, 19, 21, 24, 29, 39n73, 40, 47, 49, 57, 62, 68, 69n17, 71n25, 75, 76n39, 80, 86, 97, 104n93, 106–107
command society 9n2, 19
competition policy and regulation 159
contradictory public policy objectives 146
corporate governance 85–86, 88n58, 89n64, 90, 106, 109, 121, 154
  internal governance 109–110, 122
  external governance 107n98, 109n103, 122
corporatization 81n48, 92, 103
crime, cronyism and corruption 49, 174
cronyism, collusion and corruption 117
currency substitution 73
cyclical development 85, 174

dilution versus divestiture 86
directed lending 87, 91, 171
Djilas, Milovan 31n53
Dlouhý, Vladimír 120n123

Engels, Friedrich 12n12, 19n25
equalization 147, 149–150

Fedorenko, Feodor 41n78

financial sector 60, 77, 81, 83, 94, 95n78, 96, 98, 99n86, 106, 108n100–101, 119, 121, 124–126, 140, 159
fiscal profligacy 130, 152, 173n11
fiscal transfers 144
flow problem 66, 107, 109, 115
forced industrialization 24, 29, 51, 95
fragmentation of society 26
Franco, Francisco 35n64
Fukuyama, Francis 129

Gagarin, Jurij 40
Gomułka, Władysław 38n70–71, 39
Gorbachev, Mikhail Sergeyevich 4n6, 52–54, 55n103

Horthy, Miklós 35n64

independent central bank 73
inflation, output decline, unemployment 67–69, 76, 84, 107, 142
insolvency and illiquidity 151
institution building 2, 58, 128, 140, 142, 161

Kádár, János 39
Kaganovich, Lazar Moiseyevich 38
Kantorovich, Leonid Vitaliyevich 41n78
Kardelj, Edvard 31n53
Kennan, George 30n50
Kennedy, John F. 40n76
Khrushchev, Nikita 38, 41
Klaus, Václav 114, 120n123
Kohl, Helmut 54n103
Kronrod, Aleksandr Semenovich 41n78

Lange, Oskar 19n22, 29n45, 39n72, 40n74
legal and financial restructuring 104
legal and judicial reform 154, 156
legitimacy of the Soviet system 28
Lenin, Vladimir Ilyich 5n8, 20n25, 21, 23, 27, 36n66, 95n79
liberalization 38, 41, 59, 60–65, 66n15 67–70, 74, 75n35, 78–80, 84, 97n83, 107, 108n100, 110n105, 113, 118n121, 119, 123, 126n132, 128, 160–161, 164
  liberlization of entry and exit 61, 108n100
  liberalization of prices 62, 70n22, 79
  liberalization of employment and wages 63
  political liberalization 69
local government associations 145
local taxation 144, 147, 148

macroeconomic stabilization 57, 60, 68, 70–71, 75, 130, 131, 161n196, 164
  monetary stabilization 73n30
  fiscal stabilization 74, 75n35, 79
Malenkov, Georgy Maximilianovich 38
managed or directed democracy 170
Marx, Karl 12n12, 19n25
matrix of structural reforms in transition 57, 59–60, 84n53, 160
matrix reloaded 159
Mayakovsky, Vladimir 27
Mazowiecki, Tadeusz 80n47, 84n52
Mečiar, Vladimír 170, 171n7
Miller, Leszek 163n199
Milošević, Slobodan 100n89, 111n106, 172
Mitterrand, François 54–55n103
misallocation of resources 62, 65
models of Soviet communism
  classical Stalinist model 5, 29, 33n59, 34–35, 37, 47, 66
  Hungarian modified model 5, 12n10, 39, 42, 47
  Yugoslav model 5, 12n10, 45, 46n91, 47, 48n94, 66, 71n25
Molotov, Vyacheslav Mikhailovich 36n66, 38
Mussolini, Benito 15n17, 35n64

Nagy, Imre 38n70–71
natural monopoly 84n53, 94, 98, 99n86, 100, 101n90, 102n91, 103, 104n93, 116–118, 159
Nemchinov, Vasily Sergeevich 41n78
Neumann, Friedrich 2
New Economic Policy 21
Novozhilov 41n78

oligarchic order 168–175
open society 54, 174–175
Orwell, George 35n63

pension system
pay-as-you-go 132–137, 138n159, 162n199
multipillar pension system 137n157, 139
private pension funds 125n130, 137–140
mandatory and voluntary private pension funds 125n130, 138
Petrakov 41n78
Piłsudski, Józef 35n64
planning
central planning 10n5, 13, 14n16, 15n17, 16n19, 17n20, 42, 46–47, 72n26, 93, 95, 132n146
mandatory planning 14n14
populism 165n205, 167
privatization
mass privatization 65n12, 87, 88n58, 89–90, 114, 120n124, 121n124, 157, 160
restitution 87–89
competitive privatization 60, 80, 94, 97, 160
insider privatization 171
public finance and administration 81, 127–29, 141n164, 142–43, 151, 153
public services 142–44, 146, 151n180, 154, 165,
public utilities 45n88, 79, 81–83, 94–95, 97–106, 112, 113, 115–17, 119, 126, 160, 162
Putin, Vladimir 170

Rákosi, Mátyás 38n70, 40n75
Rakowski, Mieczysław 80n47
Reagan, Ronald 4n6, 52, 55n103
reform of the state 118, 126
regulation and supervision 109n103, 113–15, 118–119, 121–24, 125n130, 126, 128, 140, 160, 165
restoration of consumer autonomy 64
restructuring 60, 83, 84n53, 92–93, 102–106, 111n106, 112, 113, 115, 118–19, 126, 128, 158, 160, 162, 165
role of the state 85n54, 113, 125–26, 129
Rozłucki, Wiesław 120n124

scope and strength of the state 129
shock therapy 61n2, 73, 161n195,
societal solidarity 135–37, 167
Soviet communism 4, 5n8, 5n9, 11–13, 14n16, 17–18, 27, 36, 38, 40, 44, 48, 65n13, 167, 175
Soviet state 26–27n39, 49n96
Stalin, Joseph Vissarionovich 4n7, 19n22, 23, 25–27, 28n42, 31n53, 35, 36n65, 38, 46
state capture 87n56, 169n3
state ownership 20, 31, 33, 40n74, 45, 65n12, 81–82, 86, 93, 94n76, 105, 158,
state paternalism 173
stock exchange 86n55, 91n69, 96, 120, 121n124, 125n130
stock problem 66, 107, 109, 115
strategic investors 86–87, 105, 110–12
strong and fair competition 121
structural reform 6, 57–60, 78, 84n53, 100, 112–13, 115, 126, 128–29, 143, 159–64, 176
parametric reforms 134–35, 137,
paradigmatic reforms 133n149, 137, 139
sequencing of structural reforms 58, 160
critical mass of structural reforms 163–64
Strumilin, Stanislav Gustavovich 41n78
subsovereign governments 33, 60, 77–78, 100, 131, 141–44, 146, 147n173, 148–154, 165
supply-side adjustment 47n93, 64, 67–68, 74, 75n35, 80, 82, 84, 97n83, 113, 130, 161n196

tax evasion and avoidance 76, 135, 137
Thatcher, Margaret 51, 54–55n103, 82
Tito, Josip Broz 31n53, 45n89

totalitarianism 10n3–4, 15n17, 26, 28n43, 64n10
transition 2–7, 13, 51–52, 54, 55, 57–61, 63–65, 67–71, 73, 75–79, 81–87, 89, 91–93, 97–102, 105–13, 115, 117–33, 135, 137, 139–44, 146–47, 150–74, 176
transitional deficit 132, 139
Třiska, Dušan 114n113, 120n123
tribal nationalism 167
Tuđman, Franjo 100n89, 172

war communism 12n10, 19–21, 29n45, 33n58
Weber, Max 18n21, 114n111, 175n15

Yeltsin, Boris 78n43, 110n104
Yesenin, Sergei Alexandrovich 27